the *Quilter's* resource book

Maggi McCormick Gordon

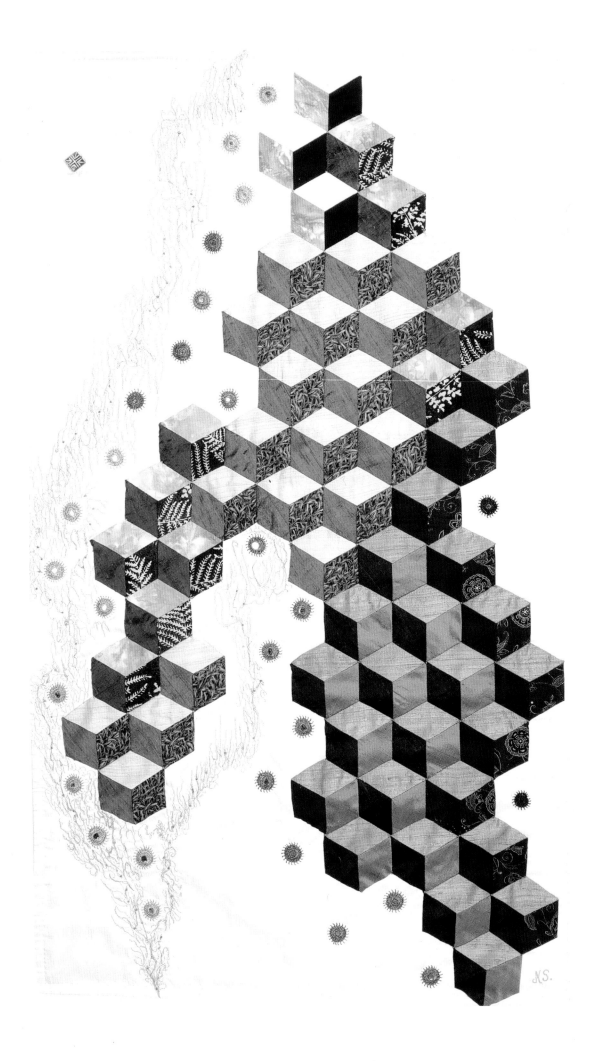

the *Quilter's* resource book

Maggi McCormick Gordon

Chrysalis

First published in the United States in 2004
by Chrysalis
The Chrysalis Building
Bramley Road
London W10 6SP

An imprint of **Chrysalis** Books Group

1 3 5 7 9 8 6 4 2

Library of Congress Control Number:
A catalog record for this book is available from the Library of Congress.

ISBN 0-681-04589-2

Designed by Lindsey Johns
Project managed by Marie Clayton
Copy-edited by Wordwork

Reproduction by Anorax
Printed and bound by Leefung, China

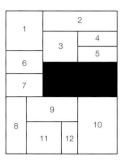

QUILT CREDITS

Front cover:

1. Star of Bethlehem (see page 84-85)
2. Contrary Wife (see page 67)
3. Windblown Tulips (see page 191)
4. Durham Strippy (see page 259)
5. Crazy Quilt (see page 129)
6. Katsuri Star Throw (see page 394-395)
7. Millie's Quilt (see page 156-157)
8. Rocky Glen (see page 68)
9. Seminole Band Quilt (see page 322-333)
10. Ralli Quilt (see page 414-415)
11. Flying Lizard Mola (see page 403)
12. Dresden Plate (see page 114-115)

Back cover: Crazy Quilt (see page 129)
Page 2: Adrift (2001) Munni Srivastava
Munni Srivastava became fascinated by the Tumbling Blocks design, and created this free-fall of colored blocks from a variety of silk fabrics. The cream slub silk background is embellished with a swathe of free-style machine embroidery.
Page 3: Star of Bethlehem (see page 84-85)

CONTENTS

INTRODUCTION

Quilts in some form have been made in myriad cultures throughout settled human history. Say the word "quilt" to most Europeans or Americans, and they will think of warm, comfy bedcovers made from multicolors and stitched in intricate patterns. But the world is filled with quiltmaking traditions that are very different from the Western idea, and even within the boundaries of North America, there are a number of quiltmaking traditions that fall outside the usually accepted "mainstream." This book has been designed partly to introduce some of the lesser-known quiltmaking genres to a wider audience, but it does not ignore the old-fashioned traditional bed quilts that our grandmothers and great-grandmothers made with loving care to provide warmth and softness in days gone by.

The generally accepted definition of a quilt is a textile made from two layers of fabric—a top and a back or backing—with a layer of padding

• Housetop variation (1998)
Mary Lee Bendolph is one of a group of African-American quiltmakers from Gee's Bend, Alabama. When a former resident of Gee's Bend send a box of old double-knit leisure suits to the community to be given away, no one wanted the rather outdated garments, so she made them into this charming variation of a Log Cabin quilt. Her daughter Essie Bendolph Pettway, also a talented quilter, quilted it in 2001, and it was part of a traveling exhibition of quilts from Gee's Bend.
Collection Tinwood Alliance

between them. Quilted textiles can be used as covers for furniture from beds and cradles to tables and sofas. They can be hung on walls, as they were in the Middle Ages to provide warmth and insulation, or as they are today, as works of art. They can also be worn. Medieval soldiers used quilted vests or jackets under their chain-mail armor, for protection and warmth, and to make the chain mail more comfortable to wear. Eighteenth-century women wore quilted petticoats that became so elaborate that the skirts that covered them became more and more abbreviated so that the undergarment could be seen and more fully appreciated. Their menfolk wore quilted and embroidered waistcoats of outstanding beauty and workmanship under their jackets. Even in today's centrally heated societies, many people dress in quilted coats and jackets to ward off the outdoor cold.

Three techniques

The making of quilts usually includes three broad categories—patchwork, applique, and quilting. When most people think of a quilt, they have an image of a patchwork quilt, in which various pieces of material have been stitched together to make a design that is appealing to the eye. Patchwork designs are by far the most common among antique quilts, but there are also vast numbers of appliqué quilts, in which pieces of fabric are applied to a larger piece of background cloth in patterns, some traditional and some from the mind of the maker. Quilting is the stitching that holds the layers of a quilt

together, and is often used in combination with patchwork and/or appliqué, as well as being used alone to create a pattern of texture on a plain piece of fabric.

The top and back of a quilt can each be a single piece of fabric, or pieced from a few, or many, smaller patches of material, which can be new or just usable scraps from old garments or other textiles. The top, plain or patchwork, can be decorated with elaborate appliqué work, or charming naive folk art. It can be patched from a random selection of scrap fabrics, or designed with a particular set of fabrics into a highly geometric piece of work. It can be embellished with beads, embroidery, ribbons, sequins, or old bottle caps. The back can be one large piece of fabric, or it can be pieced from any smaller pieces to hand. Or it can even be a separate quilt top, made into a double-sided quilt.

Quilts can be lightweight, made simply from two layers of fabric without the padding, called batting or wadding, in between. They can be heavy, padded in some cases with an old blanket or an even older quilt. Or they can be somewhere in between, traditionally with a layer of cotton or wool carded and spread evenly throughout the quilt, and today with various synthetic battings, which are bought by the yard and may contain some cotton in the mixture. In fact, the quilting itself is a result of the cotton or wool padding used in old quilts—the stitching was necessary to keep the fibers from shifting, which would have left lumps in the corners and no warmth in the middle.

Quiltmaking traditions

Quilts made in the Western European tradition—including North America and the Antipodes—are generally regarded as "typical," but the spread of quiltmaking goes much wider. Even traditional quiltmaking in western Europe, which emcompasses forms usually regarded as "American," and practiced in many parts of the New World, covers a vast variety of fabric artefacts. When we leave the confines of Europe, there are dozens of fascinating quiltmaking traditions that bear looking at more closely. Quilts in the Asian subcontinent, which includes India, Pakistan, Bangladesh, and the Southeast Asian countries, might seem at first glance unnecessary in these hot and humid areas. But there are within these subtropical lands places that are at high altitude where the temperature is often cool, or even cold, for example, and quilts are used to sleep under, as well as on top of when they become sleeping mats. They are also used to screen doorways, keeping out the heat or the drafts or the insects. Many traditional quilts made in these areas are created from multi-layered cotton fabrics taken mainly from old saris or worn household textiles.

In another part of Asia, an equally ancient and interesting form of quilting is practiced in Japan. Sashiko is the name given to the stitching that decorates and holds together the layers of garments, accessories, and household textiles. These pieces are traditionally stitched on several layers of cotton fabric that is usually, but not always, dyed deep blue with indigo. The stitching is generally done with white thread, and the highly geometric nature of the patterns used creates textiles of beauty and interest.

High in the mountains of Thailand, Laos, and Vietnam live a tribal people known as the Hmong who have a long tradition of making intricate pieces of patchwork and reverse appliqué for a variety of household and ceremonial uses. When large groups of Hmong immigrated to the United States after the Vietnam War, they brought with them their skills, and their wonderfully complex pieces are now known outside their isolated native lands. On the other side of the ocean, at sea level in the tropics off the Atlantic coast of Panama, another tribal group, the Kuna Indians, also makes vividly colored and elaborate pieces of reverse appliqué that they fashion into garments.

• Rice Crackers (2004)
English quiltmaker Rose Epton-Peter made this quilt in reponse to a challenge set by her quilt group. The members decided to use a photograph of the terraced rice paddies of Bali from Yann Arthus-Bertrand's book "The Earth from the Air" as a design source, and this quilt is her interpretation. Machine pieced from commercial and hand-dyed cotton fabrics, it is machine quilted. The lines of terracing are worked in acrylic yarn that has been couched by machine.

• Double Flying Geese (c. 1930)
An unknown quiltmaker created this quintessential scrap quilt from several thousand small right-angle triangles using dozens of different fabrics typical of the 1930s. Each multicolored "goose" unit is made from three triangles, all a different fabric, joined with their apexes pointing alternately up and down, and finished with a small white triangle at each end. The strips are then combined in sets of four, and white spacer blocks filled with meticulous crosshatch quilting alternate throughout the lively and beautifully made quilt.

Between Asia and Central America, in the middle of the Pacific Ocean, the tradition of Hawaiian quiltmaking has flourished for more than a century. The distinctive work of Hawaiian quiltmakers has even given the name of "Hawaiian" to the appliqué technique used to make these striking works of art.

Many of the traditional quiltmaking technique found in North America traveled there with the early European settlers, who made quilts to help keep their families warm through the bitterly cold winters they encountered. Various adaptations were made to the designs and patterns once the colonials began to settle and had time to exercise their creativity, and many interesting quiltmaking traditions developed among certain groups. One of the first groups were the Amish, who learned to make quilts from their "English" neighbors in Pennsylvania, and who took quiltmaking to new heights of beautiful utility.

A strong tradition also grew up among African slaves who were taken to the United States in huge numbers to work mainly on the plantations of the American South. Until they were freed by the Emancipation Proclamation of 1863, they lived tied to the owner of the plantation and did his bidding. Many of them were employed making quilts for the "big house," which were usually in the Western tradition, but when they made quilts for use in their own cabins, they drew heavily on their African traditions for designs and symbols.

Another North American quiltmaking tradition, which adapts European designs and turns them into wonderfully evocative works, has developed among various Native American tribes. Their designs often incorporated different symbols that are part of the ceremonial traditions of the tribe.

About the book

The book is not, however, all about ethnic traditions. It encompasses in its 250-plus photographs traditional and contemporary quilts from a variety of quiltmakers, both living and departed, who have illustrated in their work some aspect of the tradition of quiltmaking. Each of the three main quiltmaking methods—patchwork, appliqué, and quilting—is explored in the first section of the book, with instructions for trying out various aspects of the technique shown step by step, as well as basic information on getting started with quiltmaking.

The second section of the book is a fully illustrated picture gallery of quilts of various types and from various traditions, starting with the wholecloth, medallion, and strippy quilts that were widely made in England in particular, and which were adapted by American quiltmakers into some of the block patterns that we now consider quintessential quilt designs. In these sections you will find many beautiful antique quilts, often side by side with related designs made by today's quiltmakers, and covering areas of quiltmaking from signed friendship quilts to letters and alphabets, folk art, and pictorial and embellished quilts.

The final section of the book offers templates to provide ideas for designs, from patchwork blocks to quilting patterns, which can be copied and adapted for your own projects.

Happy quilting!

PART ONE

QUILTMAKING TRADITIONS

BASIC TECHNIQUES

**Sunshine and
Shadow c. 1990**
In this unusual example
of an Amish Sunshine
and Shadow quilt the
color families are kept
together quite rigidly.
The colors are also
slightly stronger than
normal, and include an
unconventional
combination of brown
and purple.

BASIC TECHNIQUES

TOOLS & EQUIPMENT

Traditionally, stitchers throughout the world have made their patchwork, appliqué, and quilted pieces without the need for specialized equipment. But today there are dozens of labor-saving devices on the market to make the process of measuring, cutting, marking, and stitching easier and less laborious than it has ever been before.

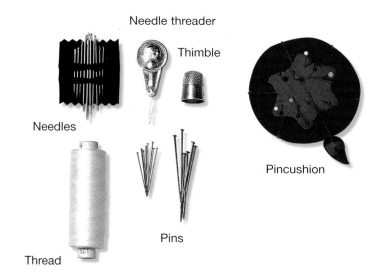

Needle threader

Thimble

Needles

Pincushion

Thread

Pins

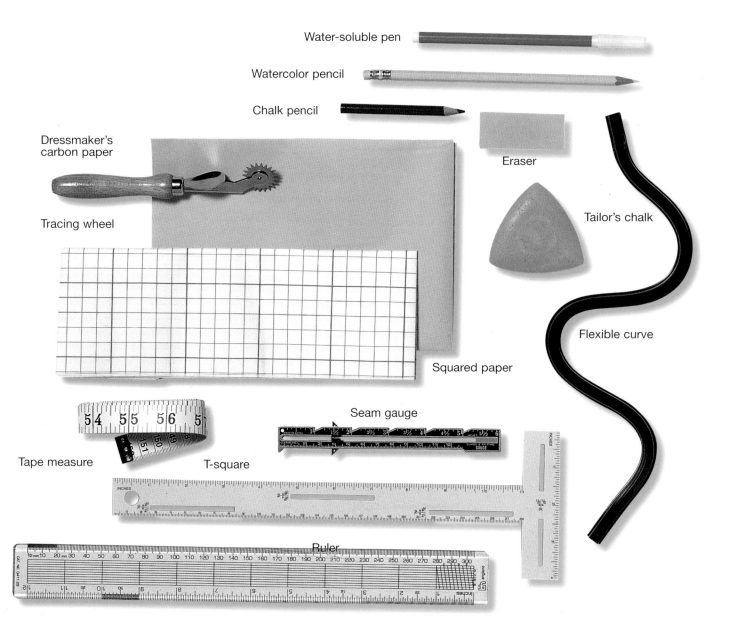

Water-soluble pen

Watercolor pencil

Chalk pencil

Dressmaker's carbon paper

Eraser

Tracing wheel

Tailor's chalk

Flexible curve

Squared paper

Seam gauge

Tape measure

T-square

Ruler

Drawing & measuring

Quiltmaking is about accuracy, and accuracy is about careful marking and measuring. Most of the measuring tools you need can be found in a desk or sewing box, but some specialized marking tools, such as water-soluble pens and quilter's pencils, whose marks are much easier to remove than traditional lead-pencil ones, are worth investing in.

Sewing

The quilter needs basic equipment for stitching, including needles, thread, both straight and safety pins—the latter can be used for "basting" the layers together ready for quilting—and thimbles.

Two types of needles are considered standard for quilters: "sharps" (ordinary sewing needles) for piecing, and "betweens" (shorter needles) for quilting. For piecing, use ordinary sewing thread to match the fabric: cotton thread for pure cotton, polyester for cotton blends, silk or cotton for silk. Most people stitch in white, cream, or gray unless the fabric is very dark. Quilting is best carried out with special quilting thread, which is heavier and stronger than ordinary thread and pre-waxed.

Many people don't like wearing thimbles, but you will probably find it useful to wear one when you are quilting large areas of fabric by hand.

There are special extra-long quilter's straight pins available with large heads that go easily through several layers of fabric and are easy to see in the work. Always keep a pincushion handy to keep a supply of pins nearby.

Templates

Ready-made metal or plastic templates come in an array of styles and sizes, and although they can be expensive, they are also highly accurate and long-lasting. The "window" sets have a solid outline with a separate see-through inner section. Some "windows" are actually cut out in the middle, with a rigid ¼" (5mm) outline so you can draw the fabric pieces using the outside edge and make paper pieces exactly the right size using the inside edge. Others are multi-sized, with ¼" (5mm) variations. A sharp craft knife and self-healing cutting mat are essential when cutting templates by hand. There are two choices of template material: plastic and cardboard. While cardboard is useful for single templates, template plastic is better for making multiple pieces or patches since it holds its shape better and doesn't drag or tear at the sides.

Tips

Fabric Grain

All fabric has three "grains," or directions of woven threads. The lengthwise threads, the "warp," are strung on the loom, with the "weft" threads crossing them horizontally in and out, under and over. The rigid edges on each side of a length of fabric are called "selvages." The diagonal grain is the "bias." The warp and weft threads remain fairly stationary under tension, but the bias, which has more give and elasticity, stretches more easily and must be handled carefully.

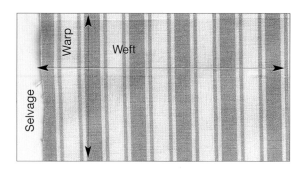

Cutting

The rotary cutter, ruler, and self-healing cutting mat have changed the face of patchwork and quilting in the past 20 years. They speed up the tedious process of cutting out by giving us unparalleled accuracy and allowing us to cut several layers at once, and the strips that we cut with them can be stitched speedily and chain-pieced. But scissors are still essential for cutting curves and templates, and for trimming and snipping threads. Keep three pairs handy: sharp fabric scissors for use with fabric only; paper scissors, which can also be used for cutting synthetic batting and templates, and small thread scissors. A seam ripper is vital for unpicking mistakes quickly. Rulers come in many sizes and shapes, from rectangles and squares in numerous dimensions, to triangles and curves that have specific uses. Most avid quilters have a selection.

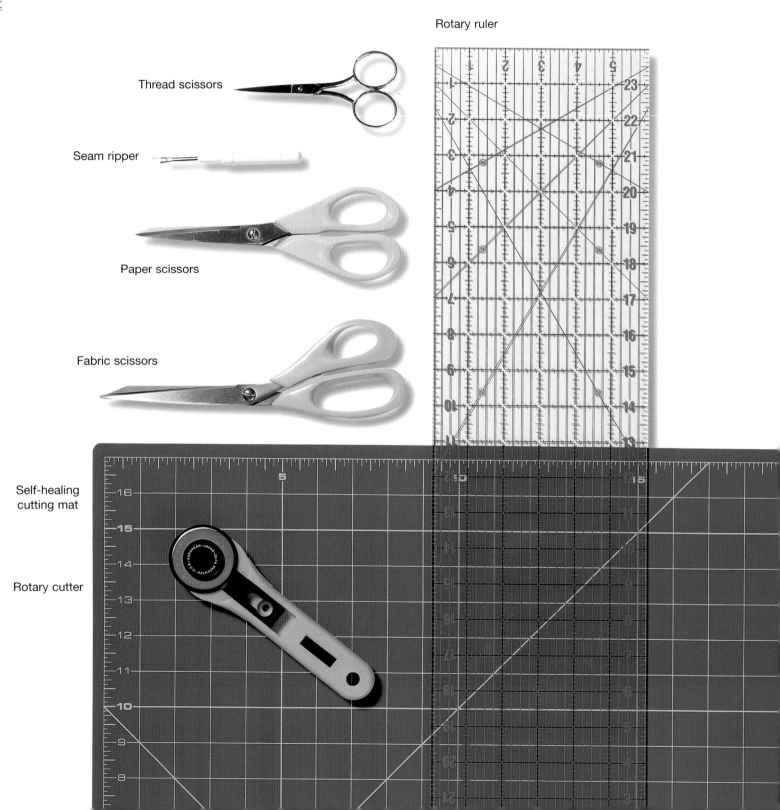

Rotary ruler

Thread scissors

Seam ripper

Paper scissors

Fabric scissors

Self-healing cutting mat

Rotary cutter

Rotary cutting

Rotary cutting is a method based on twentieth-century technology and the modern liking for speed in all things. You can use a rotary cutter for cutting fabric into strips for strip-piecing and for cutting individual patches with straight sides. When working with a rotary ruler and cutting mat, remember to align and measure the fabric with either the ruler or the mat—never both. There are many different versions of mats, rulers, and cutters available. If possible, experiment with them in classes or workshops before you buy.

Tips

Safety

Rotary cutters come in several sizes and configurations. They have very sharp blades, so remember to replace the safety guard after every use. Always cut away from yourself and use a self-healing cutting mat to protect your work surface.

Cutting strips

1 Fold the fabric along the straight grain to fit on the cutting mat. Place the ruler over the "good" fabric to avoid cutting into it, and hold it steady with one hand. Trim away the uneven edge, cutting away from yourself.

2 Turn the fabric so the ruler covers the area of fabric that you want to end up with. Using either the marked ruler or the mat to align and measure the fabric, cut strips of the desired width along the grain.

Cutting pieced strips

1 After stitching strips of fabric together, press the seams to one side. Then lay the pieced strip on the cutting mat, align the ruler across it, and cut into strips of the desired width.

2 You can either cut at right angles to the seams (*see step 1*) or diagonally at various angles, as shown here, to create short lengths for Seminole patchwork, for example.

DRAFTING AND MAKING TEMPLATES

The first stage in making patchwork is to make the patches. There are two basic methods: making templates so you can outline the shape to be cut out on the fabric, and rotary cutting. Making templates is the traditional way and is widely used for working irregular-shaped pieces, while the straight edges that can be cut quickly with a rotary cutter are easy to stitch into strips that speed up the process.

Making templates

The first step is to design and cut the templates. This book has a good selection of both block and quilting templates that you can simply trace in the section at the back (*see pages 416-445*). They do not include seam allowances, so you will need to add ¼" (5mm) all round, before you can transfer them onto template plastic ready for cutting out. However, if you are designing a quilt from scratch,

you must first draw your patchwork unit to finished size on graph paper. You will then need to trace the individual elements before you cut out the templates. The first step is to cut the template the exact size of each finished patch (*see below*). Then you must cut one with seam allowances added, known as a window template (*see opposite*), that can be used to cut backing papers.

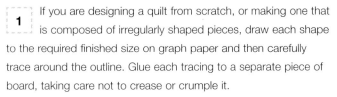

1 If you are designing a quilt from scratch, or making one that is composed of irregularly shaped pieces, draw each shape to the required finished size on graph paper and then carefully trace around the outline. Glue each tracing to a separate piece of board, taking care not to crease or crumple it.

2 Cut out the cardboard shape precisely, using a sharp craft knife and a straightedge or metal ruler. (It is best not to use plastic rulers, as it is very easy to accidentally cut into the ruler itself.) You will need to cut a seperate template for each shape in your design.

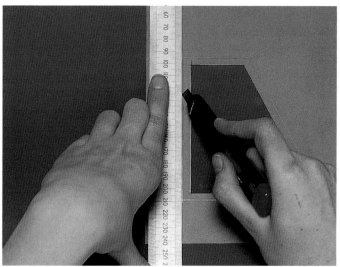

3 Lay the cardboard template on a sheet of template plastic and draw around the shape, adding ¼" (5mm) seam allowance on all of the sides. Use a quilter's quarter, as shown above, for accuracy. Then use a craft knife and metal ruler, to carefully cut out the inner "window."

4 Then cut the extended template around the outside edge. Draw around the outer section to mark fabric patches to the correct size, including seam allowances. Mark around the inner "window" to indicate the stitching line, and use the inner edge to draw any support papers.

Making Patches from Templates

In the "English" method of patchwork, fabric patches are mounted on backing paper for support during stitching. This is because many of the patches used for this method have bias-cut seams, which would stretch during assembly if they were not supported. Backing papers are cut to the finished size of each patch; fabric patches are cut along the outer edge of the window template to include seam allowances.

1 Draw the shape onto the backing paper, following the inner line of the window template. Cut a separate paper patch for every fabric patch.

2 Place the window template on the wrong side of the fabric, aligning the grain if possible. Draw around the template, inside and out, being careful not to pul and stretch the fabric. Cut out the fabric along the outer line. Pin a paper to the wrong side of every patch.

HAND PIECING

While many patterns lend themselves to the ease and security of machine stitching, others are more accurately worked by hand. There are a few traditional designs, especially among the curved patterns, which are difficult to stitch on the machine and are almost always hand-sewn.

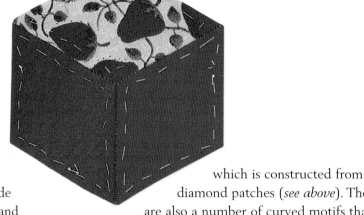

English Paper Piecing

The technique known as "English" paper piecing involves basting fabric shapes to backing papers made from fairly stiff paper to achieve the correct shape, and joining them by hand. This method is suitable for assembling patches with sharp angles or bias-cut seams, the advantage being that the papers support the fabric and prevent the seams from stretching. It was widely used in Britain and elsewhere during the heyday of Victorian quilting in the making of intricate designs, many of them worked in silk and velvet.

Although the "English" technique is time-consuming compared with rotary cutting and machine assembly, it is the usual way to assemble many traditional designs, including Grandmother's Flower Garden, which is formed from hexagonal patches, and Tumbling Blocks, which is constructed from diamond patches (*see above*). There are also a number of curved motifs that are cut and assembled using the "English" method, such as Clamshell and Double Axhead.

The first step in "English" paper piecing is to make and cut templates and to mark the cutting lines on the wrong side of the fabric (*see pages 18-19*). Window templates give you a consistently-sized seam allowance using the outer edge. You then need to cut a backing paper for every patch to the exact size of the finished patch using the inner edge of the window template. Some quilters now use freezer paper, which can be ironed in place and peeled off later, to make the backing papers.

1 Pin a backing paper to the wrong side of every fabric patch, matching the edges of the paper to the marked stitching line. Fold the seam allowance over the paper and baste it in place. Begin basting by pushing the needle through from the right side of the fabric, so that the knot is on the right side for easy removal later.

2 Place two patches right sides together and line them up carefully to make sure that the corners are level. Whipstitch the edges of the two pieces together, taking care not to stitch through the backing papers. You will need to leave the backing papers in place until all the blocks have been joined together.

3 Take a third patch and match the inside point. Working from the center out, whipstitch or slipstitch one side and then the other to complete the block. It is much easier to align each corner if you work from the center seam outward.

Straight seams

Some small patches with straight seams are fiddly to stitch by machine and these are often better stitched by hand. Patches can be joined with running stitch or backstitch. Pin your work carefully before you sew. Do not stitch into the seam allowances in case you need to trim them later.

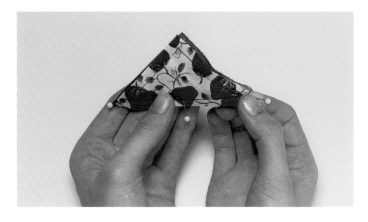

1 With right sides together, pin the patches along the straight seam, matching the corners on each piece. We have added a pin at the center; you may need more.

2 Sew along the marked seam, making sure you begin and end precisely at the corners. Handle all bias seams with care to avoid stretching the fabric.

Four-piece seams

1 Join two contrasting patches along the marked stitching line. Repeat and press the seams.

2 Pin the two units right sides together, first pushing a pin through the center seam to mark it precisely.

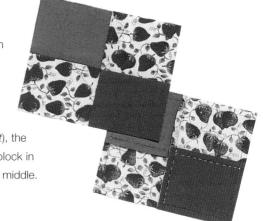

3 Working from the center out, use running stitch or backstitch to join the two units first on one side, then on the other.

4 As seen from the right side (*left*), the units have been turned into a block in which the corners meet exactly in the middle.

MACHINE PIECING

Quiltmakers have used sewing machines since early home models were introduced in the 1830s and '40s. Hand-turned and treadle machines are still widely used in many places, while electric versions have now quite often been computerized to enable them to carry out a wide variety of sewing tasks and decorative stitching.

Seam allowance

Patchwork is all about accuracy, and accuracy is all about careful measuring. This is especially important when you are stitching by machine, since if you make an error in estimating the size of a seam allowance that you need, it can result in blocks of differing sizes that do not fit together. Most machines can be fitted with a special foot that measures a precise ¼" (5mm) seam, but if you do not have one, you can mark the foot plate on the machine with a piece of masking tape at the correct distance from the needle and use it as a visual guide when stitching.

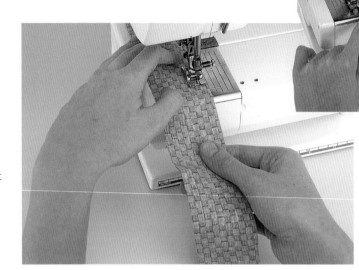

1 Here, two strips are being joined with right sides together on the machine. There is no need to pin or mark stitching lines, but it is vital that your seam allowances are even and that your stitching line is straight.

Joining pieced units

Pieced units are formed by joining several strips together along their length and then cutting them into short units. Here, two pieced units are being joined together with the colors alternating. To reduce bulk, it is very important to press the seams of each unit in opposite directions, before you start to join the units together.

1 Press the seams of each unit to one side. Place two units right side together so the pressed seams face in opposite directions; align seams and stitch carefully ¼" (5mm) from the raw edge.

2 The joined unit, shown here from both front and back, has evenly-matched rows with squared-up corners at each meeting point.

Chain piecing

This is a quick and easy way of stitching, since it allows you to sew in a continuous line, feeding prepared patches through the machine one after another without breaking the thread. If the technique is repeated at each stage in making a block, the piecing process is speeded up. Here, four sets of two-patch blocks are being joined together to create a chain of units. The chain is held together by short threads, which are cut apart once all the elements have been pieced together.

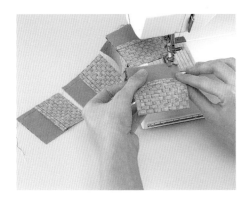

1 Place piles of units within reach and feed through the machine one after another, without lifting the foot or breaking the thread.

2 Cut the threads that hold the chain of units together once they have all been pieced.

Curves

Careful preparation and pinning is essential when stitching curved patches together by machine. The process is made more tricky by the bias-cut seams, which require careful handling to avoid stretching. It is a good idea to mark the stitching line on the wrong side of the fabric before you begin.

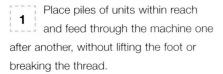

1 Placing pins at right angles to the curved edge, pin the patches right sides together, first in the center, then at each end, then in between.

2 Stitch along the marked line, removing pins as you go.

3 Press the seam toward the concave edges so that it lies flat.

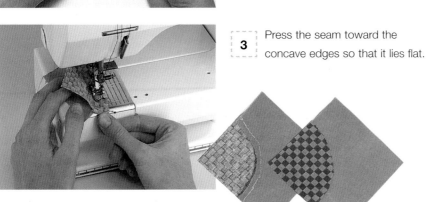

Tips

Unpicking seams

Sometimes you may need to unpick a stitched seam, either because you made a mistake or because the construction method involves sewing a series of seams that are then manipulated before one or more are opened up again. To avoid damaging fabric, use a seam ripper. Clean away bits of thread before re-stitching.

Ripping One Side

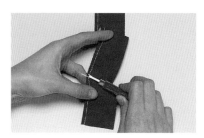

Holding the seam taut, insert the point of the seam ripper into every third or fourth stitch and break the thread.

Hold the bottom layer and pull the top layer gently to separate stitches.

Ripping Down the Middle

Holding the seam open, insert the ripper between the layers and break the thread. Gently pull the seam apart and repeat.

SASHING AND BORDERS

When all the blocks for a quilt are completed, they must be joined together. Some blocks are joined edge to edge, creating secondary patterns, while others need to be separated by narrow strips of fabric called sashing. Borders usually consist of a narrower inner one combined with a wider outer one.

Sashing

Sashing strips are used to separate blocks to emphasize the pattern in the block itself. They can be horizontal or vertical, or they can run diagonally if the blocks are set on point. Sashing is necessary on sampler quilts, and also on any design where the individual blocks need to be given a separate identity or emphasis.

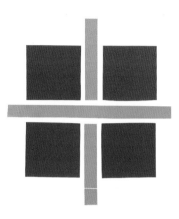

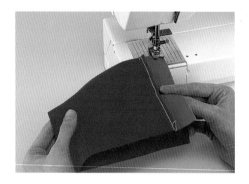

1 Cut sashing strips, ideally a little longer than the block to be sashed, to the chosen width plus seams.

2 Join a short strip to one side of the block, then join the next block to the other side of the strip.

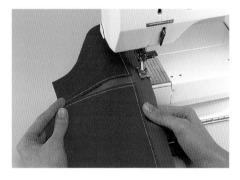

3 Open out the sashed unit and press seams to one side.

4 Stitch a long strip to the long side of the sashed unit, then join the remaining unit on the other side.

5 Open out and press seams to one side. The sashing strips form a perfect cross at the center.

Corners

Adding corner squares to borders or sashing will enhance a quilt beyond measure. Careful color planning is vital. Strong colors can be used to jazz up a plain or simple design, while complementary shades are very useful for drawing all the elements of a complex pattern together.

1 Cut strips for the borders and squares the same width for the corners. Stitch one square to each strip.

2 Line up the first strip so the seam is ¼" (5mm) from the top edge. Insert a pin 2" (5cm) from the top.

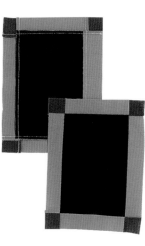

3 Working around the sides of the quilt in a clockwise direction, add the remaining strips, pressing the seams each time.

4 When you get back to the beginning again, incorporate the first square, continuing with the initial seam.

5 Note how the seams meet on the right side. On the wrong side, see how the seams are pressed in the direction indicated by the construction.

Straight Borders

The width of the border depends, of course, on the quilt itself. Its overall size, and the size and complexity of the blocks will set the tone for choosing borders. Inner borders are usually narrower than outer borders, which can be up to 4" (10cm) or more wide.

Top to bottom

Straight borders are added to the top and bottom (short) edges first. Side borders are then cut and added to each long edge.

Round and round

Start on any edge, 3–4" (7.5–10cm) down from the top corner. Apply the first strip, which must overhang the top edge of the quilt by at least the width of the strip. Add the second, third, and fourth strips, working in a counterclockwise direction. Finish by opening out the first strip and continuing the line of the stitching, catching in the end of the fourth strip. Square off all the corners if necessary.

Pieced borders

A well-executed pieced border gives a quilt extra pizzazz and flair. From left to right, Seminole chevrons, Flying Geese, squares, two-tone patches, and Prairie Points.

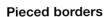

THE FOUR B'S OF QUILTING

The four Bs of quilting—batting, backing, bagging, and basting—are stages between finishing the quilt top and beginning the quilting. Batting is the fabric used to interline a quilt, backing is the fabric used for the back of the quilt, bagging is a way of finishing the raw edges, and basting is the stitching that holds the layers of the quilt in place before it is quilted.

Batting

Batting is the padded material used in the middle of the quilt to provide warmth and softness. Originally consisting of old blankets, remnants of fabric, or combed wool or cotton fiber, its modern equivalent is available cut to size or in rolls that can be measured like fabric. Synthetic polyester is the most widely used, with cotton and cotton/polyester blends also popular. Wool and silk versions are available, usually by special order.

Basting

Basting is used to hold the layers of the quilt together for quilting. It is done vertically and horizontally, and sometimes diagonally, with rows 4" (10cm) apart, and can be stitched or safety-pinned. Baste bound quilts before quilting; baste and quilt bagged quilts after bagging.

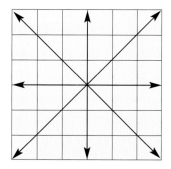

1 Always baste from the center outward, as is shown in the diagram above.

2 Sandwich the layers together and smooth out creases. You can insert safety pins at 4" (10cm) intervals.

3 If you prefer to thread-baste, take large, slanted running stitches, through all layers. Use a small spoon to press the layers together and catch the tip of the needle as it emerges.

Tips

Basting Spray

Basting spray is a relatively new product. It is a spray-on adhesive that will wash out easily, which can be used to "baste" quilt layers together without the need for any pins or stitching. It is quite simple to use and can save quite a bit of time, but make sure that you cover surrounding areas so they do not get a coating of adhesive.

1 Lay the batting flat and spray it all over with one light coat. Lay backing on it, right side up, and smooth carefully.

2 Repeat with the quilt top on the opposite side, wrong side to the batting. Try to spray evenly all over the surface.

Turning corners

There are times when you are sewing on a machine that you need to change direction sharply without breaking off threads—when you reach a corner, for example, or when you are machine-quilting a design that requires a sharp and precise change of direction in the quilting. To keep the thread continuous, you can raise the presser foot without lifting the needle out of the fabric, and turn the work to a different angle.

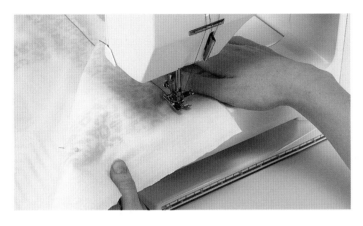

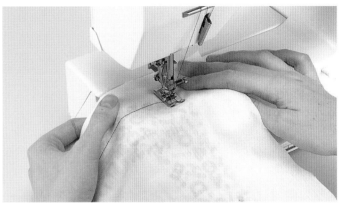

1 When you reach a corner, stop the machine a seam width from the perpendicular edge, leaving the needle in the fabric. Lift the presser foot, and turn the work at a right angle to the seam you have just stitched.

2 With the needle still in the fabric, lower the presser foot and continue stitching along the next seamline. This method is the same for all machine sewing.

Bagging

Although most quilts are quilted and then have their edges finished with a narrow binding, it is possible to join the three layers first by stitching them around all the edges, leaving a gap for turning them right side out. This procedure—bagging—must be carried out before the piece is quilted.

1 Lay the batting flat and place the quilt on top, right side up. Place the backing fabric right side down on top and smooth the wrinkles. Pin and stitch around the outside edges, leaving a 5–10" (20–25mm) opening for turning.

2 Cut away excess batting and backing fabric, trim the corners to reduce bulk, and turn the quilt right side out through the opening. Turn the raw edges of the opening to the inside and press. Slipstitch the opening closed.

Tips

Backing

Backing fabric usually matches or coordinates with the quilt top, and should be of a weight and weave that are easy to quilt. Most stores sell sheeting in extra-wide widths, which is ideal for backing a quilt. If neccessary, you can join several widths of fabric together. To avoid having the seam down the center, place a full width of backing fabric in the middle and a narrower panel on each side.

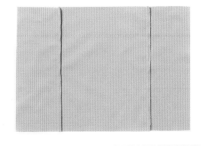

BINDING

Binding the edges is the final stage of making a quilt. Basic binding techniques are Single and Double Binding—applying narrow strips to the edges of all three layers at once; Edges to Middle; and Back to Front—folding the backing over to the front edges and stitching.

Single binding

This is the most common method used to finish the raw edges of a quilt. You can either buy prefolded binding to complement your quilt, or you can make it yourself. To do this, simply cut strips of fabric 1–2" (2.5–5cm) wide and then join them all together into very long lengths.

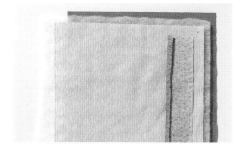

1 Mark a point in each corner ¼" (5mm) in from each side edge. Press a ¼" (5mm) seamline along one long edge of the binding strips. Trim the layers carefully.

2 Place the binding right side down on the quilt top, aligning the unpressed edge with the raw edge of the quilt. Stitch in place, starting and finishing at the marked point.

3 Open out the stitched binding and pin a new strip along the adjacent edge. Stitch between marked points, taking care not to catch the first strip in the stitching line.

4 When all the edges have been stitched, turn the binding to the quilt back to cover the raw edges and pin carefully in place.

5 When you reach a corner, fold the cut edge at the end of each strip to the inside and square off the corner. To finish, pin and slipstitch around all of the edges.

Double binding

This method makes a version stronger than a single binding because it involves using double-thickness strips of binding. It is ideal for quilts that will be laundered frequently, especially baby quilts.

1 Cut strips twice as wide as the finished binding plus ½" (10mm) seam allowances. Fold in half lengthwise, wrong sides together, and press flat.

2 Mark, pin, and stitch as for Single Binding, sewing along double thickness raw edges of the binding. Turn the folded edge to the back and slipstitch in place to finish.

Edges to middle

For this technique, the batting is cut slightly smaller than the backing and quilt top. The raw edges of the backing are folded over the edges of the batting to enclose them, and the edges of the quilt top are folded to the inside. The edges of all three layers can then be stitched down.

1 Cut the batting ¼" (5mm) smaller all around than the backing. Fold the backing edges over the batting and pin. Turn the edges of the quilt top under and pin.

2 Secure in place with a double row of top stitching. The first row should be ¼" (5mm) from the finished edge; the second row should be ¼" (5mm) in from that.

Back to front

Here, the batting is cut the same size as the quilt top, but the backing is cut larger all around. The edges of the backing are folded to the front and make a strong, neat edge.

1 Turn ¼" (5mm) to the wrong side on all edges of the backing. Center the quilt top and batting on the backing. Fold a miter at each corner and carefully trim the seam allowance.

2 Fold the pressed edges of the backing to the front of the quilt and pin in place. Stitch neatly by hand, or machine stitch along all sides. Slipstitch the miters to finish.

Tips

Mitering corners

Mitering is an attractive way of finishing a corner with a 45-degree angle. It is used in quiltmaking most often on borders and binding.

Mitered corners must be neat and precise. Smooth, even mitered corners give a professional finish to the edges of a quilt. Accurate pressing can help you achieve a sharp line along which to work.

1 Cut strips longer than the quilt sides, plus twice the border width. Mark a point ¼" (5mm) from the corner of the quilt and apply a strip in each direction, starting at the mark.

2 Fold back each strip to a 45-degree angle and press to mark the fold (*top right corner*). Working from the right side, pin along the fold to hold the seam in place.

3 Turn to the wrong side and re-pin at right angles to the fold. Match the two folds precisely and stitch from the inner corner to the edge. Trim the ends.

2 PATCHWORK TRADITIONS

Hexagon Crazy Quilt with Log Cabin Stars c. 1890
The dark-outlined stars on this magnificent Victorian quilt are made from six diamond Log Cabin blocks. The lavishly embellished Crazy Patchwork hexagon blocks set between them are beautifully worked with myriad embroidered motifs typical of the era, including a number of different flowers as well as birds and other animals, a good-luck horseshoe, and some household objects like the red vase and the teapot. Many Kate Greenaway-style children, like the two on a seesaw seen here, appear on quilts of the late nineteenth century.

STRIPS & SQUARES

LOG CABIN

• This attractive Log Cabin quilt is constructed of a selection of wool and cotton fabrics, with a wide woven plaid border. It was made by an unknown quiltmaker in around 1860. Extra strips of fabric have been added at the top and bottom inside the border, presumably to make the whole thing longer. The large center squares in various shades of red enliven the otherwise somewhat sober colors. Minnesota Historical Society

Strips are among the earliest shapes to be incorporated into quilts, and they are used with great effect to make the pattern known as Log Cabin, and all its variations. No one knows where the design originated. Mummies in ancient Egyptian tombs have been discovered wrapped in cloths constructed in the log cabin pattern, and quiltmakers on the Isle of Man, an autonomous territory in the Irish Sea between Britain and Ireland, have long created work in the Log Cabin design. Called Rooftop locally, the blocks were traditionally stitched to a square of backing that gave stability to the thin strips in the pattern, and presumably also added a layer of warmth for the harsh climate of the island.

Quiltmakers in Britain were making the pattern at the beginning of the nineteenth century. Quilt historian Jean Dubois tells in her book *Patchwork Quilting with Wool* of one Englishwoman, Mary Morgan, who immigrated to the southern United States in the 1830s with a Barn Raising log cabin quilt.

The pattern is found in quilts made in England's West Country—Devon and Cornwall—as well as the North of England, especially in County Durham, Northumberland, and the Scottish borders. Most likely the pattern for the early examples found in Canada was taken there by Scottish settlers who went from the Hebrides Islands to Quebec, where the winters were just as harsh and probably even colder, and the warmth of quilts helped ward off the icy blasts carried on the Arctic winds across the Canadian plains.

American tradition holds that the pattern's name is associated with the 1859–60 presidential campaign of Abraham Lincoln. Certainly Honest Abe's background as the son of settlers who lived in a log cabin was an important part of the president's bid for office, but Log Cabin quilts had been around

for quite a while before Lincoln's election.

Both before and after the Civil War large numbers of Log Cabin quilts were made in the United States, and the pattern's popularity carried into the late nineteenth century. Indeed, during the 1870s, Log Cabin quilts were so widely made that the organizing committees at many county and state fairs created specific categories for displaying and judging them.

Early versions were usually made from wool, both warm and easily accessible in all the places where we know the pattern existed. However, as the design's popularity increased, other fabrics, from cotton to silk, satin, and even velvet, were used. Victorian quiltmakers also used ribbons, usually made of silk, instead of fabric for the strips.

Constructing a Log Cabin block

The basic Log Cabin design is worked by positioning strips of fabric in a particular sequence around a central square of cloth. The strips get longer as each round is added, and they are laid one after the other like the logs used to build a traditional log house. When the block was made in the Isle of Man, tradition says that it represented the constructing of a roof. And in at least one African-American community—Gee's Bend, Alabama—the widely made pattern is called Housetop.

Traditionally, the center square was made of red fabric, supposedly representing either the chimney or the hearth, the center of the home. Some old examples have yellow centers, said to represent a lantern in the window, while others are dark. Perhaps the light had gone out in the maker's life.

In the regular block, two adjacent sides are made with pale fabric and the other two are dark, giving a finished square divided diagonally into light and dark values.

• The multicolored Courthouse Steps blocks in this quilt, which dates from around 1890, have been made in a variety of silk and cotton fabrics. Each strip was folded lengthwise before it was stitched in place—a technique often found in older quilts, and which makes them quite thick.

• This beautiful Barn Raising Log Cabin quilt was made in Whitestone, New York, by Mary Jane Smith (1833-69) and her mother, Mary Morrell Smith (1798-1869) for the daughter's trousseau, from cotton, wool, and silk between 1861 and 1865. Because her bridegroom died of pneumonia the day before the wedding, and both Mary Jane and her mother three years later, the quilt was never used. It is the oldest quilt in the collection of the American Folk Art Museum in New York City, a gift of Mary D. Bromham, a grandniece of the younger maker.

There are, however, a number of versions of the block, some of which have different color values opposite to one another.

There are various ways to make a block. The oldest known method has a foundation square of plain fabric, usually muslin (calico) or homespun, on which the hearth square is centered. Strips are stitched onto the foundation by hand or machine around the center, usually two light, and then two dark (or vice versa) working either clockwise or counterclockwise until the block reaches the desired size. Some strips, especially on older quilts, are doubled lengthwise; others are made from a single layer of fabric, a method

known today as "stitch and flip." As each strip is added, it is pressed to the right side, hence the name of the technique: press-piecing. In fact, quilts made in the Log Cabin design were often known as "pressed quilts."

An up-to-date version of foundation fabric can be used to make quilts of quite amazing accuracy. It is possible to purchase interfacing that comes with a grid already marked on it, so the fabrics can be added using the grid as the stitching lines.

Modern quiltmakers tend to use a chain-piecing technique to make Log Cabin quilts. This method involves cutting squares and strips with rotary cutting equipment and

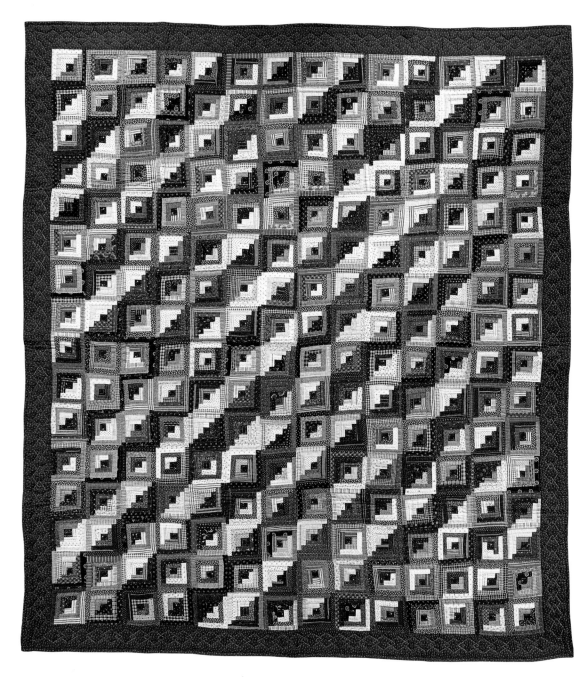

• This Straight Furrow Log Cabin from about 1875 comprises 224 blocks. The red centers are a mere 1" (2.5 cm) square, and each block has only three rounds of scrappy strips. The piece is framed by an unusual wide blue border. Look for the "superstition" block in the middle left-hand section, a deliberate mistake introduced into many quilts of the time on the principle that "only God can make something perfect."

• The quilt opposite, made c.1850, is a good example of the Barn Raising set. The black and gray cotton strips used for half of each block create a dark background for the brightly colored strips on the light sides, each with its typical red center. The quilt has narrow black binding edges and a dark brown print back. Minnesota Historical Society

machine-stitching a number of blocks, one stage at a time. This technique is widely used to teach beginners the basics of speed piecing in workshops, so many quiltmakers have a Log Cabin quilt that was made quite early on in their careers.

Another popular construction method is a quilt-as-you-go technique, in which the strips and center squares are worked on a foundation of both batting and backing. Because the blocks are already quilted once the strips are in position, they can quickly be joined together into a finished piece of three layers without the requirement for any further quilting.

Variations

There are a number of well-known variations to the standard Log Cabin block, made by varying the sequence of adding strips, their width, the shape or position of the center, or by adding small shapes at the end of each strip.

Courthouse Steps, or White House Steps (*see page 35*), is constructed by adding strips of equal length to opposite sides of the center and alternating lights and darks. This gives a design with steps along the diagonals. If the center is black, tradition holds that it represented the judge in his robes.

Regular blocks usually have strips of the same width, but they can be cut "thick and

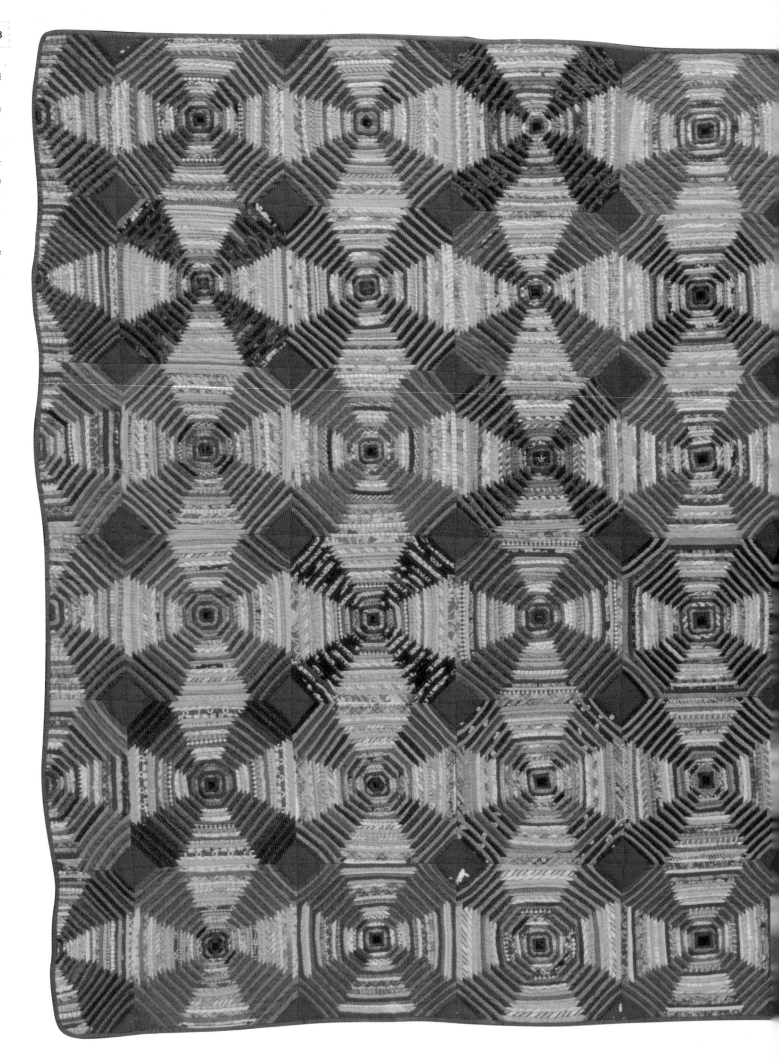

thin" and alternated in the block. If two adjacent strips are wide and the other two narrow, they create a design known as Asymmetrical or Off-Center Log Cabin, which makes a pleasing visual, but not an actual, curve.

If the center square is turned "on point," or with its straight edges diagonal to the sides of the block, the resulting block is called Hung Center Log Cabin. Best worked on a foundation, the finished block will need to be squared up by trimming the ends of the strips.

Placing the center square in one corner of the block creates the Chevron or Echo Log Cabin design (*see page 42*), when strips are added to two sides of the square instead of the usual four.

When strips of different color values are alternated row by row, with, say, four dark strips, then four light, the variation is known as Cabin in the Cotton. Another similar version varies the width of the strips, as well.

If small squares the same width as the strips are added at the end of each new strip, or every second one, a more complex pattern known as Cornerstones, or Chimneys and Cornerstones, develops with a diagonal line of contrasting color running through each block.

Other shapes can be used as the center of the block. Rectangles, triangles, diamonds, pentagons, hexagons, octagons, and irregular straight-sided pieces are found in variations of Log Cabin designs, but keep in mind that many of them work best if they are mounted on a foundation.

The variation known as Pineapple or Windmill Blades is more complex than the regular design and it must be planned and pieced with great care. It consists of eight strips in each round, four parallel with the four sides of the center square, and four contrasting ones in each corner. If the corner strips are decidedly smaller than the horizontal and vertical ones, a further variation that is commonly called Flying Geese Pineapple results.

An interfacing-weight backing is available that comes already marked up with a grid of horizontal, vertical, and diagonal lines, and this can make the piecing of Pineapple blocks rather quicker and far more accurate.

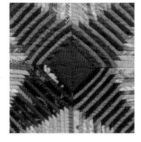

• Made in the 1850s by Rebecca Moore Herrick, this multicolored Pineapple quilt contains very narrow cotton, wool, and velvet strips left over from home dressmaking. This pattern, also called Windmill Blades, has been beautifully fashioned mainly from red, black, and shades of brown. A narrow grayish binding on three sides becomes a dark print on the fourth edge. The quilt is backed with a blackish-brown cotton print.
Minnesota Historical Society

• This highly graphic modern-looking Windmill Blades quilt was in fact made in the last quarter of the nineteenth century. The blue fabrics are all prints and almost all different, which makes the consistency of tone throughout the quilt all the more interesting. Made in Ohio, it is lightly quilted.

Setting patterns

One of the main reasons for the enduring popularity of the Log Cabin pattern is its versatility when blocks are joined together, or "set." Because there are so many ways in which the individual blocks can be combined, the variations in the design—in the form of secondary patterns—are virtually limitless. Log Cabin blocks are traditionally joined edge to edge, without sashing to interrupt the emerging pattern created by the choice of set.

If blocks are placed with dark sides adjacent to each other and light sides likewise next to one another, the resulting pattern is called Light and Dark, or Sunshine

and Shadow, or Sunshine and Shade (*see page 98*). Squares of contrasting light and dark form a regular pattern across the quilt.

In Barn Raising (known in Kentucky as Light and Dark Paths), light and dark sides are set into adjacent rows so the center of the quilt is a square on point of one value surrounded by concentric diagonal rows of the opposite shading (*see page 34*). If the blocks themselves are set on point throughout the quilt, the concentric rows become squares or rectangles.

The Straight Furrow setting, with its blocks placed so that diagonal lines of dark alternate with light, is reminiscent of plowed fields. If light sides touch light and dark ones are next

• This Pineapple quilt made between 1880 and 1900 by Ada Hapman (Mrs. William) Kingsley (1859-1939) of South Windsor, New York, or Athens, Pennsylvania, was never used because, according to her granddaughter, it was the only one she made from silk. She must have saved scraps over a long period, but the planning she did is evident in the use of three shadings instead of the usual light and dark. The dark horizontal areas are made from a consistently even fabric, while most of the vertical darks are brighter and more scrappy. The exception is the last up-and-down dark bar on the extreme right, which turns abruptly into the brighter palette toward the bottom. The light areas also contain many brights, but the tones work beautifully. The black scalloped ice-cream cone border is alternated with brightly colored strippy triangles. Collection of the American Folk Art Museum, New York Gift of Margaret Cavigga

to dark, the rows are truly straight (*see page 37*). If all the blocks face in the same direction, the rows are still clearly diagonal, but the effect is jagged.

There are dozens of Zigzag setting patterns, from Streak of Lightning, to Lazy S and Z. Remember that many of the individual block variations can also be used in most of the setting patterns.

Fabrics and finishing

Color values are crucial to making a successful Log Cabin quilt. The contrasts between lights and darks can be hard to judge, so fabrics need to be planned carefully, especially if you are using scraps. Solids work

beautifully, and patterned fabrics are also widely used, but remember that the pattern on large-scale prints will probably be broken up in ways that alter the color balance. Geometric patterns such as checks, stripes, and plaids depend on their own internal color contrasts, which may make it hard to assign them a value. Use them with caution.

Because there are so many pieces in a Log Cabin quilt, they can have a busy feel, and embellishment is rarely found. The main exception is in Victorian examples with embroidered centers, often floral motifs.

Quilting is generally minimal on Log Cabin quilts. Because there are so many seams in the piecing and because intricate quilting patterns

• Chevron, or Half Log Cabin, is made with the starting square in one corner. This unusual example from the last quarter of the nineteenth century shows a variety of cotton fabrics typical of the era, with a mixture of red and gold squares, and small-scale prints for the strips, which show well-planned arrangements of color values. String has been used to tie the layers together in the corner of each block.

• The highly unusual silk Victorian-style quilt opposite is Triangular Log Cabin, with each block of color constructed around an equilateral triangle, usually made of the same fabric as the strips. The triangle blocks alternate dark and light around dark hexagons, and the piece is bordered by a wide band of olive green velvet. The backing is a red and green floral print. Minnesota Historical Society

would be lost in the design, many modern quiltmakers prefer to quilt simple patterns by machine. Tying with thread, string, or yarn is another popular option, and was widely used on old quilts. Quilts made on foundation squares need not be quilted at all, and many old examples have been made with no batting. Such quilts had body and warmth, and were often used as bedspreads, and summer-weight covers, as well as table covers or throws. If Log Cabin quilts have borders, they are usually narrow and rather plain. However, Victorian examples sometimes had ruffles, lace, or fringe edgings, much of it handmade. The edges were often finished simply by turning under the raw edges of the top and the backing, and stitching them together.

• This simple Four-Patch pattern has a variety of names, Double Pinwheel, Yankee Puzzle, and Big Dipper among them. The consistency of color—bright red and navy blue—is maintained effectively in spite of the use of a number of different prints of both. The quilting is finely worked: a simple cable decorates the borders, and the individual pieces in each unit of the blocks have been outline-quilted. On the sashing, rows of flying-geese triangles start in the center of the block and point toward the corners, where they meet to form Xs. Because this block is fairly easy to construct and can be done with speed-piecing methods, it is still popular even today, more than a century since this quilt was made.

FOUR-PATCH

The Four-Patch block is one form of block patchwork, sometimes called American block patchwork, which did not actually originate in the United States, but which both flourished and grew as an American tradition from the middle of the nineteenth century. Many of the traditional designs in block patchwork were known and worked in Britain during the period when the American colonies were being settled, but the examples that have survived are found mainly in the borders that make up the "frames" of late eighteenth- and early nineteenth-century medallion quilts, in which a large center

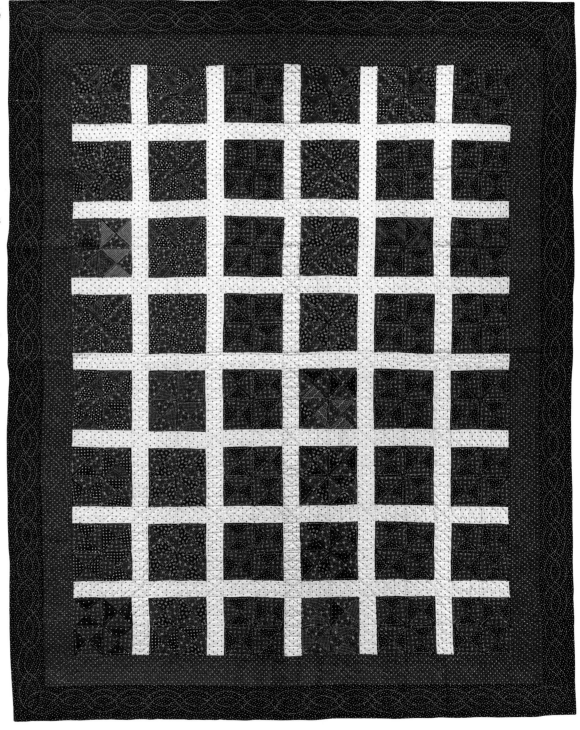

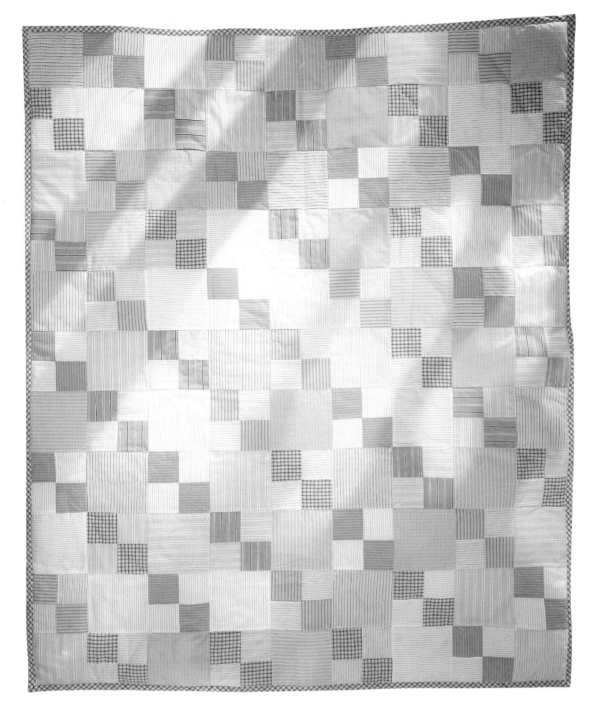

• The fabrics used in this cotton quilt from the 1990s are all old men's shirts, stripes and plaids, recycled to make simple four-patch blocks that alternate lights and darks. The Four-Patch blocks are in turn separated by plain spacer blocks cut from striped shirts and turned in different directions, and together with the bias-cut gingham binding, enliven the piece in subtle ways. The layers are quilted in the traditional utilitarian way: each corner of the blocks has a tie made of mercerized cotton.

square or rectangle is "framed" by strips of varying widths and contrasting patterns and colors to make up a full-size quilt.

When the early colonists arrived in North America, an ocean away from their European homelands—mainly Britain, Holland, France, Germany, and Spain—they had to make do with what they had brought with them, what they could grow and produce themselves, and what could be imported from their mother countries. Journeys from Europe were long and perilous, and the price of fabric—all of which had to be carried across the Atlantic—

reflected this fact for years after the first settlers set foot on the American mainland. In addition, during the English colonial period, it was illegal for private citizens in the colonies to own either spinning wheels or looms, so fabric was both extremely scarce and exorbitantly expensive. Thrifty housewives saved every tiny scrap cut from dressmaking projects, and both worn-out clothes and household linens were hoarded to be mined for the good bits that could be cut out and used again. Also, most homes were small and cramped, and many of them

• Ten different small-scale prints have been used to make this Windmill baby quilt, which is composed of twelve Four-Patch Pinwheel blocks that alternate with quarter-size Hourglass blocks. Placing the reds and blues adjacent to one another creates the pattern of the blades whirling in the breeze. Two narrow dark blue borders are finished by a bright red binding.

• The dramatic colors of the Pinwheel blocks in this small quilt are reminiscent of the East. Quilts with simple geometric designs similar to the one on this late twentieth century quilt have been made in India and Pakistan for centuries. Bright, highly contrasting colors are part of the textile heritage of the area, and each one carries its symbolism. Red is the color of love and saffron yellow evokes the earth. Colored blocks alternate with black and white ones arranged in diagonal rows.

were occupied by large extended families, so there was often very little space to keep large sewing projects on hand.

Some of the patterns that were often used lent themselves to being assembled as blocks over a period of time. They could be stored much more easily like this, until enough blocks had been assembled to make a whole quilt, and combining the larger pieces could be done fairly quickly. When the lands beyond the Appalachian Mountains were

opened up to American settlers, and especially after the Louisiana Purchase of 1803 added much of the land west of the Mississippi River to the fledgling country, thousands of pioneer families headed west, carrying familiar techniques and a redoubled need for thrift with them. Storage space was, if anything, even more precious on the frontier, and new fabrics were almost nonexistent, so blocks became the staple of American quiltmaking.

• Made between 1875 and 1900, this cotton quilt in a pattern called Goose Tracks has been color-planned with great care. Each corner of every block is made from a different fabric, but when the blocks are joined, each corner meets three others made of the same fabric. The white sashing with the bright pink corner squares separates the blocks and makes the pattern more complex and interesting. Each piece is outline quilted, with a simple cable quilting border.

• The cotton quilt opposite was made around 1930–49 either by Margaret (Mrs. Ernest) Larsen Larson, or by her grandmother, Martha Larsen of Saint Paul, Minnesota. The design consists of four triangles of two fabrics. Solid, floral, geometric, and paisley prints are all used, but there is no batting. Minnesota Historical Society

Four-Patch blocks

Many of the best-known traditional patchwork patterns are blocks based on square or rectangular grids that contain units of shapes. Blocks can be put together in combinations of four, five, seven, nine (or even more) "patches" using familiar geometric shapes—squares, rectangles, diamonds, triangles—or irregular pieces, for which you may need a template.

The simplest of these designs is the Four-Patch, which uses four units, sometimes identical, sometimes not, to make each block. Blocks are then combined to create patterns with evocative names like Pinwheel (*see page 48*), Hourglass, Crosses and Losses, Yankee Puzzle (*see page 44*), Broken Dishes (*see page 53*), and Fox and Geese, to name but a few. Many Four-Patch patterns are made from sixteen units, in which case they are often called Double Four-Patch.

As always, the contrast between light and dark values determines the effectiveness of the pattern. Values can be determined by visual texture as well as by color, and fascinating contrasts can occur when plain fabrics are put next to patterned ones, or when different shades or tones of the same color are juxtaposed. Because a color's value can be determined in part by the color next

to it, a color that looks quite light in isolation can appear much darker set next to a much paler shade.

Alternating colors cause a grid pattern to emerge when blocks are combined. If the blocks are turned on point, a diamond grid is created. When plain "spacer" blocks are used between each pieced block, a different effect is achieved. The same rules of color and setting together of blocks apply to the other similar grids—Five, Seven, and Nine-Patch—as well. Middle of the range values can also change the look of the fabrics set next to them. Curved blocks can also be set in several different ways, and again the same color rules will apply.

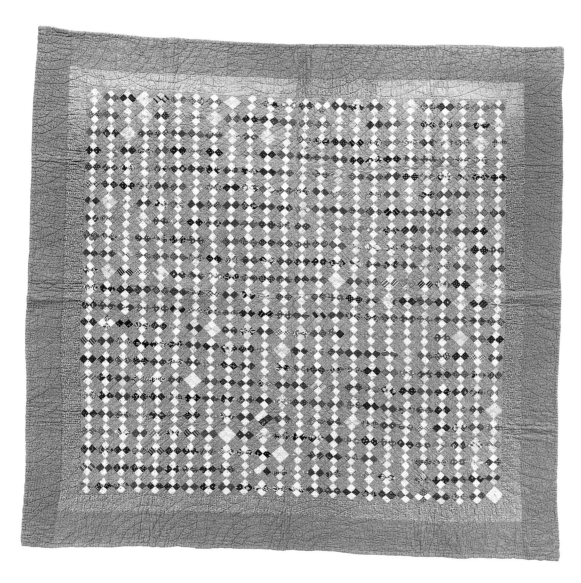

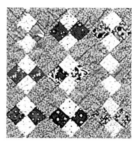

• This lively late nineteenth-century quilt contains 552 light-and-dark Four-Patch blocks made from a selection of dark prints combined with white or cream light units. The blocks are turned on point and alternated with the same number of double-pink plain squares. Mottled double-pink fabrics, printed in two shades, were very popular during this period. The quilting is simple: straight diagonal lines across the blocks, and fans that tie the two borders together.

Block construction

The basic Four-Patch is probably the simplest patchwork block of all, and many children through the ages have learned to sew by making Four-Patch blocks. The block consists of four squares of the same size stitched together two-by-two into a larger square. These blocks can be strip-pieced by stitching two strips of fabric together along their length, then cutting the resulting pieced strip into new strips across the width and joining these rectangular units in a different order, usually with the colors reversed, to make an overall grid of alternating squares of color.

Four-Patch blocks can be used as corner squares in sashing and on borders, and blocks can also be joined into strips and used to make both sashing and borders. Very effective Strippy quilts can be made by using strips of Four-Patch blocks alternating with plain strips, and they can also be used to make the center of Log Cabin blocks.

Variations of basic Four-Patch

The units in Four-Patch blocks (and in the other types of grid) can be divided into smaller squares or bars, squares can be cut in half or quarters along the diagonals to create right-angle triangles, and simple squares can be set on point with four triangular corners to make a square inside a square. These combinations can then be reassembled into even more complex combinations that provide vast numbers of possibilities for new designs. Most can be strip-pieced using modern equipment and techniques that let us create beautiful machine-stitched versions, or they can be sewn in the time-honored traditional way—by hand.

Drafting patterns for Four-Patch blocks is relatively easy. You will need squared graph paper, a ruler, a pencil, and an eraser. You can either draw a single block, and then take measurements from it to rotary-cut and strip-piece blocks, or you can make templates to

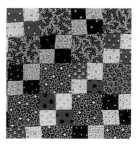

• Double-pinks have been combined with another color—acid green—that was widely used around 1885, the period when this quilt was made in New York state. Four-Patch blocks have been set edge-to-edge to make the diamond center and alternated with green spacer blocks in each corner. More Four-Patch blocks set on point make the pieced border.

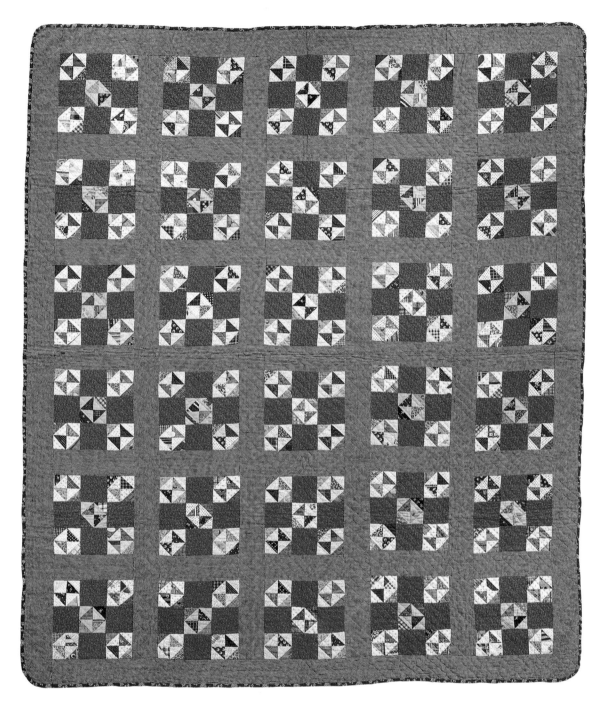

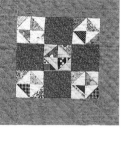

• Four-Patch Broken Dishes blocks made from scraps are combined with plain blocks into Nine-Patch units in this Double Square quilt made between 1875 and 1900. The random fabrics that make up the Four-Patch units are nevertheless carefully chosen, and the brown sashing and border work with the red spacer blocks to make a coherent background for the piece. A typical brown print binds the quilt.

• British quiltmaker Rose Epton-Peter of Poole in Dorset has used two sizes of Four-Patch block in combination with corner triangles and nine-patch blocks to make this lovely Amish-style quilt. The randomly placed plain fabrics in bright jewel colors and black are echoed in the inner and outer borders, and the strong diagonal lines of the piece create a lively feel.

use as patterns to cut out the individual pieces. Exactly the same methods can also be used to make all the Five-, Seven-, or Nine-Patch patterns. Balancing the sizes of the various components of the block, and of the blocks themselves, is the key to creating the most successful design.

Four-Patch blocks can be quilted in a number of ways. Simple outline or in-the-ditch quilting can be used to hold the layers together, especially on quilts made from busy fabrics, where an elaborate quilting pattern would be completely lost. Grids or lines that cross the diagonals or go straight through the middle of the four units can be utilized to add texture. Plain and unpieced Four-Patch units can contain individual quilted motifs, as can the spacer blocks that are sometimes used to separate pieced blocks. Borders on Four-Patch quilts—wide or narrow, pieced or plain, light or dark—offer a way for quilters to show off their skills, but should always complement the overall feel of the quilt—as should all the quilting patterns used, curved or straight, single or double lines.

• This Japanese-inspired throw by British quiltmaker Janet Haigh contains a variety of blocks—Four-patch, Nine-patch, and Mosaic—as well as appliquéd "noble" medallion shapes. The noble motifs on kimonos worn by actors in Japanese **No** theater indicate male characters in the highly stylized traditional plays performed by **No** companies, in which all the roles are performed by men. The two Nine-patch blocks shown are variations of the Ohio Star pattern.

• British quilter Magie Relph made this lively machine-pieced and quilted Nine-Patch wall hanging from African prints and striped shirt material to explore curved seaming, after she had attended a workshop taught by Colin Brandi. She calls the quilt "Free Fallin'."

NINE-PATCH

Like the Four-Patch block, the Nine-Patch has myriad variations and very widespread appeal to quiltmakers. The history of Nine-Patch parallels that of other traditional quilt blocks, with its main difference being the number of squares in the grid. There are probably more Nine-Patch patterns around than any other configuration—most likely because of the variety afforded by the wide number of possible combinations.

Like all patchwork, both the choice and juxtaposition of color is the crucial element in the success or failure of a Nine-Patch design. On the whole, strong contrasts tend to work best, although many beautiful quilts in muted colors do exist. Historical examples are often made from scraps, and they provide fascinating chances to study both the use of color and the history of fabric, since such a quilt may have been made over an extended period using a selection of fabrics collected at different times. Patterned fabrics can be combined with plain ones in endless combinations, using many colors, or—especially graphic to the modern eye—just two. There are numerous antique quilts made from only two colors—often blue, red, or black combined with white or

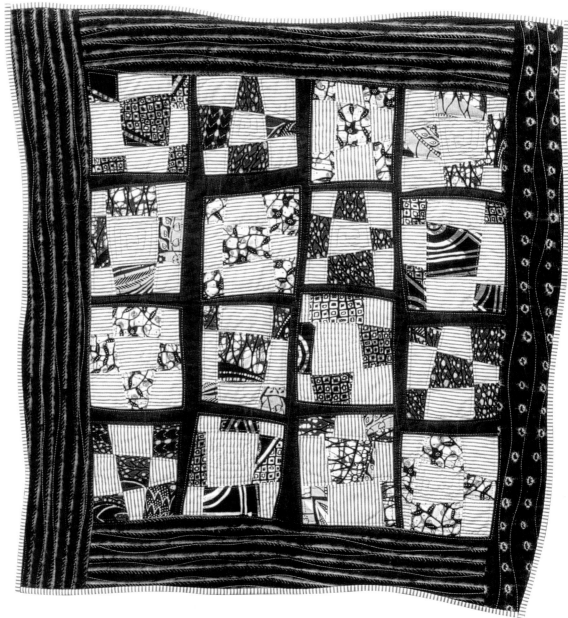

• All the blocks in this Nine-Patch Amish quilt are set on point, with pieced blocks alternating with plain spacer blocks. As the outer corner units of the Nine-Patch blocks are the same color as the spacers, the darker middle and center squares become crosses that seem to float above the background. The pieced blocks are outline-quilted, then quilting has been worked across the diagonal of the light blue corner units in each block to create secondary squares of pattern.

• This Nine-Patch linsey quilt from about 1850 is made from garment scraps of coarse handwoven linsey-woolsey, woven with a cotton warp and wool weft. The dark colors are typical of the time, when linsey was used to make men's clothing, while striped fabrics were often found in women's skirts. Quilts of Tennessee

cream—that are wonderfully striking. Different fabrics may have been used in these quilts, but with a consistency of tone that carries off the overall design beautifully.

Some blocks work best set edge to edge with no spacing between them, while others deserve to be set apart from their neighbor with either sashing strips or plain spacer blocks. Many of the most effective patterns are made by alternating two different types of pieced block to create the quilt. Sashing the blocks can create an entirely new pattern, and most block quilts need a border or two to contain them.

Developing complex patterns

While many different patterns were worked in the new territories of the young United States in the mid- to late-nineteenth century, the eastern seaboard of the country was becoming more stable and economically secure, especially after the Civil War of 1861-1865. As the older areas of the country became more settled and manufacturing and trade increased, quiltmakers could spend more time creating new, interesting designs. Many of the block patterns that we today consider traditional became popular, and myriad variations were developed by the

• Double Nine-Patch blocks are set on point, spaced and bordered with sharp green in this quilt from c.1885. The Double Nine-Patch blocks are quilted, like the rest of the piece, with straight lines in a grid. Because the blocks are on point, the stitching is worked through the diagonal of each square. Beamish Museum

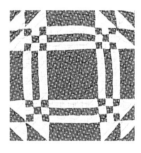

• Patterns of squares, triangles, and bars all contribute to the complexity of this design, known as either Goose in the Pond or Gentleman's Fancy. The use of many blue fabrics, combined in a way that denotes a scrap quilt, makes a highly graphic piece made between 1890 and 1910 seem fresh and very modern, especially against the stark white background of plain spacer blocks. The blue stripe of the inner border is not found anywhere else on the quilt.

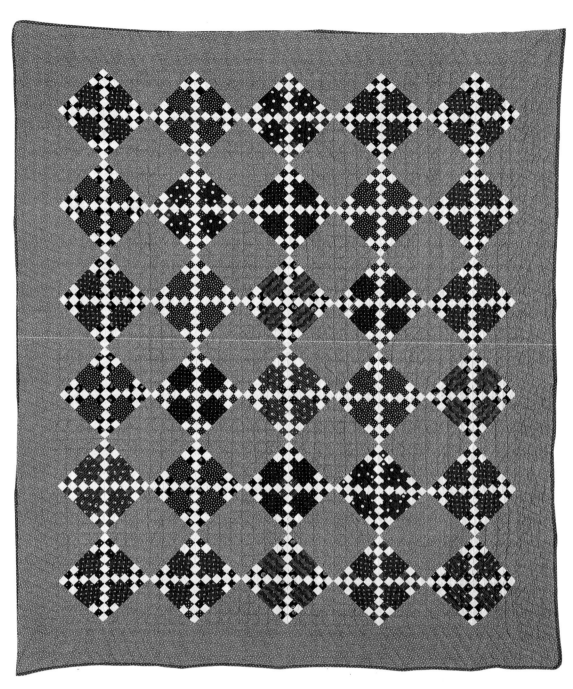

quiltmakers of the time. Drafting patterns was relatively simple, as true today as it was in the past, and—as any quiltmaker who experiments will know—even just switching the lights and darks in a block will sometimes create an entirely new design.

Basic Nine-Patch

The basic Nine-Patch block is based on a simple three-by-three grid of squares. Because the number three divides evenly into so many other numbers—for instance, 6", 9", 12", and 15" are all frequently used as block sizes in patchwork quilts—the Nine-Patch is an extremely popular configuration. It is much more versatile than Four-, Five- or Seven-Patch, but the same principles of design and overall balance still apply to all.

A Nine-Patch block can either be made from individual squares, or it can be strip-pieced by joining three strips of fabric lengthwise into one wider strip, with twice as many of one configuration as of the other. Strips are then cut across the width of the new pieced strip and combined in a particular order to make a block with nine units, which will speed up cutting and assembling the blocks considerably. In its

• This Amish-style wall hanging made in 1997 by Carol Clay shows what happens to a Shoofly Nine-Patch block when darks and lights are switched. The same four colors are used in each block, but the effect is different in each because of the way the different fabrics are placed. Simple quilting is in keeping with the feel of the piece.

• Made by Minnie Smith McLeod c. 1930, this hand-pieced, hand-quilted patchwork quilt is a basic Nine-Patch. It has 2½" (6cm) squares, with each block made up of five light pink squares and four squares of multi-colored scraps. The edges are machine hemmed and the border and backing are a strong pink polished cotton. Minnesota Historical Society

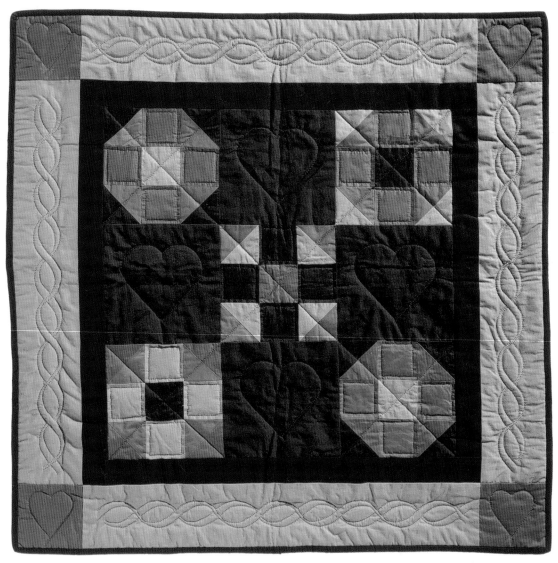

simplest form, the block is made up of three squares in alternating colors, which creates a cross-shape. If five of these blocks are combined with four plain squares to create a Double Nine-Patch, alternating the pieced and the plain, diagonal chain patterns can be created—for instance, Single Irish Chain is often made from alternating plain and Nine-Patch blocks. If only the center square of a Double Nine-Patch is pieced, with the other squares of one or two alternating plain fabrics, then the design appears to "explode" outwards from the center. An emphasis on light colors in a block will make it leap out of the overall design; an emphasis on darks will make that section appear to recede, or merge into the background. A large number of patterns, including Puss in the Corner, Patience Corner, and Homeward Bound, can be devised using Nine-Patch blocks

fashioned only from squares. Even something quite simple—like reversing the light and dark fabrics in a design—can have a very dramatic impact on the overall effect. The size of the blocks and their position within the quilt can also be manipulated for effect—many of the most surprising and impressive results occur spontaneously, without any particular regard for color placement.

Variations

As in blocks made in the other types of grid, the units that make up Nine-Patch blocks can be subdivided into other shapes, from smaller squares or rectangular bars to triangles made by dividing squares into right-angle triangles by cutting along the diagonal one or more times. Triangles can be added to corners to create octagonal effects, and units can be

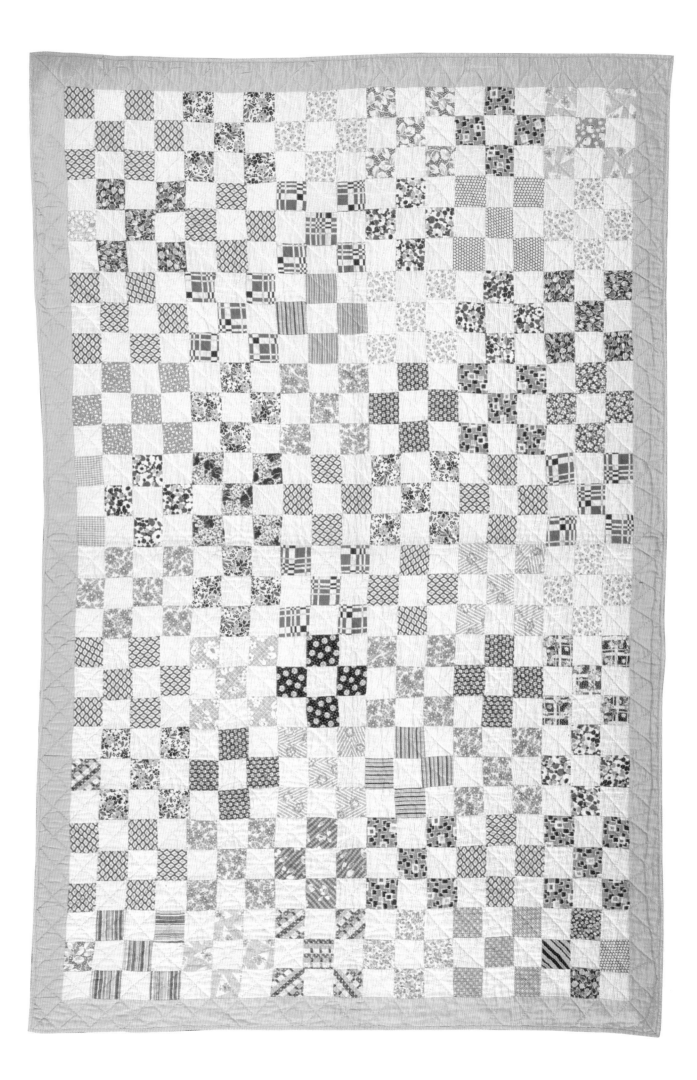

• This outstanding example of an Amish quilt, made in about 1930, has all the elements. Small Nine-Patch blocks made from a random selection of plain scraps are alternated with larger plain red spacer blocks to make bright-colored Double Nine-Patch blocks, which are then set on point and in turn alternated with larger spacer blocks and setting triangles in a lighter, rosier red. The inner pieced border has tan squares set on point with black setting triangles and light reddish-pink corners, while the wide outer border is the same red as the plain blocks in the Double Nine-Patches. The quilting is superb, too, with a plain straight grid on the Double Nine-Patches, an intricate looped design in the large spacer blocks, pumpkin seeds in the inner border, and fabulous running feathers in the outer border. The Heritage Center of Lancaster County

repositioned by color to make new configurations. Units are usually all the same size, but a number of patterns are assembled from units of different sizes in which the corner sections, for example, may be smaller than the central units, or the center section may be little more than strips of fabric, with much larger squares in the corners.

Simple Nine-Patch blocks that are set on point with spacer blocks can create a very lively and interesting quilt. Many of the star patterns—like Ohio Star, for instance—are Nine-Patch blocks, and Nine-Patch blocks are also the basis for many pictorial and representational patchwork blocks. Nine-Patch and Four-Patch variations were the only patterns permitted by the Nebraskan Amish, who followed very strict limitations in their quiltmaking, but they were also popular in other Amish communities in Ohio, Pennsylvania and Indiana.

As with the other grid blocks, Nine-Patch blocks can be subdivided, which can create quite highly complex patterns. Many of these patterns also combine Nine-Patch blocks with, say, Four-Patch ones. Such combinations are often referred to as Double-Square patterns, and can be made as four Nine-Patch blocks or as nine Four-Patch ones.

Quilting

The size and complexity of a finished block will determine the type and amount of quilting you add, with outline or in-the-ditch quilting often being used within a Nine-Patch block to avoid taking attention away from the pieced blocks themselves. Spacer blocks used to alternate with pieced blocks also provide a good background for quilting or for other embellishment, as do the borders on many Nine-Patch quilts. A simple grid, either vertical and horizontal or diagonal, is another good option for many Nine-Patch patterns.

Project: REGULAR LOG CABIN BLOCK

Chain Piecing

Chain piecing is a "production line" way of making identical blocks quickly. With fabric pieces close at hand, stitch two pieces together. Without lifting the presser foot, place two more pieces in position and continue without cutting the threads.

1   For each block, cut a center square (ours are 1½" or 4 cm). Cut a selection of 1½" (4 cm) wide strips.

2   Lay the first strip (ours is light) right side up on the machine. Stitch center squares, one after another, along the length of the strip. Repeat to make the required number with a ¼" (5 mm) seam.

3   Cut each unit apart carefully; you can either use scissors or a rotary cutter and ruler. Press the seams toward the center square.

4   Place the second (light) strip right side up on the machine as in Step 2. Lay one stitched unit along the length of the strip, with the center square at the top. Chain piece units as in Step 2.

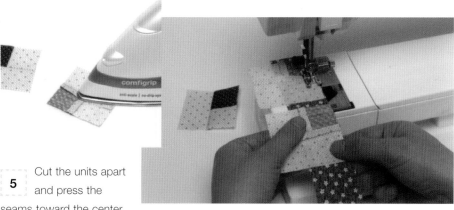

5 Cut the units apart and press the seams toward the center.

6 Place the third (dark) strip right side up on the machine as before. Place the stitched unit with the right side facing the strip and the newest strip nearest you. Chain piece as before. Cut apart and press the seams toward the center.

7 Add the fourth (dark again) strip the same way. This completes the first round of strips.

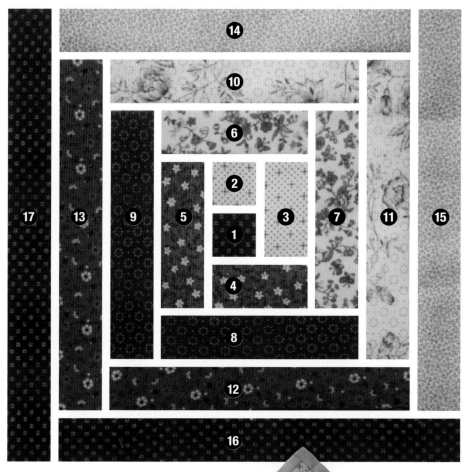

Piecing sequence for one block

8 Add the fifth strip—the beginning of a new round—the same way, right side up with the stitched unit right side down and the newest strip nearest you. Since we started with a light strip, the fifth one should be another light fabric.

9 Trim the edges as shown. Be sure to line up the raw edges carefully and do not stretch them as you work.

10 Following the sequence in Steps 2–6, continue adding strips, alternating two light, then two dark strips until the block is the desired size.

• Made by Mrs. A. R. Robertson in the first quarter of the twentieth century, this Contrary Wife quilt top is made from a myriad of multicolored cotton scraps, some of which appear to be fabrics from between 1880 and 1910. It has a four-square repeat with two triangle square units alternating with two squares to make each Four-Patch block; the arrangement of the colors gives a strong diagonal line across the entire quilt. Minnesota Historical Society

• The quilt, made by Patricia Archibald of West Lothian in Scotland, uses half-square triangles to create a stylized poppy design.

TRIANGLES & DIAMONDS

There are a number of different kinds of triangles. Geometrically, the most familiar is probably the equilateral, or 60-degree, version, in which each angle measures 60 degrees and all three sides are exactly the same length. Then there is the isoceles triangle, in which only of the two sides and two angles are the same. Irregular triangles are just that—all three sides and all three angles are different.

The most familiar and widely used triangle in patchwork is the right-angle isoceles triangle. Because squares and rectangles can be divided into right-angle triangles with a simple slash across their diagonals, they are used to make many patchwork designs, both simple and complex. In addition, they can also have two sides cut on the straight grain of the fabric, making them much easier to work with than any other type of triangle, all of which have only one side that can be cut on the straight grain. Both the other sides will therefore, by definition, be on the stretchy bias and difficult to keep in shape. The simple Four-Patch pattern known as Broken Dishes is derived solely from right-angle triangles. When the blocks are combined, the effect is supposed to be of a pile of broken dishes on the floor. Simple Nine-Patch blocks such as Ohio Star and Shoofly also make use of the right-angle triangle.

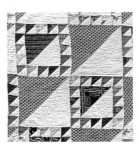

• The seller's tag on this beautiful version of the traditional Lady of the Lake design identifies it as Rocky Glen, but that pattern has a sawtooth edge around only two sides, not four as in the Lady of the Lake block. Here, the blocks are of random scraps, with the white fabric consistent throughout, alternated with squares made from two large white and light brown right-angle triangles. The several red fabrics give sparkle.

• The Bounding Betty quilt shown opposite was made by Emma Dongus Laudenschlager (1871-1941) in around 1880. The blocks are made up of two different-size isoceles triangles in an hourglass shape, and are set on point at alternate levels, which creates a strong zigzag effect.
Minnesota Historical Society/Part of the Joyce Aufderheide collection

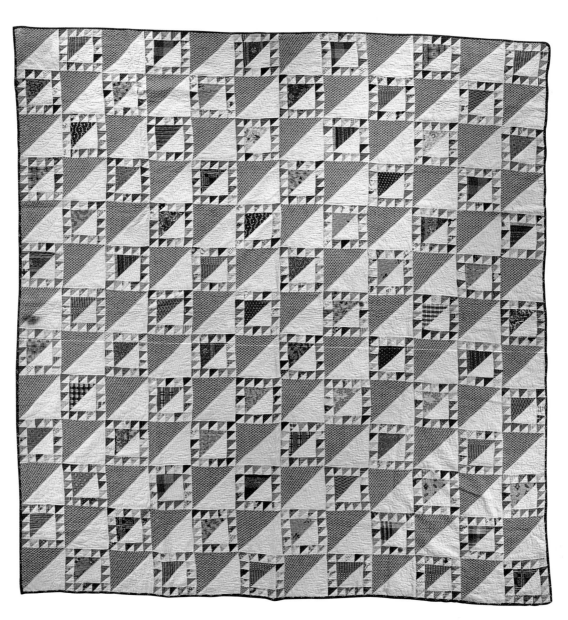

The true diamond shape—as opposed to a diamond created simply by setting a square on point—can be used to make some of the most exciting of all patchwork pieces. Two of a diamond's edges can be placed on the straight grain, but two will be on the bias, and so liable to stretching and distortion unless great care is taken as you work with them. As with triangles, there are two versions of diamond shapes: the 45-degree and the 60-degree. The 60-degree diamond can most easily be described as two equilateral triangles that are set side by side, while a 45-degree, or long, diamond is effectively two isoceles triangles, set base to base.

Both triangles and diamonds are widely used in star and sawtooth patterns, as well as in many one-patch "mosaic" patterns.

Drafting shapes

A drawing compass should be used to draft both diamonds and most triangles. The exception is the right-angle triangle, also called the half-square or triangle-square, which is easily made by cutting a square across the diagonal. Cutting a square will create an isoceles version with a base longer than its two sides. If you use the same technique to halve a rectangle, you get the two long irregular triangles that occur in a number of patterns. If you cut a square twice, once along each diagonal, you end up with four quarter-square triangles. Measurements for these shapes can appear tricky, but there is a simple formula that you can follow. Your original square should be cut ⅞" (18mm) larger than the desired finished measurement

• This quilt, called Tropical Tessellation, was made by nine Round Robin group members in Berkshire, England. They designed their quilt after seeing a similar one by quilter Jinny Beyer. The design is based on a 60° diamond subdivided into six strips. The depth of color in each block and the proportion of red to green, gives the impression of hothouse flowers in bud, half open, or in full bloom. Free machine quilted petals and leaves enhance the design, and flower centers are defined with embroidery thread. Royal Berks Hospital collection

if you want two half-square triangles. Add 1¼" (3cm) to create quarter-square triangles. It is best to draw the pattern of a finished long triangle on paper first and then add the seam allowances to determine the exact measurements of the original rectangle.

To draft other triangles and diamonds you can either use a special quilter's ruler with the various angles marked on it, or you will need paper, pencil, straight ruler, and a compass, and your basic geometry skills. Start by drawing a circle marked with 60-degree intervals, which can then be joined with the straightedge to make a series of equilateral triangles and 60-degree diamonds. For 45-degree diamonds, draw two sides of a 45-degree angle to the correct length and then use the compass, set to the length of each side, to mark the point of the opposite 45-degree angle.

All these versions of both shapes, and any irregular shapes you use, will need

to have the seam allowances marked on the template.

Cutting and stitching shapes

There are a number of ways to cut triangles and diamonds. You can cut strips of fabric to the correct width, including the seam allowances, and cut the desired shapes from them using a special quilter's ruler. This is a good way to make sure you maximize the potential for keeping as many edges as possible on the straight grain of the fabric. For right-angle triangles, you can cut strips into squares or rectangles and then into triangles, or you can cut separate shapes as you work. Shapes can be drawn on the fabric and cut by hand, a long, laborious task if you are making a full-size quilt.

Another way to create right-angle triangles is to place two squares of different fabrics right sides together and mark a diagonal line on the wrong side of one

• Nosegay is a traditional block formed from triangles. It is found on many 1930s quilts, usually in combinations of yellow, mint green, and light purple. This modern version by Estelle Morin of Levallois-Perret in France is made in earth-colored silks.

piece. Stitch ¼" (5mm) from the line, on both sides of the line, and then cut carefully along the marked line. Press the seams, and you then have two finished squares, each made from two right-angle triangles. You can also use this method to make both quarter-square and long triangles as well. However, do not cut the units apart until you have stitched all the seams. Another method involves cutting strips, marking squares and diagonal lines on them, and then stitching the diagonals as described before. Or you can draw a set of squares and diagonals on a larger piece of cloth and stitch as before. Just make sure before you start sewing that you don't stitch the sides of the units instead of the diagonals. One of the great advantages—

in addition to the speed—of using this method is that the bias edge of the shapes is much less likely to be stretched as you work.

All other triangle and diamond shapes should be stitched with great care and with as little handling as possible. Many of the patterns based on these shapes can be stitched by machine, but the traditional hand method known as English paper piecing (*see page 20*) creates a beautiful piece of work.

Seminole Patchwork

Triangles and diamonds are created in profusion—together with the occasional square—in Seminole patchwork, which was developed by the Seminole tribe of Native Americans. The fabric created by this method

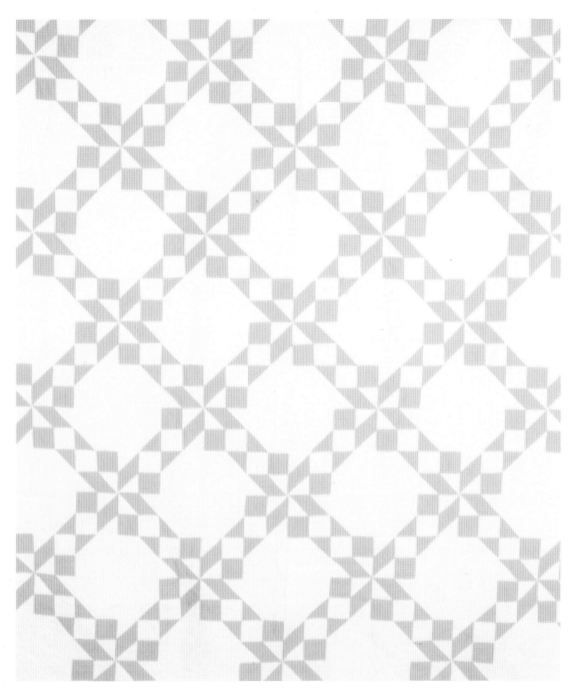

• This windmill flower design was created by Christine Moulin of Soisy-sur-Seine in France. Flashes of golden yellow and tomato red solid colors in the triangular blooms provide a foil for the many busy floral prints, and large and small quilted petal shapes link the blocks and the simple triple border on three sides.

• Purchased by its present owner in Minneapolis, Minnesota, this 1930s variation of Clay's Choice combines triangles into diamonds to create the pinwheel and alternates the yellow-gold and white windmill-and-squares blocks with octagons, quilted with heart motifs. Each patchwork piece is outline-quilted, and the border is quilted with five-point stars enclosed by squares. All the quilting is worked by hand in white. Minnesota Historical Society

of double strip-piecing is seldom seen on full-scale quilts, but it is widely used for clothing, especially jackets, vests, and skirts, and for bags. Long strips of bright fabrics in several solid colors, and in varying widths, are sewn together and then the strips are cut, usually at a sharp angle, and re-sewn into new patterns, which are most often diagonal in nature—chevrons, diamonds, and double chevrons.

Historians believe that the technique first began to be developed around 1900, when women on the reservations in Florida—to which the remnants of the tribe had been moved after two wars with the United States

government had been lost and many of their members sent to reservations in Oklahoma—acquired early sewing machines. They soon began creating clothing, both for themselves and as items for sale. Several reservations continue to make both garments and accessories commercially today.

Non-Native quiltmakers have adopted the Seminole pattern to create brightly-colored geometric wall hangings and pillow covers, among other items (*see pages 322-325*). The design can also be used to create wonderfully intricate and exotic-looking borders on other types of quilt.

• This quilt is called Bristol Stars because it was inspired by the design of a marble floor in Bristol Cathedral in England. Made in 1999 by Judy Mathison of Sebastopol, California, it is a masterpiece of color planning and execution. It is foundation pieced, which gives sharp and accurate points to the large number of triangular pieces in an astonishing variety of sizes and shapes. The shading and subtle variety of the colors is outstanding, as is the quilting, which was worked by both hand and machine.

• The last quarter of the nineteenth century saw a vast number of blue and white quilts being created, and Ocean Waves designs like this stunning example were widely made. In this version several different dark blue fabrics, all with close-set dotted patterns but in several different shades, were used to make the small triangles.

• Tumbling Blocks, or Baby Blocks, is a traditional diamond pattern made from small pieces that is often used by frugal Amish quiltmakers. In this 1980s baby-quilt version, there were enough scraps in the basket to keep the colors consistent, and the unusual green and terracotta borders also depended on the leftover fabric that was available at the time.

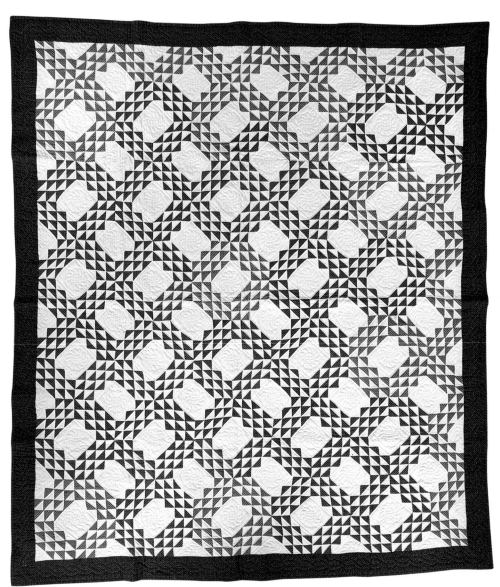

Setting triangles

Triangles have another important use in quiltmaking, as setting, or filler, pieces. When quilts are put together with the square blocks set diagonally, or turned on point, right-angle setting triangles can be used to fill the spaces around the piece to make the edges straight. Each setting triangle will be half the size of the block itself, but when measuring and cutting them out remember that seam allowances must be added first. Because it is likely that the straight grain of blocks that are set on point will run on the diagonal, the quilt is much more liable to stretch out of shape than one that is set straight. To stabilize the edges, cut the setting triangles with the base on the straight grain to support the edges of the blocks and give a smooth side to which to attach the borders.

Similarly, when creating a design using hexagons, the edges of the quilt can be straightened up by inserting isoceles triangles. The hexagon itself can be viewed as being made up of three diamonds joined together—as illustrated in the Tumbling Blocks pattern on page 77—so the filler triangle will either be half the diamond lengthwise, as shown across the top of this quilt, or half the diamond crosswise, as shown down the sides. When you are working out how geometric patterns will fit together, try using graph paper, which comes in both square and isoceles grids, and can also be colored in to show how the design might look. Alternatively, cut out the shapes in paper first and play around with them to see what happens.

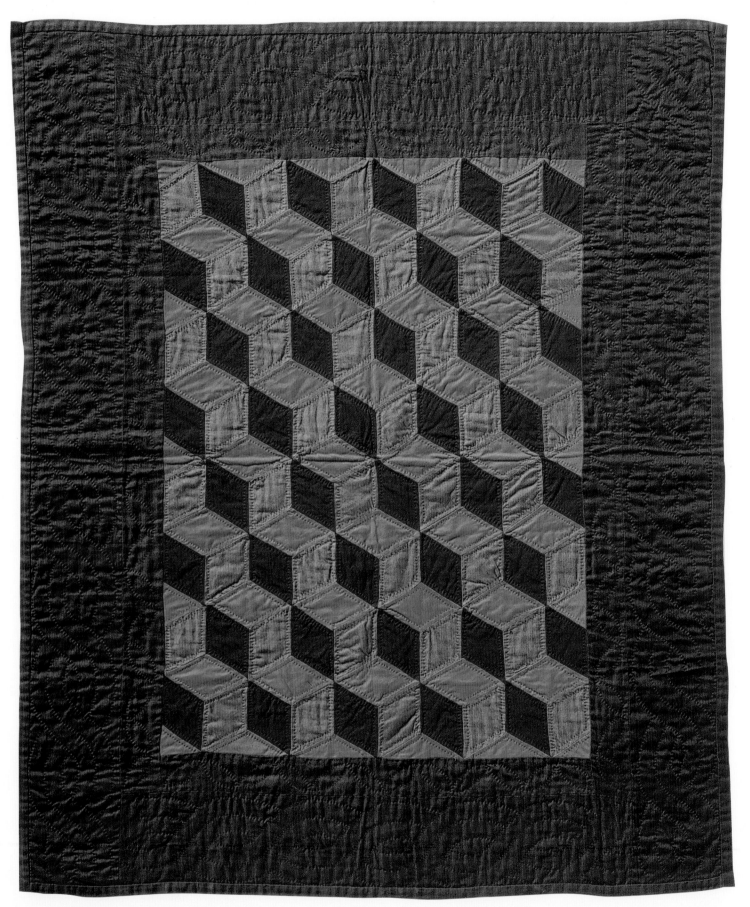

Project: TRIANGLE BLOCK

Making triangle squares

This small quilt, made up only of squares and right-angle triangles in two contrasting colors, is the perfect size for a baby's crib. Since only small pieces of the contrasting fabric are needed, it works very well as a scrap quilt, and the pattern is also effective when only one contrasting color is used throughout. It makes an ideal pattern for the beginner.

To make this as a full-size bed quilt instead, increase the number of Shoofly blocks: you will need perhaps 24 blocks for a single bed and 36 blocks for a double.

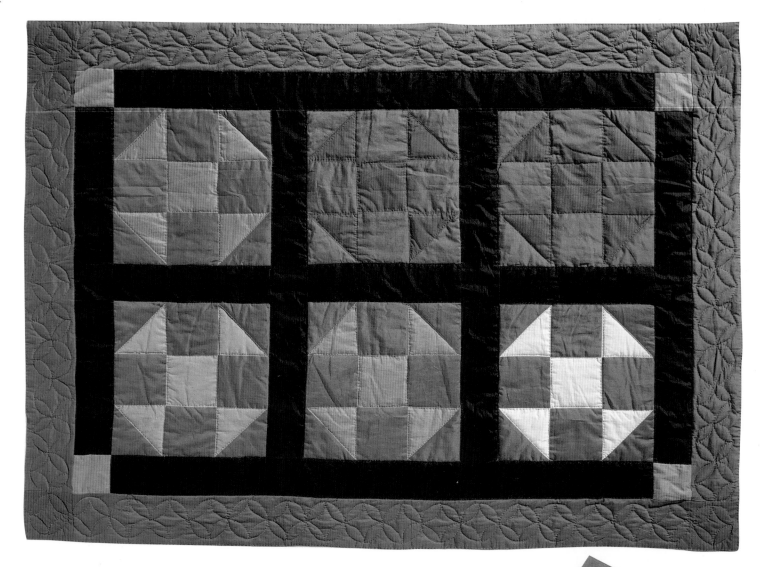

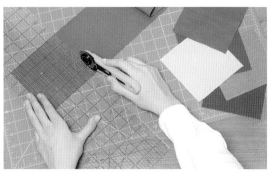

1 Use a rotary cutter, ruler, and mat to cut out the squares for each block from the contrasting colors you have selected, and the turquoise background color.

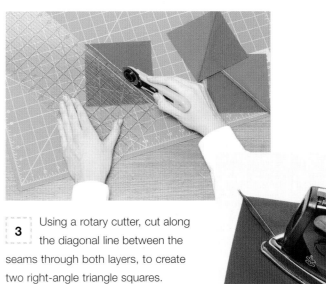

2 Place one 5" (13cm) square of each color right sides together. Draw a line across one diagonal on the wrong side of one square and use it as a guide to stitch a ¼" (5mm) seam on each side of the line.

3 Using a rotary cutter, cut along the diagonal line between the seams through both layers, to create two right-angle triangle squares. Inset: Press the seams to one side.

4 Before stitching, lay out the squares to check their position (inset). To make each Nine-Patch block, stitch two strips with triangle squares (A) to one background square (B) and one strip of background square (B) to two opposite sides of a plain contrasting square (C).

5 Sew the three strips together, matching ¼" (5mm) seams carefully and positioning the triangles correctly. Press the seams to one side.

6 The Shoofly block is now complete. To make the full quilt, repeat to make five more blocks in the same way, using the other five colors.

STARS

• This wonderfully complex Seven Sisters quilt from Oklahoma was made around 1875. The pattern is a traditional mosaic design composed of interlocking diamonds that create the seven six-point stars that appear inside each large hexagon shape. The central star of each group is also surrounded by a hexagon, while the pink setting triangles create a large star around the big hexagon.

• The simple LeMoyne Stars in this quilt have been created from a scrap bag of fabrics typical of the 1870s when it was made. Some of the stars have been cut in a way that creates an interesting secondary pattern; other fabric choices seem totally random. The green used for the spacer blocks is also typical of its time.

Stars appear in the firmament of quiltmaking probably more than any other pattern. There are patchwork stars, appliqué stars, and quilted stars. They can have as few as four points, and as many as the maker of a large Mariner's Compass can fit in—certainly as many as 64. Most modern sampler quilts have at least one star design among the blocks, and beautiful quilts have been made containing a sampler of many different star patterns. Dozens of patchwork patterns have the word "star" in their names, and there are many designs that are star-shaped but which are not called stars.

Because a number of star patterns are made from small pieces of fabric, many of the existing traditional star quilts are pieced from scraps. Stars can also be large enough to be

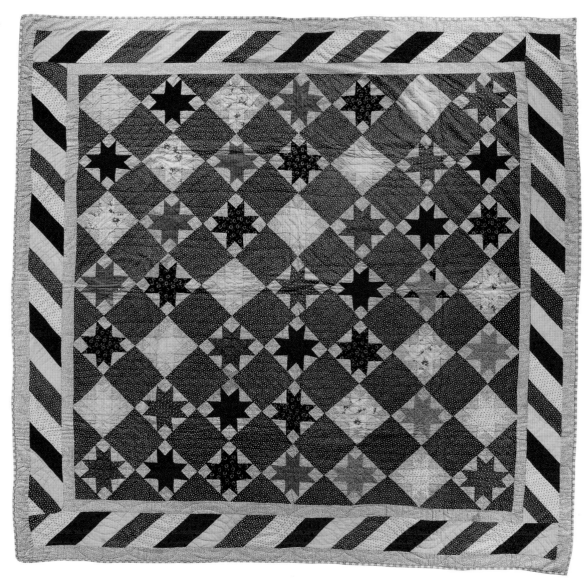

• Dating from between 1860 and 1870, this Variable Star quilt has an obvious "superstition" block, since the stars are arranged diagonally by color except for the center of the bottom row. The dark green spacer blocks create a subtle background for the bright stars, and the same fabric is used in the pieced border. The yellow border fabric has been used for some stars, but the red print occurs nowhere else on the quilt.

• This All-American Star quilt was made in New York between 1940–45, at the time of World War II. It patriotically displays thirty blue stars within red stars and the choice of both plain and polka-dotted cotton fabrics makes the design appear three-dimensional. The white areas have been quilted in a diamond or kite-shaped pattern. American Folk Art Museum/Gift of Cyril I. Nelson

placed in the center of medallion quilts, and come in all sizes in between.

Star points can be made either by using triangles or by using diamonds. Patterns can vary immensely, from the very simple, four-pointed versions, such as Friendship Star, which is made using half-square triangles, and Periwinkle, which uses long triangles (*see page 68*), to a vast number of eight-point stars, which are relatively straightforward to draft by simply using graph paper and a ruler. Most, although not all, of the eight-point patterns are based on triangles. There are also various types of six-pointed stars using both diamonds and triangles, for which you will need a drawing compass if you wish to draft your own designs. Some of the more complicated star designs can be quite tricky to piece.

Four-point stars

While the Friendship Star is probably the simplest of star patterns, it is not the only version. It is made from a Nine-Patch block, as are many star patterns. Its closest variation is the Nine-Patch Star, which has half-square triangle patches in the corner units that give the star pattern a feeling of spinning through space. The pattern called Blazing Star, or Mother's Delight, and its best-known variation, North Star, are variations of more complex four-pointed stars. Made as Four-Patch blocks, both are based on long triangles that face each other and are made from alternating contrasting fabrics. The Laced Star uses both small and large long triangles to create an interlaced four-pointed star design. Based on diamonds, the Barbara Bannister Star block is intricate and tricky to piece.

• The complicated
patterning created by the
Star of Bethlehem design
has a kaidescopic effect,
with all the elements, from
the elongated diamond
pieces to the radiating
bands of color, adding
to the feeling of swirling
light and shadow. This
American quilt, dating
from the latter half of the
nineteenth century, is
made more complex by
the four smaller stars in
the corners and the half-
stars tucked between the
top, bottom, and side
points of the main star.
The unknown quiltmaker
has used color brilliantly:
there are two versions of
the corner stars, with the
ones diagonally across
each other carrying the
same coloration. The pink
ones match the coloring
of the central motif to the
pink row of diamonds,
the dominant yellow of
the other two does not
appear elsewhere. Both
the quilting and the
piecing is done with great
skill. Each diamond shape
is outline-quilted inside
the seamline, and the
inset areas of the smaller
stars have concentric
rings of stitching.
Milwaukee Art Museum/
Gift of Richard and
Erna Flagg

Eight-point stars

Variable Star (*see page 83*) and Ohio Star, both Nine-Patch blocks, are among the simplest of all eight-pointed star patterns. Both depend on contrast in the colors between the points and the background, and are easy to draft using little besides graph paper and a ruler. They are also simple to cut from strips and to chain-piece, so they are popular projects for beginner-level workshops. There are literally dozens of variations of the basic Ohio Star based on nine equal squares, and even more made from dividing the block into sixteen equal squares.

Another group of eight-pointed stars are based on 45-degree diamonds (*see page 70*). They range from the LeMoyne, or Lemon, Star (*see page 80*), which is made from eight diamonds with filler squares in the corners and triangles in the side edges to square up the block, to the Lone Star, or Star of Bethlehem (*see page 85*), which begins with a central LeMoyne Star and radiates out in concentric rings of color to create a dramatic pattern that pulsates.

Like a giant LeMoyne Star, the Star of Bethlehem has filler squares and triangles to complete the quilt, which are large areas that are just crying out to be quilted. An even more elaborate pattern than this is the Broken Star (*see page 88*), or Carpenter's Wheel, in which triplets of diamonds radiate from each point of the Lone Star.

The LeMoyne Star, according to tradition, was named for the two brothers, Pierre and Jean-Baptiste LeMoyne, who founded the city of New Orleans in the early eighteenth century. The Lone Star has an equally illustrious history. The symbol of the independence of the Republic of Texas, the Lone Star was incorporated into the state flag when Texas joined the union in 1845.

Both these star patterns offer an example of how names can change according to geographical location. As the LeMoyne Star design traveled north, where the LeMoyne brothers were less well-known, the name became corrupted to Lemon Star. The Lone Star was widely made in places other than Texas, and was known as Star of Bethlehem in Pennsylvania and Star of the East in Missouri.

• This Lone Star quilt with appliqué and a chintz border was made by an unknown quiltmaker in the middle of the nineteenth century. The large star is composed of small diamonds of small-scale print fabrics arranged in concentric rings around the red-orange eight-point star in the middle. The white background areas—squares in the corners and triangles in between the side points—are embellished with beautifully executed broderie perse motifs cut from the same chintz fabric that has been used to make the 8" (20 cm) border. Notice that the colors of the fabrics used to make the star are echoed in the pattern of the chintz. Quilting is relatively simple: sawtooth on the border, diagonal rows in the appliquéd areas, and outline on the star. Minnesota Historical Society

• Made in Hastings, Minnesota, in the 1930s, this quilt is beautifully planned and executed, from the arranging of the colors to the superb quilting of individual wreaths in each of the white background blocks. Called Broken Star, the pattern needs careful handling, and the meticulous piecing of this midwestern quilt makes it a masterpiece.

• This Prairie Star quilt in navy blue and white cotton was made in the late nineteenth century by an unidentified Ojibwe woman, in Redwood Falls, Minnesota. It was quilted much later, in 1976, by Irma Schroer, of New Ulm, Minnesota. Minnesota Historical Society/Part of the Joyce Aufderheide collection.

Star-pattern names

The names of most patterns are lost in antiquity, but sometimes a design is closely associated with either a person or an event. This is the case with a number of star patterns. Tippecanoe and Tyler Too, for example, is a complex Four-Patch design named for William Henry Harrison, the territorial governor and a general, who defeated the Shawnee tribe at Tippecanoe in the Indiana Territory in 1811. Harrison was nicknamed "Old Tippecanoe," and although he was defeated in the 1836 presidential election, he ran again as the Whig Party candidate in 1840 with John Tyler as his running mate. The slogan was coined, and became associated with a thoroughly undignified campaign, but Harrison and Tyler were elected and Whig quiltmakers subsequently created many quilts using the pattern. Harrison, who was 68 when he was elected, was the oldest man to assume office until Ronald Reagan was elected 140 years later. He was also the first to die in office. Only a month after his inauguration he succumbed to pneumonia, which developed from a chill he caught while out walking on a bitterly cold day. He was succeeded by Vice President Tyler, and the slogan became a catchphrase of American history.

At the next election in 1844, the Whig candidate was Kentucky Senator Henry Clay, a famous orator and statesman. Clay lost the election, but his memory lives on in the star pattern called Clay's Choice, which is also known as Harry's Star and Henry of the West.

Dolley Madison's Star (*see page 91*) is a complex Nine-Patch pattern named for the wife of the fourth president, James Madison. Dolley Payne Todd was a Quaker widow who

• Called Star of the East, this pattern is constructed using the same basic method as the Lone Star (*page 86-7*) or Broken Star (*page 88*), and is similar to the Prairie Star block on page 89. Dated around 1875, this quilt uses a number of different printed fabrics, especially among the blues, all typical of the era in which it was made. The binding is a different shade of blue from the navy blues used elsewhere.

married Madison, then a congressman, in 1794. When her husband became secretary of state under President Thomas Jefferson, who was a widower, Mrs. Madison assumed the duties of hostess in the then-unfinished White House. She, of course, continued as official First Lady when Madison was elected in 1809 and presided over a growing capital city. However, the British army raided the city in 1814 during the War of 1812, and the president's mansion was burned—along with the Capitol and other buildings. Mrs. Madison oversaw the packing of state papers and priceless documents, including—according to legend—the Declaration of Independence and Gilbert Stuart's iconic painting of George

Washington, before she escaped into the woods of Virginia and safety. Her heroism and her reputation as the most gracious lady in the land won her a place in the country's history, as well as in the hearts of quiltmakers throughout the land.

Six-point stars

Stars with six points can be created from equilateral triangles or 60-degree diamonds. These patterns can be drafted using a drawing compass and assembled in a similar way to the eight-point stars made from 45-degree diamonds. They are frequently made by the English paper piecing method (*see page 20*) and can be combined with both hexagons and

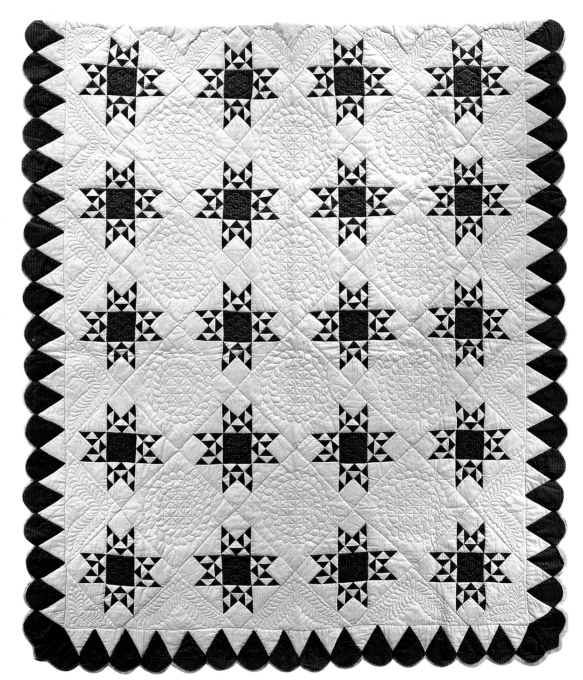

• This beautifully pieced and quilted Dolley Madison's Star made in about 1920 was never bound. But the piecing of the pink and white star blocks with many small triangles and the ice-cream cone border is meticulous, and the quilting—a feathered wreath in each plain white spacer block and a running feather filling each setting triangle—is superb. The small roses in the center square of each star have been worked in a matching pink thread.

equilateral triangles to create wonderful designs. Among the patterns are Eisenhower Star, Tea Box, Ozark Diamonds, and Savannah Star—which is created by adding an equilateral triangle to each side of a hexagon.

Mariner's Compass

One of the supreme tests of a quiltmaker's skill, the Mariner's Compass is a highly intricate star pattern consisting of concentric rings of pointed starbursts radiating out from a central circle. It looks much like the elaborate compasses used by mariners since the early days of sail, and has traditional associations with the coast of New England, according to quilt historian Carter Houck. Certainly the ships transporting the pilgrims from Europe to North America during the late seventeenth century would have carried such instruments.

Some Mariner's Compass quilts are made using six-, ten-, or twelve-point stars, but most are based on multiples of eight. To be classed as a Compass pattern, the block should have at least sixteen points, and many have 32 or even 64. As the rows move out and the number of points increases, the points grow ever sharper and more difficult to piece.

• Feathered, or Sawtooth, Star is a pattern that must be pieced with precision, especially when the contrasts are as strong as the red and white shown on the right. The piecing on this quilt, made in about 1920, is beautifully done, while the color placement is slightly eccentric in places. The straight-line quilting is worked white on white and red on red.

• This blue and white cotton Feathered Star dates from 1850-60 and was perhaps made in New York state. The name of the quiltmaker is unknown, but the initials E.C.B. appear in the center of the bottom. The quilt is cleverly arranged from thirty-five blocks in three different designs surrounded by a frame of half-blocks. The plant forms on the border are appliquéd in place. American Folk Art Museum/Gift of Cyril I. Nelson

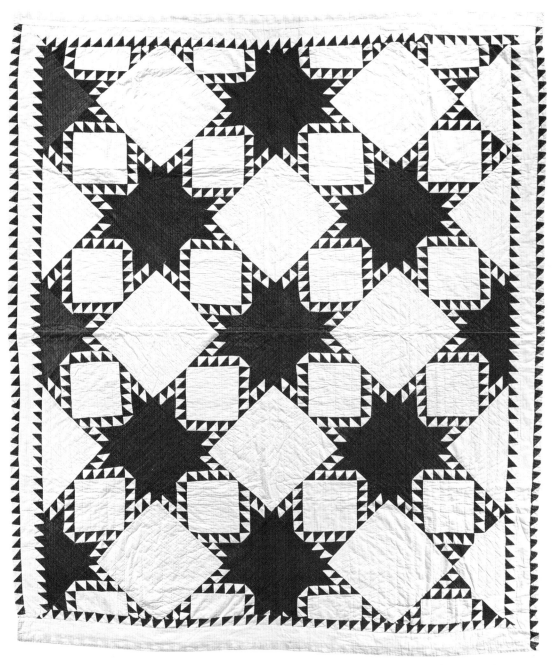

Feathered stars

In the Feathered Star design, the pattern still features a star shape, but the edges of the motifs are "feathered" using rows of tiny triangles in alternate light and dark colors. This pattern can also sometimes be called Sawtooth Star. The strips of feathering triangles would usually be placed with the base of the triangles nearest the star, as in the quilt on page 93. In the quilt shown above, the triangles are placed with one side against the star, so the effect here is of a starburst edging with a red outline. Sawtooth Star is quite often the central medallion in the frame quilts that were popular on both sides of the Atlantic in the early 1800s.

Blue and white, and red and white, color combinations have both been widely used in many areas of the decorative arts throughout history. The blue and white quilts of the early nineteenth century were probably influenced by popular coverlets made of indigo blue wool woven with white cotton or linen. These eighteenth-century textiles date from before the emergence of the blue and white quilts. Red and white compositions were widely made after the invention of a colorfast dye known as Turkey red, which meant that the colors did not run into each other if the quilt was washed.

Project: EIGHT-POINT STAR BLOCK

Making a star block

The brilliant jewel colors of this baby quilt are typical of the work of Amish quilters, as is the center square with its seven separate borders which alternate between light and dark color settings. The corner squares in the second border anchor the center, and the bright-colored sawtooth border—number four—gives the piece a zing.

The central medallion is an eight-point star variation of a traditional pattern called Evening Star. The eight-point star appears in many forms, especially in Star of Bethlehem quilts, made from myriad diamond-shaped scraps, and Ohio Star designs, which look much like Evening Star, but are based on a Nine-Patch block instead of the Four-Patch block used in the example shown here.

The borders alternate between dark and light colors, so the dark narrower strips have the effect of emphasizing the brighter hues. Above and below the sawtooth border are additional strips of deep indigo that lengthen the quilt in these directions, and make it rectangular rather than square.

The quilt has been quite simply quilted by machine-stitching along each of the seam lines, but there is plenty of scope for adding more elaborate hand quilting if you wish to do so—especially along the wider, unpieced borders.

1 Make a square template measuring 3⅞" (9.8 cm). Place the two contrasting colors of the fabric that you have chosen for the eight-point star right sides together and mark with 6 identical squares.

2 Using a ruler, draw diagonal lines across the squares from corner to corner. NB: You only need to mark the top layer of fabric as, with this quick-piecing method, you stitch both layers together.

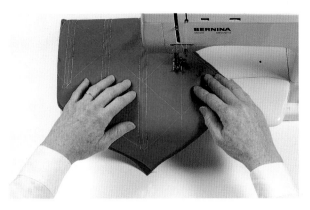

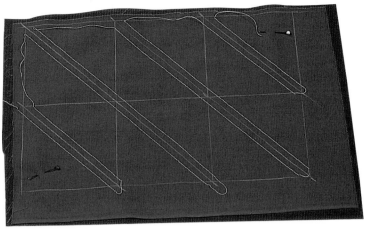

3 Align the presser foot along the diagonal line and stitch a ¼" (5mm) seam first on the left-hand side, then on the right-hand side of the line. Do not cut the thread at the end of each line: simply sew along one side of the diagonal, swing the material around 180 degrees, and sew along the other side.

4 When you have finished stitching, your piece of fabric should look like this. As you will see in the stages that follow, this method is far less tricky and time consuming than piecing the individual squares of the center design one by one!

5 Carefully trim away the outer edges of the block along the marked lines. You can do this with a rotary cutter and ruler, if you have one, or with scissors.

6 Cut along the marked diagonal lines between your stitching lines to produce 12 triangles. Open out the triangles and press the seams to one side. You should have 12 pieced squares in total. Cut four plain squares the same size as your pieced squares.

7 Arrange the pieced and plain squares in your chosen combination. Join the squares together first into rows, then into a block, matching seams carefully. Or make four Four-Patch blocks and combine them into a Double Four-Patch. Press the long seams to one side.

8 The first border band is four strips 1½" (4cm) wide; the second four strips 3½" (9cm) wide with a 3½" square at each corner; the third four strips 2½" (6.5cm) wide; the fourth four strips of pieced triangle patches joined into rows formed from 8 pieced squares, with an unpieced square at one end of each strip. The fifth band is two strips 3½" (9cm) wide; the sixth four pieces 1½" (4cm) wide; and the seventh is four pieces 3½" (9cm) wide.

MOSAICS & GEOMETRICS

• Grandmother's Flower Garden blocks arranged in concentric rings by color have turned this quilt, made in New England in the nineteenth century, into an exciting hexagonal trip around the world design. The "garden paths" that run between the blocks and the rows are made from a light orange print fabric, and show the obvious planning done by the unknown quiltmaker. She obviously ran out of fabric to make the hexagon blocks in the corner match, but she has found material of an equivalent tone to create a harmonious design. Flower Garden blocks have also been used in the border, but they are themselves bordered by squares that are almost at odds with the center of the quilt and lack the same precision: the top left and bottom right corners of the borders have needed to be trimmed to fit. University of Nebraska-Lincoln

Mosaic patterns occur in almost every culture. Around the Mediterranean, from Europe and Africa to the Middle East, ancient sites yield floors, pavements, walls, and ceilings of mosaic. In Pompeii volcanic ash preserved vast areas intact until the city, which was buried by a catastrophic eruption of Mount Vesuvius in A.D.79, was rediscovered in the mid-eighteenth century. The ancient Greeks were making mosaics before the birth of Christ, and their skills were passed down to the Romans, who were among the most prolific of the mosaic makers. Roman mosaics can be found in all the areas colonized by the empire, and the technique was widely used in the Byzantine Empire. Islamic cultures have fine examples of the mosaic-maker's art in mosques and other buildings; and in the New World, the Mayan and Aztec civilizations made mosaics of great beauty. Many examples from all these cultures survive, and the designs have

• Filled with typical late-nineteenth century fabrics, this Boston Commons quilt from about 1880 is composed of nearly 1,000 tiny squares, each one about 1½" (4 cm). Related to Trip Around the World, the pattern is also known as Postage Stamp, and it is easy to see where the name came from when we look at this quilt. The fabrics almost certainly came from the quiltmaker's scrap basket, but the consistency of tone that has been employed in each round of squares is superb. The quilting is simple: a square grid that cuts through the diagonal of each patch, thus avoiding the seams that occur so frequently. The rounded corners of the border are an unusual feature.

been put to other uses, from tiles and tabletops to needlework patterns.

The ancient trade routes around the various Mediterranean areas that are rich in mosaics point to a prolific interchange of design ideas. There are many regional variations—examples in Venice are different from other areas of the Italian peninsula that are rich in mosaic work, such as Florence, Naples, and Pompeii—but patterns are often related to one another.

The intricacy of Islamic motifs found throughout the Arabic world is unequalled. Most are made in brilliant shades of tropical colors, and many gleam with gold-colored pieces. Here, too, variations are found in different regions, but relationships exist. Arabic patterns are always abstract, in keeping with Islamic strictures against graven images.

Mosaic patterns.

Most mosaics are based on small geometric shapes such as triangles, squares, diamonds, hexagons, and octagons, laid out in combinations to form intricate patterns. While some mosaics portray a scene, or have a pictorial image in the center with geometric borders around the edge in the manner of medallion quilts (*see pages 242-255*), others

have repeating patterns that rely on the juxtaposition of lights and darks for their effectiveness. It is easy to see the transition from the hard glass and stone materials of ancient mosaics to the soft fabrics of the quiltmaker's art. Many of the most intriguing quilt designs use only one shape, but have thousands of pieces, laid out in careful arrangements of color to balance the areas of light and dark.

Triangles, both right-angle and 60-degree versions, can be joined into rows and the rows into quilts of stunning beauty, with names like 1000 Pyramids and Birds in the Air. Squares can be arranged into concentric bands around a center piece, each row a different color, into the quilt designs called Sunshine and Shadow, or Trip Around the World (*see page 105*), or Boston Commons (*see page 97*). Diamonds arranged into sets of three, with a light, a medium, and a dark shape joined together, are used to create one of the most three-dimensional and interesting of all mosaic patterns, known as Tumbling Blocks (*see page 106*), or Baby Blocks, or its variation with nine diamonds called Inner City (*see page 107*). Pentagons are only occasionally used in mosaic patternmaking—because they do not abut each other on all sides, they need an inset triangle between shapes.

Hexagons

The six-sided hexagon is one of the most versatile of all geometric shapes. It can stand side by side with other hexagons of the same size, or be combined with other shapes such as 60-degree diamonds or triangles into designs of amazing complexity. Its versatility certainly helps to account for its enduring popularity as a quilt pattern at a time when speed cutting and piecing is so important, since it is still first and foremost a design that works best for most quiltmakers as a hand project. Various ways of piecing hexagons successfully by machine have been devised, but the pieces are generally cut and joined by hand.

Hexagon quilts have been made at least since the eighteenth century, with many intricate early examples worked in silk or fine cotton. Many of the medallion quilts worked on both sides of the Atlantic had one or more borders made from hexagons. Hexagon quilts are shown on pages 96, 102-3, 104 and 105.

• The Sunshine and Shadow pattern is considered one of the quintessential Amish quilt designs, but in fact was not widely used among the quiltmakers of the Plain People until the early twentieth century. This example from about 1940 is an outstanding piece, with its seventeen different colors—which are typical of the Amish community around Lancaster, Pennsylvania—shading in and out of light and dark in a diamond shape. Quilting worked in a diamond grid accentuates the diagonal effect and means that the quilter does not have to stitch over too many seams.

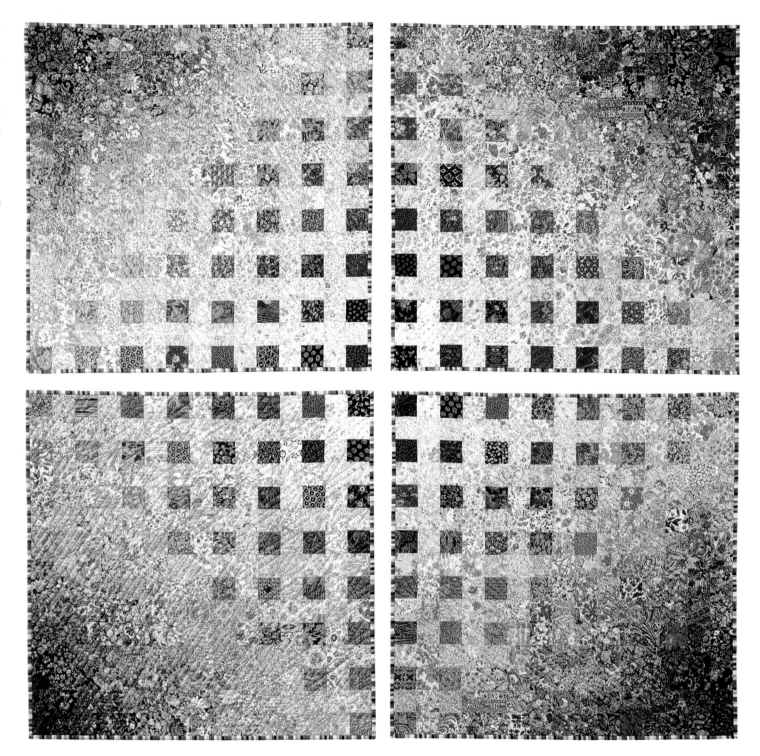

Grandmother's Flower Garden

The best-known hexagon quilt pattern is doubtless Grandmother's Flower Garden (*see page 102-3*), also known as French Bouquet or Flower in the Field, an old Welsh name. By 1835 the design, called by its American Colonial name of Honeycomb, was so popular that a pattern was published in the February issue of *Godey's Lady's Book*, a popular women's magazine that featured fashion, needlecraft, and home decoration. Some experts believe that almost every woman who made quilts during the first half of the nineteenth century made at least one hexagon quilt, and many of them survive today. And many of today's quilters will admit to having an unfinished hexagon piece tucked away in a drawer or chest. Some of them even intend to finish the quilt someday…

The options for creating hexagon quilts are limitless. Most Grandmother's Flower

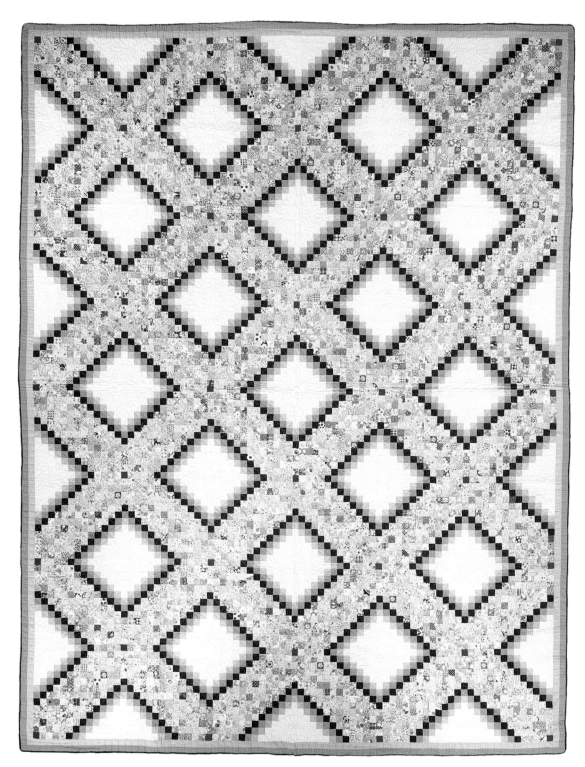

• There are several thousand pieces in this quintessential scrap quilt. Dozens of fabrics, mostly light and medium-light in value, have been used, separated from the white spacer blocks with three carefully planned and executed rows of green squares graduated in shade from dark forest green to very pale. The small squares are quilted with a diamond grid with a rose in each spacer.

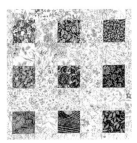

• The subtle merging of patterns makes the four panels opposite, called Seasonal Gardens and made by English quiltmaker Deidre Amsden in 1998, who pioneered the watercolor technique used. The darker squares in the center represent formal gardens with flowerbeds and paving. Just as the countryside has few hard edges and little rigidity, defined shapes break down toward the edges.

Garden quilts are assembled from rosettes consisting of a central hexagon surrounded by two more rings of the shape, in many cases a plain row followed by a patterned one. When the supply of rosettes is considered to be large enough, each one is usually outlined in another fabric, generally a plain and light-colored one—although very dramatic results can be also be achieved when a dark fabric is used instead.

If more hexagons are added to opposite sides of a rosette, an elongated version occurs. Pictorial blocks can be created if the colors are arranged carefully. Hexagons can be joined in rings to make hexagonal Trip Around the World patterns, or in rows to make straight, wave, or diamond settings. Six-pointed stars can be surrounded by contrasting diamonds to make complex hexagons, which can be used in any pattern based on six-sided designs.

• In this traditional Grandmother's Flower Garden design, the yellow flower centers are surrounded by rings of plain hexagons, which are in turn bordered by flower prints typical of the 1930s, when it was made. Each rosette is outlined in white and joined to its neighbor by a row of small green diamonds that make a path through the quilt. Equilateral triangles are used at the points of each rosette.

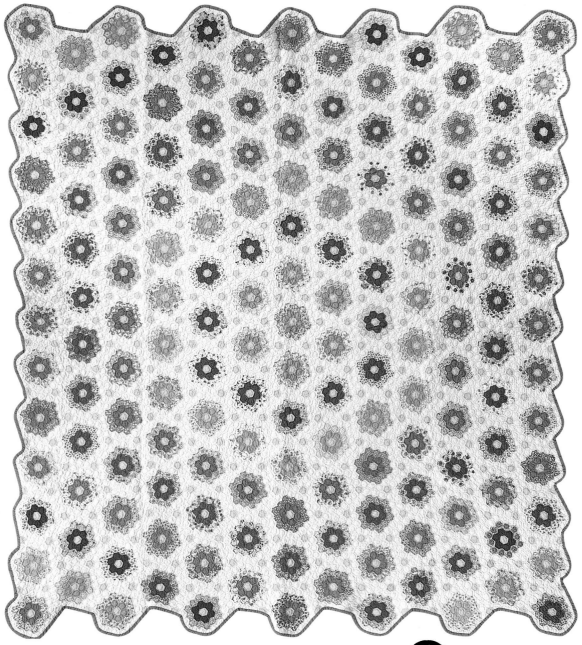

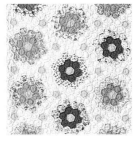

• This Hexagon Trip Around the World with Stepping Stones is made up of 4–5,000 individual hexagons. The basic pattern is Grandmother's Flower Garden, but the rosettes are organized from the center outward like a traditional Trip Around the World. Each rosette has a bright yellow center; the same fabric has been used to create a regular pattern of "stepping stones" between the background rosettes. The binding outlines each finished shape along the edge.

English paper piecing

Mosaic patchwork patterns are traditionally worked using the method known as English paper piecing (*see page 20*). The technique involves cutting out a supply of identical shapes the finished size of the piece from heavy paper, and basting fabric shapes cut slightly larger to them. Particularly useful for triangles, diamonds, and hexagons, which each have at least two sides that cannot be cut on the straight grain of the fabric, the method stabilizes the edges, which are then whip-stitched together into the chosen pattern. The technique seems

• The quilt opposite was made in 2002 by four members of The Weyward Quilters in Surrey, England, to raise money for a hospice. Hexagon rosettes form the flowers in the hexagon basket; the diamond border around the basket is made up of hexagonal lozenges, and there are more rosettes in each of the corners.
Collection of Vera Moles

• This quilt, called "Rise & Shine, Inner City," was made in 1997 by Martha W. Ginn of Hattiesburg, Mississippi. The basic block is called Inner City and is made from trapezoids, placed here into color-coded "neighborhoods" that are each quilted in a different style—from expanding spirals into straight-line and geometric patterns— as the shading changes.

• This Tumbling Blocks quilt was made by an unknown quilter around 1907. The fabrics used are satin and velvet, and it has a wide double border of two different shades of dark blue. The backing fabric is plain white muslin (calico). Minnesota Historical Society

time-consuming in today's fast-paced world of rotary cutting and chain-piecing, but it provides accuracy that is hard to duplicate, especially on difficult or delicate fabrics. When all the pieces have been sewn together, the papers are removed and the top can be completed in the chosen way. The project to make a block at the end of this section involves the paper-piecing method (*see page 108–109*). The technique can be time consuming, but the accuracy it offers is hard to achieve by any other method so it is well worth the effort. When the fabric shapes are cut, motifs in the pattern of the cloth can be arranged to appear in the center, and stripes can be set to create interesting secondary patterns within the quilt.

English paper piecing has been used for several hundred years, and a number of quilt tops have been discovered with the papers still intact behind the fabric. In the past, quiltmakers used any convenient supply of paper—including old letters, newspapers magazines, and catalogs, and these unfinished treasures can often yield vital clues that can help to date and identify the source of the quilt, as well as the maker.

Project: BABY BLOCKS PLAYMAT

English paper piecing

This small quilt would make a perfect present for a new baby, with its pretty pink and blue color scheme, and its pattern so closely associated with the nursery. It can be used as a crib quilt for a newborn and then as a playmat once the baby is more mobile, but be sure to finish it carefully as it is bound to get lots of hard wear.

Entire quilts can be made from tumbling blocks, but the pattern also works well when it is appliquéd to a background as we have done here. Creating a pyramid emphasizes the diamond shapes on which the pattern is based, and using small groups of floating blocks gives the piece a playful feel appropriate to a young child.

Many people prefer using natural fibers for both fabric and batting in quilts made for children. If you use cotton batting, be sure to wash it first to allow for any shrinkage. This background fabric is widely used for sheets and dust ruffles, and should stand up to heavy laundering.

The machine quilting, a simple outline around the appliquéd shapes, is adequate to hold the layers together securely, but there is plenty of scope for more elaborate quilting if you wish.

1 Trace the diamond template from page 416 and cut 171 shapes from plain paper. To make cutting easier and quicker, use a rotary cutter and ruler to cut the fabrics for your blocks into strips 2" (5cm) wide. You will need approximately three or four full-width strips of each color.

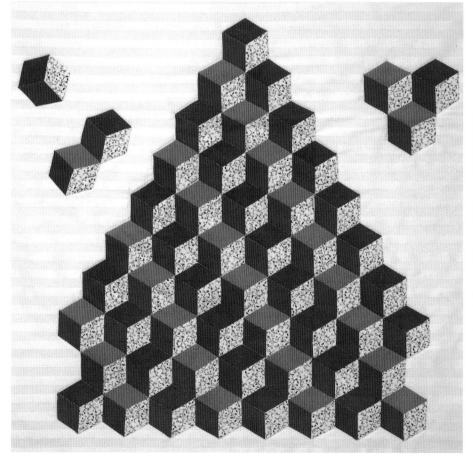

2 Trim one end of each strip at a 60-degree angle. The rotary ruler should include this marking. Cut the rest of the strip into 2" (5cm) diamond-shaped lengths. Repeat to create 171 diamonds in different fabrics.

3 Center a backing paper on a fabric patch, wrong sides together. (The fabric patch should be ¼" (5 mm) larger all around than the paper.) Turn the fabric edges over to the wrong side and baste in place on the backing paper, fingerpressing at the corners before stitching them down. Knot the basting thread on the right side so it is easier to remove later. Prepare all the fabric patches this way.

4 The first stage in assembling the Tumbling Block is to join two contrasting diamonds to make a pair. Place two fabric patches right sides together and overcast or slipstitch neatly along one edge. Make sure the seamlines are in the correct position as you work. The "tails" that protude at each end of the unit will be hidden by the final stitching.

5 Starting in the middle and working out in each direction, overcast or slipstitch the next diamond in place to complete the block. Make 57 blocks in total. Do not remove the backing papers until after the quilt top is complete.

6 Place your completed blocks on a surface and decide on an arrangement. We have alternated blocks of light and dark pink diamonds to create diagonal bands of color throughout the quilt. To assemble the pyramid, start by joining the blocks into strips of 2, 3, 4, 5, 6, 7, and so on, joining the units along one edge only.

7 Then join the strips together to create a tower of blocks. Start at the base of the pyramid with a strip of 8 blocks and join it to a strip of 7 blocks. Continue piecing the blocks together in this way to complete the tower.

CURVES

• In this bedspread, the traditional Grandmother's Fan pattern has been given an oriental flavor. Japanese "cloud" fans alternate with typical pieced fans made from eight blades cut from a wonderful assortment of small-scale print fabrics. The appliquéd fans are made from a selection of upholstery fabrics with gently curved cloud shapes applied along the top and bottom of each fan shape. Each fan is mounted on a blue background and outlined with herringbone-stitch embroidery in the style of a traditional crazy quilt.

Curving shapes give movement and liveliness in a way that cannot be matched by straight lines. Curved designs in quilts are among the most beautiful, but they are often intricate and can be tricky to piece. Curves are found more often in appliqué work than in patchwork, but there are many patterns for quiltmakers who prefer to piece their blocks, including a number that are made from only two simple shapes. Many curved patterns work best when they are sewn by hand, but with care it is possible to machine-piece some of the designs, at least in some stages, to speed up the process. In some cases, the technique known as English paper piecing is an ideal, if time-consuming, way to work. Because curved edges are highly vulnerable to stretching, each piece of fabric must be handled with great care.

Patterns like Double Wedding Ring and the Fans and Plates, in their many variations, provide quiltmakers with a good way to use up the contents of their scrap baskets, especially when there is consistency in the background fabric. Others, such as Drunkard's Path (*see page 117*), Orange Peel, and Robbing Peter to Pay Paul, are most effective when a limited palette is used.

Double Wedding Ring

One of the best-known of the curved quilt patterns is Double Wedding Ring, an example of which is shown on page 118–9. The design first shows up on quilts made in the 1920s, and reached its peak of popularity in the 1930s, when there were numerous patterns with templates published in magazines and newspapers. Precut kits were also available. There is no evidence linking the pattern with a wedding tradition in earlier times, when quilts were made in large numbers for and by brides—in fact the name probably comes from its interlocking circles of fabric pieces.

It is firmly associated with quiltmaking during the Great Depression, when it undoubtedly became a favorite because it afforded hard-pressed quiltmakers, hit by the worldwide economic downturn, a chance to create a beautiful design that relied heavily on scraps. A challenging pattern usually attempted by more experienced quiltmakers, it is also often worked in the various Amish communities, with many wonderful traditional examples containing jewel-colored plain fabrics set on a dark blue or black background, as well as those backed with cream or white.

Fans and Plates

Known in Victorian times as Fanny's Fan, the pattern usually called Grandmother's Fan, and the related Dresden Plate (*see pages 113 and 114–5*), are two groups of curved patterns with dozens of variations that have remained popular since their heyday in the 1920s and '30s. Because, like Double Wedding Ring, they work well using scraps, they are firmly associated with the Great Depression era, and many surviving examples are fashioned from the printed fabric sacks in which staples like sugar and flour, as well as chicken feed and seeds, were purchased.

Fans appear in many guises, from the traditional Grandmother's Fan in one corner of a block to Wagon Wheel with four fans, curves facing out and divided by a narrow cross of sashing. Snake in the Hollow has two fans, in opposite corners, with blocks joined so that the diagonal bands of color snake sinuously across the quilt. Two fans joined point to point in the middle of the block make a wonderful pieced butterfly. Dresden Plate is effectively four fans placed in a circle in the center of the block.

The edges of both Fans and Plates can be as varied as the blocks themselves. They can

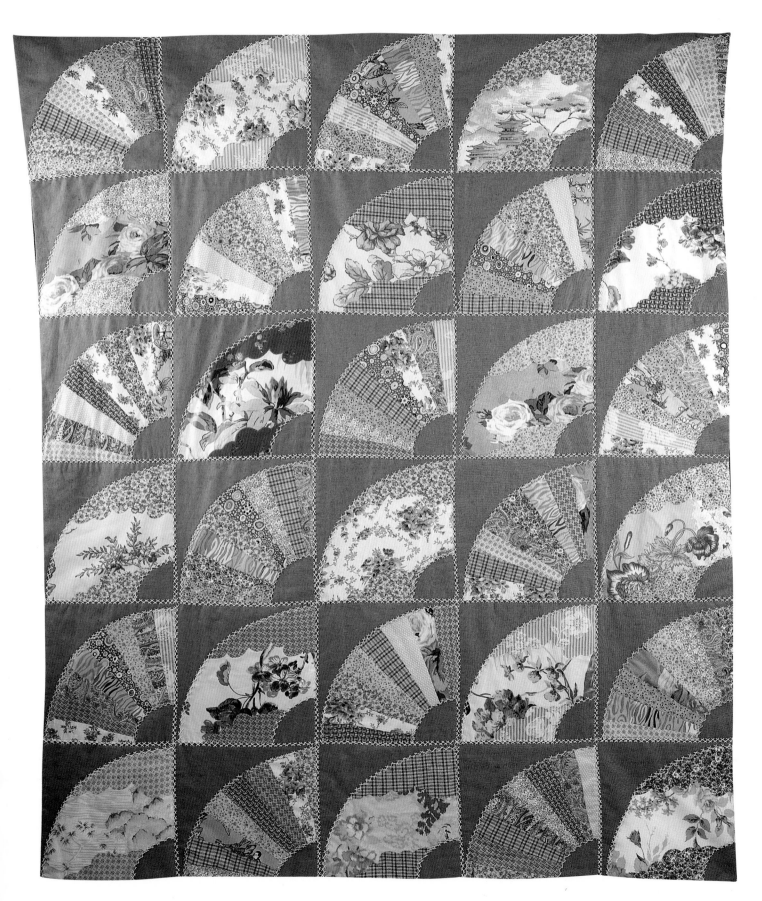

• This Dresden Plate variation has curved "petals" made, as with so many quilts of this type, of random scraps. Some of the scraps are floral, but a lot of them are stripes, checks, and even plaids that appear to be shirt material. Many of the colors have faded since the quilt was made between 1930–40, but it retains a lively effect of pinwheels whirling in the wind. The center of each flower is appliquéd in place, and the bright pink ice-cream-cone border displays the same random choice of scraps.

be cut flat, tapering into each other smoothly. They can be rounded or pointed, and these types can be mixed and alternated with very great effect.
The borders found on many traditional Dresden Plate quilts are, for some reason, often quite elaborate, ranging from ice-cream cones and applied circles to half-plate versions that match the ones featured on the quilt. The plain, and usually very light-colored, background areas on both Fans and Plates are relatively large and so lend themselves well to being quilted.

Robbing Peter to Pay Paul.
The curved patterns that go by the name Robbing Peter to Pay Paul are constructed from units made of two simple pieces in strongly contrasting colors which, when joined, look like a square with a bite taken out of one corner. Complex and interesting versions can be made from more than two colors, but most historical examples have only two, and the strongest color contrasts provide the most striking quilts. Red and white combinations are popular and highly graphic. Blue and white is another widely seen mix,

• Many of the fabrics used in the 1940's Teabag quilt shown opposite—stripes, checks, ginghams, and small-scale prints—have been used more than once, but the random way the sections have been combined means they never feel repetitive. Outline quilting has been used throughout.

• The multicolored fans in this fancy Dresden Plate design, which was pieced around 1930, are made from an enormous number of different scraps, most of them floral prints entirely typical of their era. The segments have rounded ends, while the yellow pieces that occur at the compass point positions, all made from the same fabric, are pointed. The top is heavily marked, and there may have been some delay between when the top was made and when the quilting was worked.

• This variation of Drunkard's Path is unusual—looked at one way it seems to be a diagonal row of hearts, seen another it could be close ranks of plain blue-and-white butterflies. The individual pieced squares are quite small and there are many seams, so the quilter has chosen a simple diamond grid overall, with diagonals stitched in one direction, and intersected by vertical lines. It was made around 1920.

• The red-and-white Drunkard's Path blocks in the wonderfully graphic quilt shown opposite, which dates from around 1910 to 1920, alternate with plain white setting squares, which have been quilted with a feathered wreath pattern. This version of the pattern is truly a Robbing Peter to Pay Paul design, since half of the patches have a red "bite" taken out and the other half have white "bites."

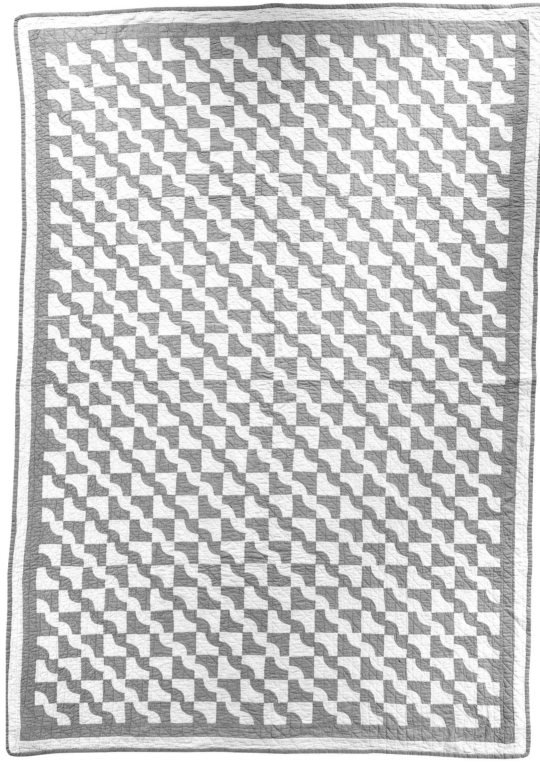

especially in quilts made in the variation known as Drunkard's Path. A group of so-called Temperance quilts dating from the late nineteenth century were made in the society's colors of blue and white by members of the Women's Christian Temperance Union, formed in Ohio in 1874 to stop the sale of alcohol.

Drunkard's Path places blocks in diagonal rows, and the curved pattern creates a twisted, staggering "path" across the quilt. The name is, however, objectionable to some, and it has many variations. Amish quilters, whose religion does not allow drinking alcohol, call the pattern Old Maid's Puzzle. Depending on the way the blocks are joined, patterns can have names like Dove, Steeplechase, Falling Timbers, Love Ring, Chain Link, Fool's Puzzle, and World Without End, among

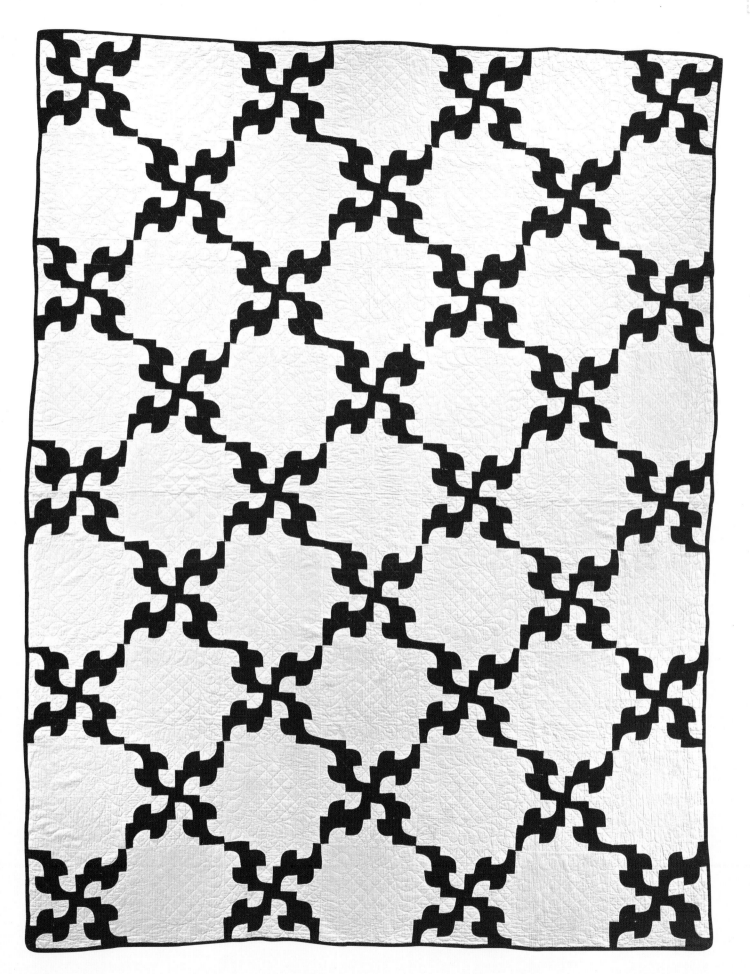

• Developed by American patchworkers in the early twentieth century, Double Wedding Ring is a challenging pattern because of the large number of pieces used and the difficulty of the curved shapes. This example was made around 1990 in Lancaster County, Pennsylvania, in colors—jewel-like pinks, reds, and blues—that are typical of the region and which seem to shimmer against the black background. Roses with leaves filling the space are quilted in the large black background areas, while the so-called melon shapes are outline-quilted and diagonal lines cross the four diamonds where rings meet. The lack of a border reinforces the curved feeling of the pattern.

others. In some variations, the units are all the same; in others the colors of the pieces alternate, with the smaller piece light in half the blocks and dark in the other half.

The design known as Orange Peel, also called Lafayette, Joseph's Coat, and Melon Patch, has a long ellipse that runs diagonally down the middle of each square unit. The group of patterns called Pincushion is a square with a shallow curve starting at each of the four corners, leaving a shape similar to Cathedral Window (*see page 138*), in the center, which can be filled with other blocks, such as a Four- or Nine-Patch. Again the colors can be alternated or each unit can be the same. When the squares are joined into Four-Patch blocks, wonderful secondary patterns emerge.

Clamshell

Clamshell, and the related Apple Core patterns, are among the most difficult of all quilt designs to piece. Clamshell is an old traditional pattern, and its simple rounded elegance gives Clamshell quilts a timeless

appeal. But the depth of its curve makes it complex to assemble, and most quiltmakers use the English paper piecing method when working it and the related designs.

Clamshell with its fully rounded half-circle is usually worked with the stems of the piece pointing all in the same direction, but the pieces can be alternated with stems facing each other to create a completely different effect. The Apple Core patterns have concave bites taken from opposite sides of a circular piece, drafted in such a way that the head of each piece fits into the side of another. Both these patterns, in all their variations, require absolute precision in cutting and piecing.

Other curved patterns

There are numerous other designs that rely on curved shapes, including a group of Knot patterns, and another set of Compass shapes made as Four-Patch blocks. Many curved patterns need to be cut using templates that can easily be traced from pattern books or carefully drafted.

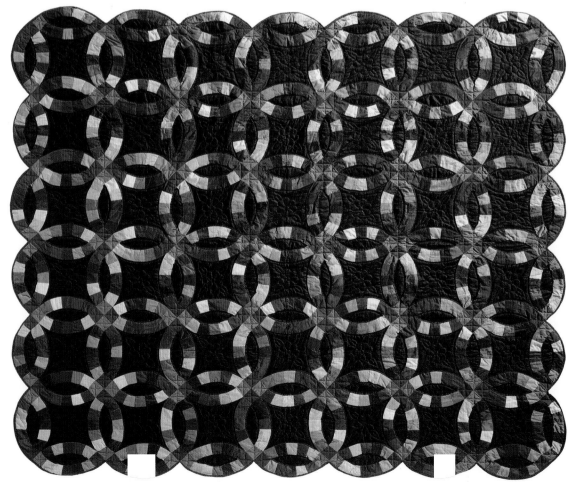

• The curves used in the Mohawk Trail block are gentle, which is just as well since this is a very difficult block to piece accurately. Based on a Double Four-patch, each section is made the same way and put together in strict order to create the block. Quilted sunflowers fill the centers of this World War I-era quilt, while lines flow through the red areas. Running feathers have been used in the white outer areas of the blocks and the border.

Making curved blocks

The meticulousness needed for curved designs begins with the marking and cutting of the fabric pieces (and the paper backing pieces if they are being used). Even pulling a marking pen or pencil across the fabric can begin a process of stretching that may create problems later. When you are cutting with scissors, hold the scissors steady and move only the fabric to cut carefully around the shape of the curve. Special templates are available for rotary cutting of some shapes. Use a small rotary cutter if possible.

Accurate marking of seam allowances is essential whether you are sewing by hand or machine. Adding a notch at the center point of each piece along the seam allowances is useful for matching. Curves are either concave (inward) or convex (outward), and once the seam allowance has been added, the outer edge of the concave piece is slightly smaller than the raw edge of the convex one.

To fit a convex curve into a concave one, match the center notches and pin, then match and pin the corners of the seamline. Ease the shapes and add enough pins to hold the shapes in place while you stitch. If you make a tiny clip in the seam allowance of the concave piece WITHOUT cutting anywhere near the seamline, the piece will be more flexible and easier to work with. The clipped edge should open enough to make the pieces fit together.

If you are stitching by hand, use small running stitches or a tiny backstitch, but make sure the needle is going through the marked seamline on both the front and back pieces each time. Finish the seam securely. If you are working by machine, you need enough pins to keep the seamlines on both pieces level. Place the flatter piece of fabric on the bottom and stitch. Ease puckers as you work. Pressing the seam toward the concave (inward) curve means you won't need to clip the convex seam allowance to make the piece lie flat.

• Called North Shore Beauties, Jennifer Cooper's original design is based on Karen Stone's New York Beauty pattern. Using graph paper and a photocopier to alter the sizes of the blocks, she then foundation-pieced the curved and triangular pieces and interspersed them with plain filler squares.

Project: CHAIN LINKS QUILT

Using templates/Working with curved seams

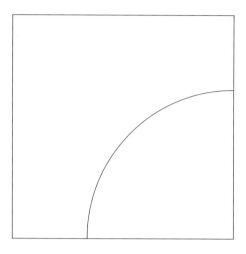

This intricate-looking pattern is a variation of Drunkard's Path. It uses the same two shapes to make squares, but the arrangement of the blocks creates a series of ever-increasing rings that can go on and on to make a large square. It can also be pieced by hand, in which case mark the seamlines from the template carefully on each patch.

Drunkard's Path and all its numerous variations—with evocative names like Wonder of the World, Falling Timbers, Dove, Love Ring, Snowball, and Fool's Puzzle, to name but a few—are all based on a square with a curved "bite" taken out of one corner—another variation is called Robbing Peter to Pay Paul.

Some of these patterns need half the blocks to be pieced in one combination and half in the other, but Chain Links uses identical blocks to create its effect. Any of the Drunkard's Path designs can be made as scrap quilts, but you must choose your fabrics carefully to keep the color values even throughout the piece or you will risk losing the pattern. The stronger the contrast, the better it will look.

In Chain Links, in particular, the balance between the dark and the light colors is crucial. We have used light corners and a dark main square, but a completely different look would occur if these colors were swapped.

1 Trace your template onto template plastic, or make templates from cardboard. Take care to position the notch precisely on each template.

2 Using a rotary cutter and ruler, cut the dark fabric into five strips 6½" (16.5cm) wide, and the light fabrics into four strips 4½" (11.5cm) wide.

3 Fold each strip in half right sides together to create a double-thickness layer. Draw around the relevant template to make 18 of each shape (9 of each color). Pin the top and bottom layers of fabric together ready for cutting.

4 Carefully cut out the shapes with scissors, paying close attention to the notches. Remove the pins. You should have 36 of each shape (18 of each color).

5 Place a large dark-colored patch right side up in front of you. Place a small light-colored "corner" patch on top, right sides together. Align the notches on each patch and insert a pin. Align the side edges and pin again.

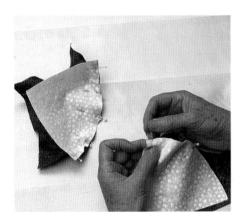

6 Add more pins along the curved edge, placing them in between the existing pins. Assemble 36 blocks in this way, aligning the notches carefully each time.

7 Stitch along the curved edge, making a precise ¼" (5mm) seam allowance, removing pins as you work. You can chain-piece the blocks for speed.

8 Press the seams on the reverse toward the darker side. If you have cut and stitched accurately, there should be no need to clip the curve.

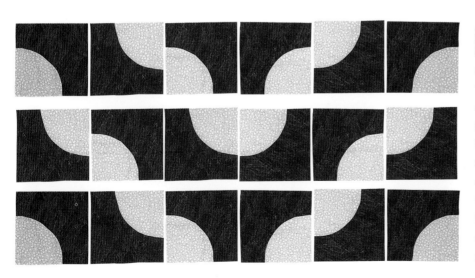

9 Lay out the completed blocks to make six rows of six. Rows 1, 3, and 5 are the same configuration, as are rows 2, 4. and 6. Refer to the illustration on the left to make sure the pattern is correct. Stitch the blocks together in rows and press the seams of each row in opposite directions. Join the rows together.

CRAZY PATCHWORK

• This crazy patchwork coverlet, made around 1890, is created with random patches of silk fabrics that have been heavily embellished with mainly floral motifs. Line stitches outline each piece and many different flowers appear, from fuchsias and rosebuds to pansies and daisies. A sunflower, a symbol of adoration, adorns the middle of the piece, surrounded by a bouquet of leaves and other flowers embroidered on the black center square. The wide black silk border is decorated with a vine of wild roses, and a scalloped lace edging finishes the piece, which has no batting and is not quilted. University of Nebraska-Lincoln

When most people think of crazy quilts, they think of genteel ladies of the late Victorian era sewing beside the fire on beautiful silk and velvet fabrics. This image has some truth, but crazy patchwork was made in towns, cities, and country homes on both sides of the Atlantic in vast profusion. And the roots of the technique go back much further. Logic tells us what historians believe—that using scraps joined randomly as they came to hand was one of the first forms of patchwork—but there is little surviving evidence since the pieces would have been roughly sewn and subjected to heavy use.

Because many of the dresses made in the last quarter of the nineteenth century were made with silk, satin, taffeta, and velvet instead of the cotton and wool homespun fabrics of an earlier time, there were no doubt copious scrap baskets in most homes, and thrifty housewives would have been loathe to throw away even small pieces. At the 1876 Centennial Exposition in Philadelphia, Pennsylvania, held to celebrate the 100th anniversary of the founding of the United States, and the first world's fair to take place in North America, a Japanese exhibitor showed work that combined fine fabrics of

• Made from hundreds of wool scraps, this beautiful quilt is dated 1891 and bears the initials IMB. There are twenty individual blocks made in a Crazy Log Cabin technique from strips of fabric stitched in a fairly random fashion around a central shape. The center of each of the blocks is decorated with a motif—a dog, an owl, a child, a good-luck horseshoe—and each strip is outlined with elaborate straight-line embroidery stitches. There are lots of flowers, all worked with the same great skill as the rest of the stitching.

different textures that were then embellished with embroidery. Some historians think that this moment may have set quiltmakers on the road to crazy patching, and many crazy quilts of the time contain a Fan block, as did the original exhibited piece.

Another part of the exposition held an exhibit of decorated household items that had been made by stitchers at the Royal School of Needlework in London. Crazy quilts existed before this time, but perhaps the Exposition helped popularize the style, first among middle- and upper-class women who had

more time to devote to decorative pursuits like needlework than they had in the past, and then among the working women who tried to emulate them.

Embellishment

The fine quilts made from expensive fabrics were almost all heavily embellished with embroidery, beads, buttons, and bits of lace and ribbon. Embroidery that covers the seams between pieces is a strong element in crazy patchwork. The needlework, which usually contains a variety of stitches, can be worked

• The beautifully executed fans and the obvious overall planning in this work are too carefully organized to make this a true crazy quilt, but the use of random patches of leftover silk fabric and the highly decorative embellishment put it into the category of "controlled crazy patchwork." Designed and made by Mary Ann Crocker Hinman (1817-1893) in New York state between 1880 and 1890, this throw or coverlet shows an oriental influence, perhaps from the 1876 Centennial Exposition in Philadelphia, Pennsylvania, where Japanese goods were introduced to the American public for the first time.

The symmetrical blocks are made in crazy style, and each block has at least one fan. The blades of the fans are embellished with feather stitch, and each fan is outlined with herringbone stitch. There are none of the pictorial motifs usually associated with crazy patchwork, but the maker has used a variety of individual embroidery stitches to decorate various areas. American Folk Art Museum/Gift of Ruth E. Avard

• Rose Garden, by French quiltmaker Estelle Morin, is created from thirty tiny 2½" (6 cm) blocks of Crazy Log Cabin. The color varies dramatically between blocks, all pieced on a non-woven foundation, so they look very different but are actually constructed in exactly the same way.

• The quilt opposite is dated 1883; its maker, Margaret A. Beattie, was born around 1860. It is made from silk and silk velvet, with twenty blocks the same size, each with a pieced corner fan. The motifs create diagonal rows, alternated to point up in one row, down in the next, controlling the design without losing the crazy quilt chaos. It is beautifully executed, and virtually every scrap has an embroidered motif. Milwaukee Art Museum/ Funded by Marion Wolfe, Mrs. Helen L. Pfeifer & Friends of Art

in embroidery floss or several strands of thread. Hundreds of motifs can be found on crazy quilts, some appliquéd in place, while others are embroidered right through the cloth. Natural forms like flowers, trees, leaves, and fruit are featured, with animals, birds, and people also very popular. Most crazy quilts contain a fan, an owl, a horseshoe, or a spider's web, and many display all these symbols of good luck.

Because they were generally mounted on a foundation fabric that gave them added stability, and since they were not usually given heavy use, many of these early crazy quilts have survived more or less intact. Many were not technically quilts, since they are neither batted nor quilted. Most would not have been laundered, made as they were from very delicate, non-washable fabrics. They were in fact often display pieces—throws or lap quilts, table or piano covers, or decorative bedspreads that were never used for sleeping under. Many were edged with handmade lace or a fringe. They are of particular interest as a group, because many of them are dated, a habit that was not widespread among quiltmakers until the current generation, and a goodly number are either signed or at least initialled or monogrammed, so rather more is known about the exact circumstances of their making than with most other groups of antique quilts.

• Crazy Log Cabin and carnival colors inspired this quilt, made by Sandra Wyman. The fabrics were hand-dyed, and the patchwork was quilted both by hand and by free machine stitching. It also includes "in the ditch" quilting along the seam lines.

• The multicolored crazy quilt shown opposite, made by Dora Timm in the 1920s, is pieced entirely of irregularly shaped patches of velvet. Sprigs of colorful embroidered flowers, leaves, and buds are scattered over the surface, and two sides have a blackish-blue fringe 6" (15 cm) long. The backing is a single piece of deep red quilted satin, which folds over the top and bottom of the front of the quilt to form a border along these edges only. Minnesota Historical Society

Transatlantic divisions

There are interesting differences between the crazy patchwork of Britain and the United States. British crazy quilts are usually made into one large, solid piece of patchwork, which is then backed and bound after the embellishment has been added. American crazy quilts tend to exist as pieces made from blocks of crazy patchwork, some quite large, that are joined to make a full-size piece. Many American examples are sashed to separate each crazy block into a self-contained unit, and these quilts are known as "contained crazy quilts." A number of American quilts have a large image in the center of the quilt portraying a famous person or perhaps a beloved pet.

On both sides of the Atlantic, crazy quilts of a more prosaic nature were made from wool and cotton. Woolen versions tended to use larger pieces—many of them left over from the tailoring of suits and coats—than those found on silk quilts. They were also embellished, sometimes with thick embroidery thread, but occasionally with heavy wool yarn. Cotton scraps were used to make so-called crumb quilts, which were seldom decorated, but were quilted to hold the batting in place. The small pieces of fabric found in many of these quilts points to their origins as true scrap quilts, made for warmth and from necessity.

Making crazy patchwork

Although some antique crazy quilts have odd-shaped pieces with curves, it is much easier to work crazy patchwork if the raw edges of the pieces are straight. Most favored techniques

utilize some sort of foundation to stabilize the scraps, from a lightweight cotton fabric or fusible webbing, to batting or fleece fabric. It is generally much easier to start in the middle of your foundation backing square, and continue working toward the edges in a convenient sequence, depending on the size and shape of the scraps you are using. Divide your scraps into different groups according to their color or tonal value if you wish to achieve a certain effect.

If you use fusible webbing, you will need to iron the webbing to the wrong side of each scrap, and then peel off the backing paper and iron the scrap directly to a foundation fabric. Continue adding the scraps one by one until the block has reached the desired size. It is then very simple to embellish the edges of the pieces to finish them neatly—although because they are already stabilized by the adhesive in the webbing, this serves a function more decorative than essential. It will be easier to embroider if you use a lightweight webbing and if you butt each piece up to the next one as closely as possible without overlapping the edges.

Stitch and flip

If you use fabric or batting as a foundation, you can work using the so-called "stitch and flip" method. A suitable scrap is placed right side up in the center of the foundation and another piece is positioned right side down on top of it. These pieces are joined and the second piece is opened to the right side. The next piece is added in the same way, and so on until the foundation has been covered with scraps. The raw edges are easier to work with if they are straight, but the pieces do not need to meet each other at right angles—in fact, in most cases, they should not. The sides should not match, but should look as if they are randomly positioned.

If you prefer to work by hand, you can baste the pieces in place with an overlap and blind stitch each one, turning under a seam allowance, in turn. Just make sure that the stitches go through all the layers, including the foundation backing, or the pieces will not be anchored and will slip or sag. Then you can embellish the piece as you wish.

• Made around 1890 by Elizabeth Devereux Enright, this pieced and appliquéd crazy quilt has six blocks. Multicolored velvet, taffeta, brocade, satin, ribbon pieces and fancy embroidery pieces are worked with brightly colored silk floss, wool yarn, or chenille. In the center of many plain colored patches are embroidered or painted flower sprays. One patch is a handpainted image of a Saint Paul Winter Carnival ice palace; one patch is an embroidered figure from a Kate Greenaway illustration. The border is a row of satin ribbons, tucked and edges folded back by a line of embroidery stitches. The backing is a dark reddish-brown flannel with a feather stitched edge. Minnesota Historical Society

• Controlled Crazy Quilt c. 1890. Hexagonal units have been constructed from scraps of cotton and combined in a crazy fashion. The pieced shapes are then trimmed to size and joined to yellow squares that produce a gridlike structure in the midst of the whirling patterns made by the red, blue, brown, beige, and black fabrics. Among a number of unusual features of this quilt are its organized nature and the total absence of embroidery.

Project: CRAZY PATCHWORK

Stitch-and-Flip Piecing

The most familiar form of the crazy quilt is a large piece composed totally of random scraps stitched together and often also beautifully embroidered. However, many of the most interesting crazy quilts were made from blocks that were squared off and then combined in a grid.

This method of making contained, or organized, crazy quilts was particularly popular in the United States during the heyday of Victorian crazy quilting. Making crazy quilts in blocks provides a way of controlling the chaos that is inherent in the style, and the patterns that result can be quite fascinating. In this quilt, for example, the yellow squares impose a regular grid on what would otherwise be a random arrangement of fabrics.

1 Using the pattern on page 417, make a template for the hexagon shape. The pattern is the finished size of the shape with no seam allowances.

2 Gather up a pile of scraps and try out various colors, or alternatively put a selection of scraps in a bag and pull them out at random.

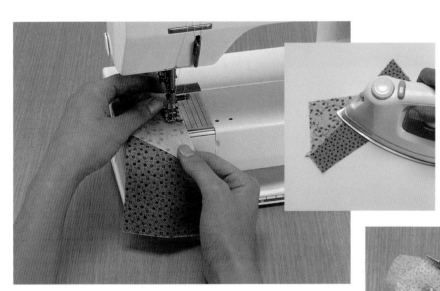

3 The scraps will be stitched together one by one to form a rough hexagon shape, with a generous seam allowance all around the outside edges of the shape. Start with the middle section, and join the first two fabrics, with right sides together. Inset: Press the seam.

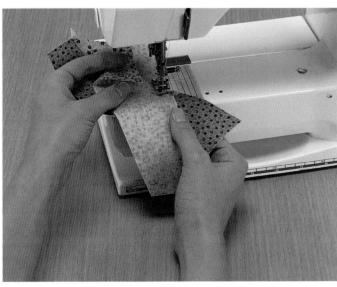

4 Stitch the third fabric to the previous two and then press. This method of construction is sometimes referred to as "stitch and flip."

5 Because many of the pieces will overhang the work, carefully trim the seam allowances as necessary.

FOLDED PATCHWORK

• This wallhanging, made by Munni Srivastava, is part of a series in the cycle of Four Seasons. The browns, grays and dull greens are contrasted with creams, white and silver, with touches of sky-blue and pale pink. The blocks are heavily embroidered and quilted, using much kantha quilting, in varying densities and stitch lengths. The deep panel at the base is made up of 49 Cathedral Window patchwork pieces in carefully graded colors. Shiny, metallic silks were used for some of the "window frames," which contrasts with the dull indigo, matt, block-printed Japanese hemp fabric used for some of the small squares at the center of the windows. Courtesy of American Craft Museum & Munni Srivastava

Most of the folded patchwork patterns have much in common with the Japanese technique of paper folding that is known as origami. Indeed, some quilt historians feel that folded patchwork actually originated in the Far East, and some of the earliest known examples of Cathedral Window are from Korea and China.

In addition to Cathedral Window, and the closely-related pattern called Secret Garden, there are an number of other well-known traditional folded patchwork techniques. The Yo-Yo, or Suffolk Puff, has been found in novelty quilts and other items since at least the early twentieth century. A design called Folded Star, or sometimes Somerset Patchwork, is a folded patchwork design that is useful for table mats and related household items, but it is not often seen in quilts. A whole tradition of Japanese folded patchwork also exists.

Folding fabric for patchwork and quilting has become a life's work for British quilter Jennie Rayment, and anyone who wants to explore the tucking and pleating that are the basis of her work should consult her Batsford book *Creative Tucks and Textures* for more information about her techniques.

Cathedral Window

The best-known and most widely worked folded patchwork pattern is undoubtedly Cathedral Window. The pattern is also called Mayflower, because there is a legend that on board that ship the first Pilgrims to land in North America made bedcovers in this way. However, evidence suggests that the technique is a modern one that was at the peak of its popularity in the 1920s and '30s. This dating to the period of the Great Depression in the United States—when quiltmaking was a way to create warm bedding from remnants and used fabrics— makes some sense. Because the pieces needed for the "windows" are small, it is a good way to use scraps, and the backing fabric most often seen is inexpensive muslin (calico).

A bedcover made in Cathedral Window is technically not a quilt since it has no batting or backing, and isn't even quilted. It does, however, have several layers, and the backing is built into these. The corners of large squares of backing fabric are folded toward the center into smaller squares, which are folded again and then stitched together. A contrasting fabric square, usually patterned, is laid over each seam of the background to hide

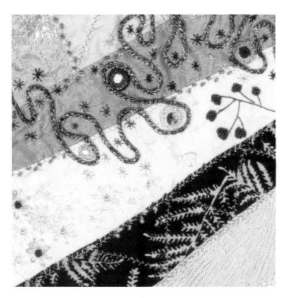

the joins. Then the folded edges are rolled over and slipstitched in place, creating an attractive curved shape along each side of the "window" square. The effect of a finished piece of Cathedral Window is indeed that of a stained-glass window. The background squares can be worked by hand or machine, but the window pieces must be secured by hand. The window squares can be cut to highlight motifs in the fabric, and colors can be graded through the piece to create lovely effects.

If the pattern is worked in reverse, with the patterned fabric basted in the center of each square before the second fold is made, the design is known as Secret Garden. When the corners have been tacked down after the second fold is made, the folded edges are rolled back and slipstitched in place to make sets of four flower-petal shapes in each square.

Yo-Yo

Another Depression-era folded patchwork design is known as the Yo-yo, or by its British name, Suffolk Puff. Like Cathedral Window, it is not batted or backed, and so is not technically a quilt, but it can make an attractive bedspread or pillow cover, and the yo-yo pieces can be strung together to make appealing soft toys in animal shapes or jolly clowns. Yo-yos can also be used to embellish quilts, either sewn on individually or in groups as flowers or berries. They can be blind-stitched in place, or applied with a decorative embroidery stitch to enhance the desired effect.

Yo-yos start as circles of fabric, which should be cut twice as large as the finished yo-yo. A gathering thread is run around the folded-under rim of each one and pulled tight, with the gathered material in the center of one side. The other side of this doubled circle will look smooth. Folding the rim of the circle

• The Cathedral Window quilt shown opposite was made sometime in the twentieth century by Mrs. Quentin (Alice Lee Palmer) Horner, a Minneapolis dressmaker. She has used cotton batiks, predominately in blue and brown, with the "window frames" in plain white cotton fabric. Minnesota Historical Society

• Suffolk puffs, or Yo-yos, can be used to make charming small soft toys, like this adorable clown with his embroidered features and big neck bow. Made by British quilter Pat Clark, the hands and feet are felt and the hair is combed yarn.

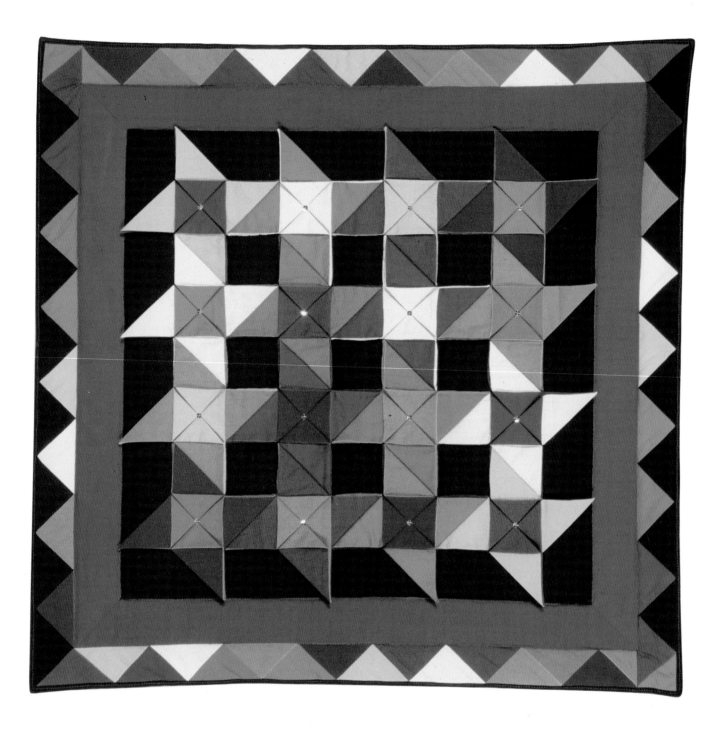

gives a hem at the same time as the gathering is worked.

Pieces are then sewn together by hand. Each circle should have the same side, either gathered or smooth, facing up. Circles are joined on four sides with short seams, so when several yo-yos are combined, there are "holes" between each one. This gives the piece an openwork look.

Folded Star

The folded star technique, which is sometimes called Somerset patchwork or LaGrange Trivet, gives an eight-point star of several layers. It is not suitable for making quilts, but works well in table mats and potholders, which need thickness; attractive cards and tree ornaments can also be created. In addition, they can be used as individual motifs on bags or pockets.

The design comes from folding squares of fabric in half and then folding the corners into the center to make a point. The raw edges of the fabric lie along the long edge of the piece. Four folded squares are laid, points inward and just touching, in the exact center of a circle of foundation fabric. They are then stitched to the foundation along the fold lines.

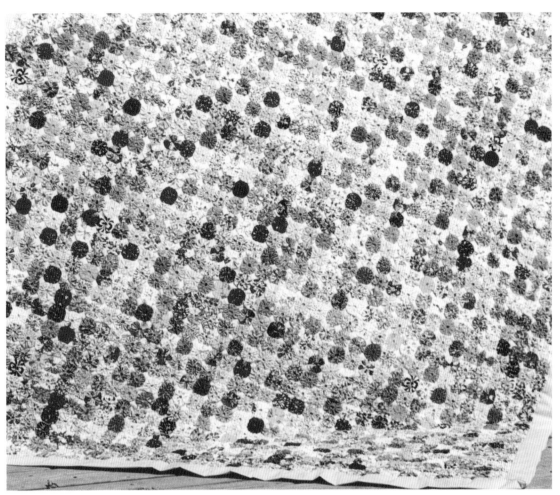

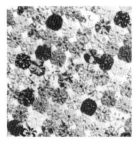

• This Yo-Yo quilt, made around 1970, is not technically a quilt since it does not consist of three layers of top, batting, and backing, and it is not quilted. Once the yo-yos, also called Suffolk Puffs, were joined, the entire piece was mounted on a backing of cotton fabric and the edges were turned from back to front to make a wide binding. The backing stabilizes the piece and makes it into a good lightweight coverlet. There are 1872 circles of fabric in the quilt, each cut by hand using a coffee can as a template.

A second set of squares in a contrasting color, eight in all, are folded, positioned, and stitched in the same way. This is repeated at least once more with another contrasting fabric. When enough layers have been applied, the piece is trimmed and either backed and bound, or incorporated into another piece of work.

Japanese folded patchwork

The technique known as Japanese Folded Patchwork is different from the other methods discussed in that the blocks contain batting. What sets it apart from other block-making is that each unit is batted separately, so when units are joined, the piece is already batted and backed.

Shapes—usually circles—are cut from fabric and the edges are pressed under. Different shapes—squares or hexagons, for example—are cut from contrasting fabric and batting. A batting shape is placed in the center of a circle and a fabric shape is placed, wrong sides together, on top. The turned-under edge of

the circle is folded over the contrasting shape and slipstitched in place creating a framed "window" similar in effect to Cathedral Window. The finished units can then be assembled into quilts or other items. As with Cathedral Window, the inserted fabrics can be cut out to highlight motifs.

Creating folded fabric designs

Many designs can be worked out initially as flat artwork on paper, but since the essence of this kind of work is in its three-dimensional quality, at some point you will have to start folding. This is where trying out designs in paper comes into its own, because you can cut and fold it easily. It is also inexpensive and easy to obtain, so it won't matter if you make a few mistakes along the way.

Folding can also be used in other ways to enhance your quilt design. Prairie points are small squares of fabric folded into triangles and used to edge a border. They can also be incorporated into the body of a quilt or used in place of piping.

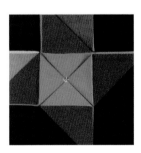

• The quilt opposite by English quiltmaker Louise Mabbs is called "Origami Winds." The detail above shows one of the blocks, which is made of patchwork triangles in bright colors. The same shapes and colors appear on the reverse, but the folded fabric adds an extra dimension to the front of the piece.

Project: FOLDED BLOCK

Cathedral Window block

In her quilt Gardening Leave, made in 2001, English quilter Jinny Jarry has used two related folded blocks to create an abstract wall quilt based on the colors of delphiniums. These folded patchwork blocks are sometimes arranged more formally to create a medallion layout with concentric rows of alternating shades, but Jarry has used this technique to create a glorious colorwash of pink, blue, and purple.

For additional interest, she chose a selection of fabrics—including hand-dyed cotton, velvet, acetate, and loosely woven silk. By combining the Cathedral Window pattern with the similarly constructed Secret Garden design, in which she inserted additional fabrics, she created a beautifully modulated piece. The blocks are made here by hand, and require careful handling to achieve precise seams.

1 Cut 6" (15 cm) square of main fabric using squared paper or a rotary ruler as a guide to keep the sides square.

2 Cut a 5½" (14cm) square of template plastic or cardboard. Then center it on the fabric square and fingerpress a seam allowance all around, to the wrong side if there is one.

3 Fold diagonally to find the center of the main fabric. Fold opposite corners to meet at center. Press each fold in place. Your patch should now be about 4" x 4" (10 x 10 cm).

4 Fold new corners into the center again and press each fold. At the center, carefully but firmly sew points down. Use matching thread, as the stitches will show. The square will now be about 2¾" x 2¾" (7 x 7 cm)

5 Repeat to create 3 more squares. Join the squares wrong (unfolded) sides together, whipstitching (oversewing) with matching thread. This seam will not show as it will be covered with "windows." (The threads can be left in the center to stitch down rolled edges later.)

6 From coordinating and contrasting scraps, cut window squares 2" x 2" (5 x 5 cm). Turn a window square diagonally over the seam edge of two main fabric squares. Position a few squares before stitching—you may want to change your original plan. Put your final selection in place.

7 Roll the edges of the main fabric over the window squares. You may need to trim them very slightly if they wrinkle when you roll the edges. Pin each side. Slipstitch (blindstitch) the rolled edge with matching thread, but don't go all the way through to the background. Make two small stitches across the rolled corners, which will give a crisp finish.

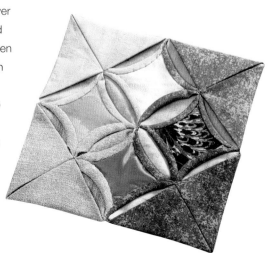

REPRESENTATIONAL

• The unusual Schoolhouse quilt shown opposite has unexpected depths created by the subtle colors, which are set off by splashes of brighter pink and yellow. Like most traditional Amish patchwoork, the design is relatively simple and based on geometric shapes—although the abstraction of early Amish quilts has been abandonded in favor of depicting an actual object, the schoolhouse has been reduced to its simplest form.

Representational and pictorial blocks have long been a part of quiltmaking. The desire to portray familiar everyday objects or to commemorate special events has led to the creation of fabric pictures by traditional and modern quiltmakers, using a variety of techniques. Many representational blocks are appliqué, or are a combination of patchwork and applied work, and creating a repeatable block design in patchwork is something of a challenge.

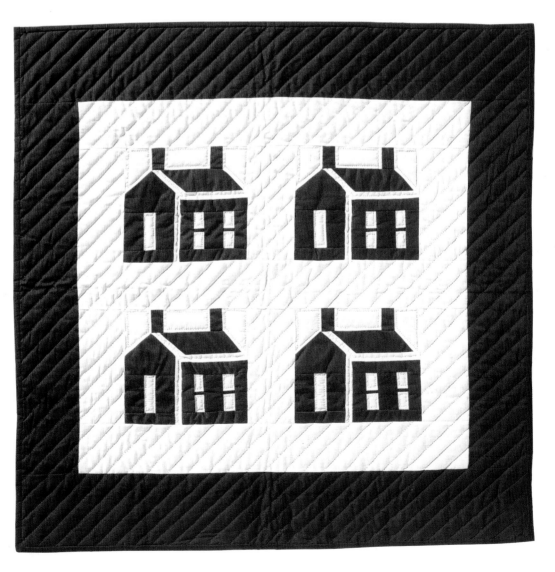

Luckily, it is one that seems to have appealed to quiltmakers for many years, and while realistic pictures such as the ones that often appear on Baltimore Album quilts (*see pages 338-343*) and traditional patterns like Sunbonnet Sue are appliquéd rather than pieced, the creativity of traditional blockmakers has left us with a good number of outstanding examples of pieced representational blocks. Modern quiltmakers continue to design pictures in fabric.

• The simple Schoolhouse quilt on the right has only four buildings, and the sashing is the same cream fabric as the background, so each one seems to occupy an open space. The main elements of each schoolhouse are outline quilted, while the border and sashing are quilted with evenly spaced diagonal lines that unite the elements.

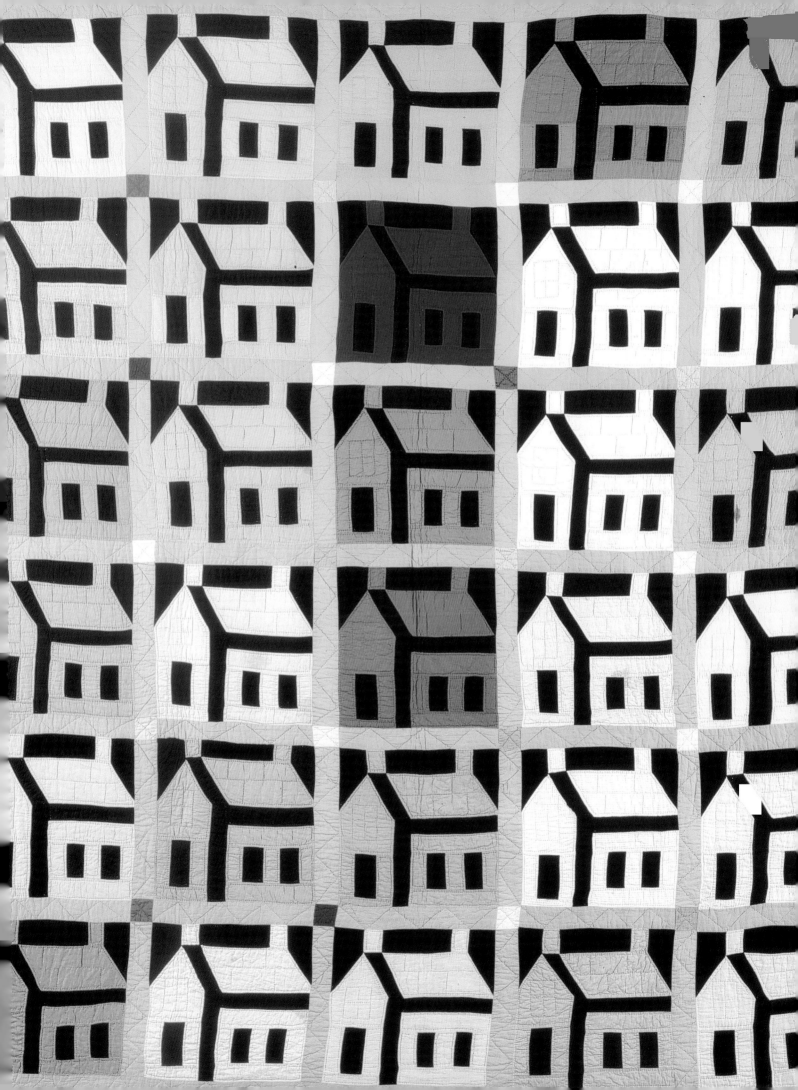

• The combination of colors and the small scale of the printed fabrics are typical of this quilt's date—1890—but the overall impact is modern. Repeating letters to create a pattern is not a nineteenth-century tradition, but the quilt's owner, Patricia Cox, couldn't resist it when she bought it as a top. She designed and commissioned the quilting, which she feels stabilizes and helps to preserve old tops.

• The repeating Kimono design opposite makes good use of recycled fabrics from old Japanese robes. Two types of block make up the quilt: some blocks contain one print and one solid fabric, while others are made from two different prints. Each block is different, but the various indigo fabrics tie the piece together. The pieced sashing is striped, with red corner squares.

Houses and other buildings

Among the best-loved of all picture blocks is the traditional Schoolhouse or Little Red Schoolhouse design. It has a large number of variations; in fact, entire books have been written about the block. It is generally designed to be made using templates to cut the pieces, and many of the shapes are quite intricate. In this category there are versions of schoolhouses, homes, churches and other public buildings, as well as barns.

Designing a Schoolhouse block is an interesting exercise for quiltmakers looking for a challenge, since creating a realistic effect usually requires joining acute angles. Houses in House blocks often look much like a child's drawing of a house, facing front. Adding a steeple or a belfry can easily turn a schoolhouse into a church or city hall.

Letters and alphabets

Letter shapes—learned of course in schoolhouses along with numbers—are another type of representational block. Alphabets were used as learning aids on needlework samplers for several hundred years, especially in the days when girls did not attend school, and some early quilts contained lettering, usually in the form of Bible verses. But using letters and numbers as the design

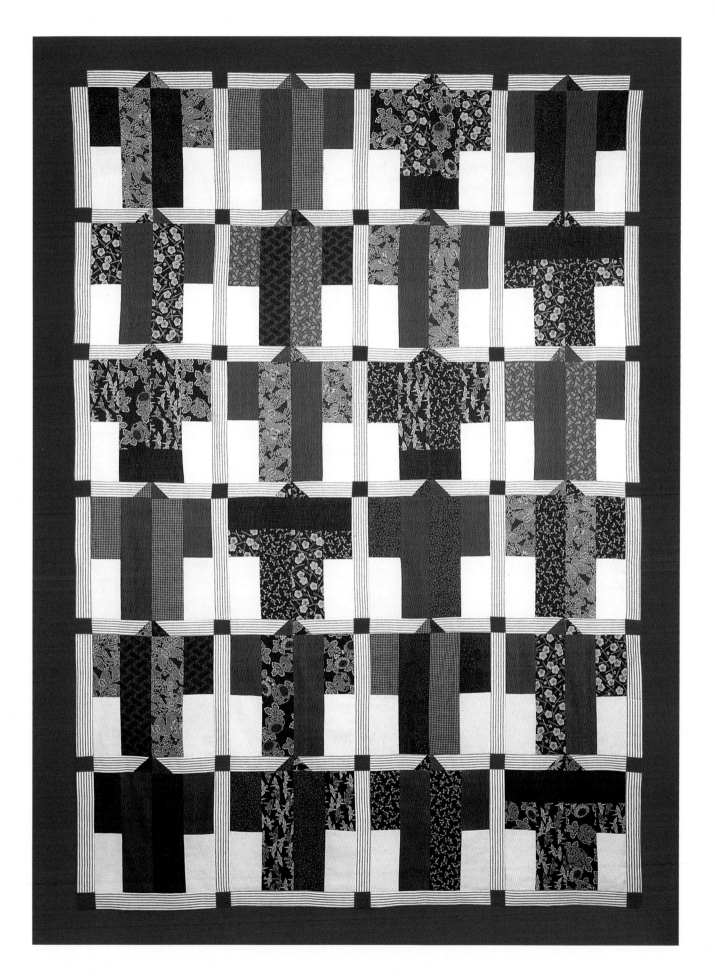

• The background of this small quilted piece consists of strips of graded tones of blue, with blocks containing multicolored kites flying in rows upon it. The small-scale prints are Japanese and the red tails are bias strips with narrow bows that have been anchored to look entirely natural.

• The quilt opposite, made in the last quarter of the nineteenth century, is a pattern called Basket of Chips. The use of random fabrics, mainly brown, beige, and olive green for the baskets and an interesting multicolored selection of tiny triangles for the "chips," which range from navy blue with dots to double pink—both typical of their time— makes this the quintessential scrap quilt.

feature on quilts really came into its own in the early twentieth century. A few alphabet quilts appeared late in the previous century, but the form was first popular in the 1920s. Patterns in different typefaces were published in newspapers and magazines, and many were sold by companies that created needlework designs for patchwork, appliqué, and quilting, as well as embroidery and cross stitch. Surviving quilts vary from repetition of the same letter to full alphabets, and others have letters arranged as monograms and to spell words, especially to write both verses and quotations. Many of the latter type are religious in nature.

While there are hundreds of appliquéd examples of alphabet or letter quilts, there are also many patchwork block versions. Creating a block alphabet is fun and a good exercise in differentiating similar shapes.

• The stylized butterflies that flit across the white surface of this quilt, called "Life is a Butterfly" by its maker, Anne Hardcastle, are made from a variety of red print fabrics. They are pieced using a carefully planned Log Cabin construction and set in a way that gives a random feel, but is anything but.

• Representational blocks are often based on trees. This one, variously called Tree of Paradise, Christmas Tree, and Tree of Life, works well as a scrap pattern as shown by the quilt opposite made in the 1930s. By alternating the light and dark values of the leaves, the maker has created a masterpiece of liveliness.

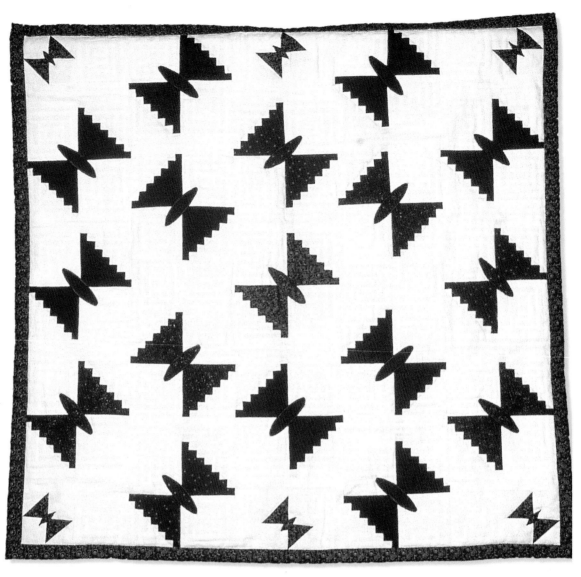

Goods and chattels

Almost any item can be turned into a patchwork pattern. Ships, trains, planes, automobiles, bicycles—all have been the subject of quilt blocks. So have teacups, teapots, goblets, clothing, and spools, as well as tables and chairs, and any other household item. Machines, from those that sew to those that dig, can also be stylized into successful representational blocks.

Baskets

Another popular—and varied type—is the Basket block. Many sampler quilts, made from blocks that are all different but tied together by color or theme, contain at least one Basket block. In most versions, the basket itself is made from triangles of various sizes, although parallelograms are sometimes found. Sometimes there is a "handle" made

from right-angle triangles, or triangle or diamond shapes fill the area above the basket to represent flowers or other things contained within (*see page 149*). Assembling the blocks usually requires care since many of the pieces are triangles or diamonds and therefore have bias edges liable to stretching.

There are many traditional names for Basket blocks from Bread Basket, Fruit Basket, Grape Basket, and Tea Basket to Colonial Basket, Tulip Basket, Pieced Baskets and Basket of Scraps—sometimes known as Flowerpot. Carolina Lily, or North Carolina Lily, is a complicated block designed, as are most Basket blocks, to be set on point. Its complexity comes with the three pieced lilies on long thin stems that rise out of the basket.

As with other representational designs, there is a vast variety among Basket blocks, which were popular through much of the

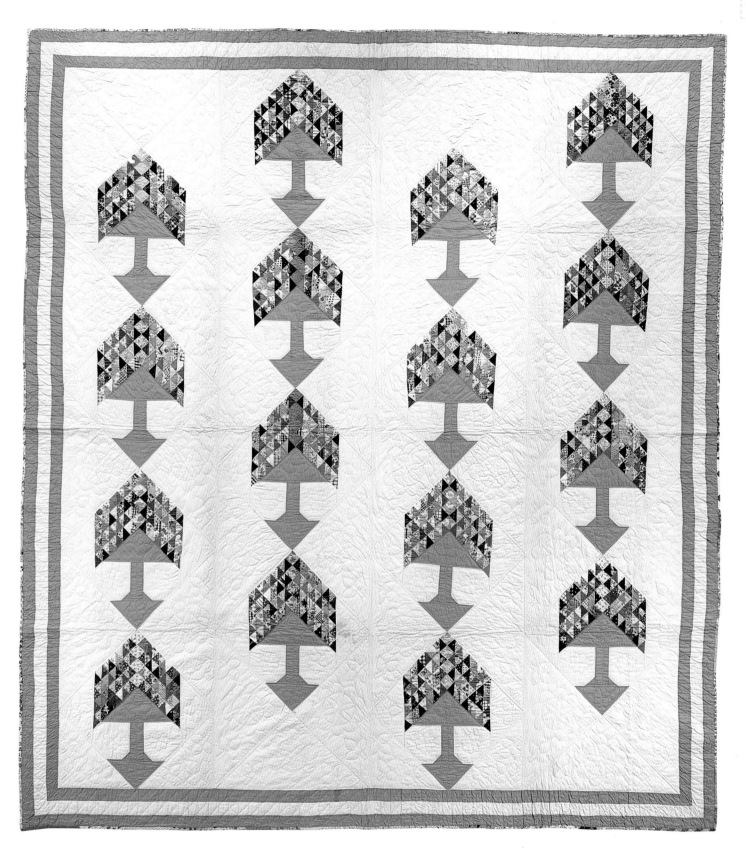

nineteenth century and remain so today. Although the patterns usually seen in Amish quilts are not usually pictorial, both Basket and Schoolhouse blocks are widely used by Amish quiltmakers—perhaps because they represent values that are important to the Amish community—and the designs do lend themselves to being made from the traditional solid-colored fabrics found in Amish work.

Plants and animals

Almost any botanical or zoological subject can be turned into a representational block

• This stunning map quilt, dated 1886 in Roman numerals embroidered on the boundary between Oregon and Washington, was constructed using the crazy quilt method from silk velvet and brocade. Each state is outlined with embroidery, as are the "Y" shapes that make up the busy background, but the application of further embellishment is uneven. Five states have been given symbols—flowers in Illinois, Iowa, and Wyoming; a spider's web in the corner of Colorado, and a large star in Texas—but no one knows whether these states were particularly important to the quiltmaker. She has outlined the entire country with a strip of brown fabric applied with herringbone stitch on each edge, and added the Great Lakes in dark blue, with the major rivers—the Ohio and the Missouri flow into the mighty Mississippi, while the Potomac runs down to the Atlantic on the east coast—beautifully worked in light blue ribbon. American Folk Art Museum, New York/Gift of Dr. & Mrs. C. David McLaughlin

with the clever use of a grid. Flowers are perennial favorites, with lilies, tulips, and roses high on the list of popular motifs. Leaf patterns such as Maple Leaf, Sweet Gum Leaf, Tea Leaf, Clover, and Ivy, and tree blocks like Pine Tree, Tree of Life, and Tree of Paradise are also widely seen, and all these designs have myriad variations.

Animals—from butterflies and other insects, bats, and birds to elephants and donkeys—can be devised, and the human figure can be stylized into a recognizable block shape.

Patriotic icons

Flags and other patriotic motifs are found on quilts, and were particularly popular in American quilts during the late nineteenth and early twentieth century. At one point there was a craze for Donkey blocks and Elephant blocks which hinted to the world the maker's political leanings toward either the Democratic or the Republican party.

Patriotism in the United States took a back seat following World War II, but resurfaced with great impact in numerous pieces designed after the attacks of September 11, 2001. Many older designs have been adapted and incorporated alongside new techniques in work commemorating those who died in the catastrophic events of that day.

Out of the box

In addition to patchwork quilts made from pictorial blocks, there is a body of work that defies categorization. The crazy-quilt map on the right is one good example. It is highly representational, a pieced-work quilt, and a truly unique piece.

Other American map quilts have surfaced, providing interesting information about when they were made. The date can often be determined by which states have been included. Some quilts depict only one state. British map quilts also exist and remind us of the old counties and their traditional names. Some map quilts are appliquéd, while many are pieced.

Project: BASKET BLOCK

Turning a block on point

Baskets, of course, come in various shapes and sizes, and many of them are turned on point. This version can be assembled as a Double Four-Patch block and it is bound using the back-to-front method. Fifteen of these blocks could be combined to make a single bed quilt.

Cutting

1 Cut out the pieces required (*see inset*). You can cut all the smaller squares from a strip of fabric, measuring each carefully.

2 For the basket, cut seven 4¾" (12cm) squares in various colors. Cut each one in half across the diagonal to make 14 right-angle triangles.

3 Cut one rust and one black 8½" (21.5cm) squares. Use a square ruler to make sure the edges are equal.

Stitching

4 Chain-piece the smaller triangles together into squares. Join one of each contrasting color to rust; one light blue to black; one purple to black, one dark blue to green. Inset: Press all seams to the darker side.

5 Lay out the pieced squares together with the 4⅜" (11 cm) rust squares before you combine the pieces (see inset). Join the pairs first, then join the paired strips to make three Four-Patch units.

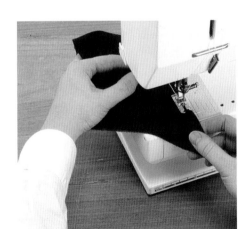

6 Next, join the large black and rust triangles to make the fourth unit of the block—the bottom of the basket.

7 Join the pieced squares in pairs with a ¼" (5mm) seam, following the layout (see left). Then join the pairs as shown into the finished block.

8 To set the block on point, cut two black 11½" (29cm) squares and cut them in half diagonally. Join one of the resulting triangles to each side of the basket block and press the seams.

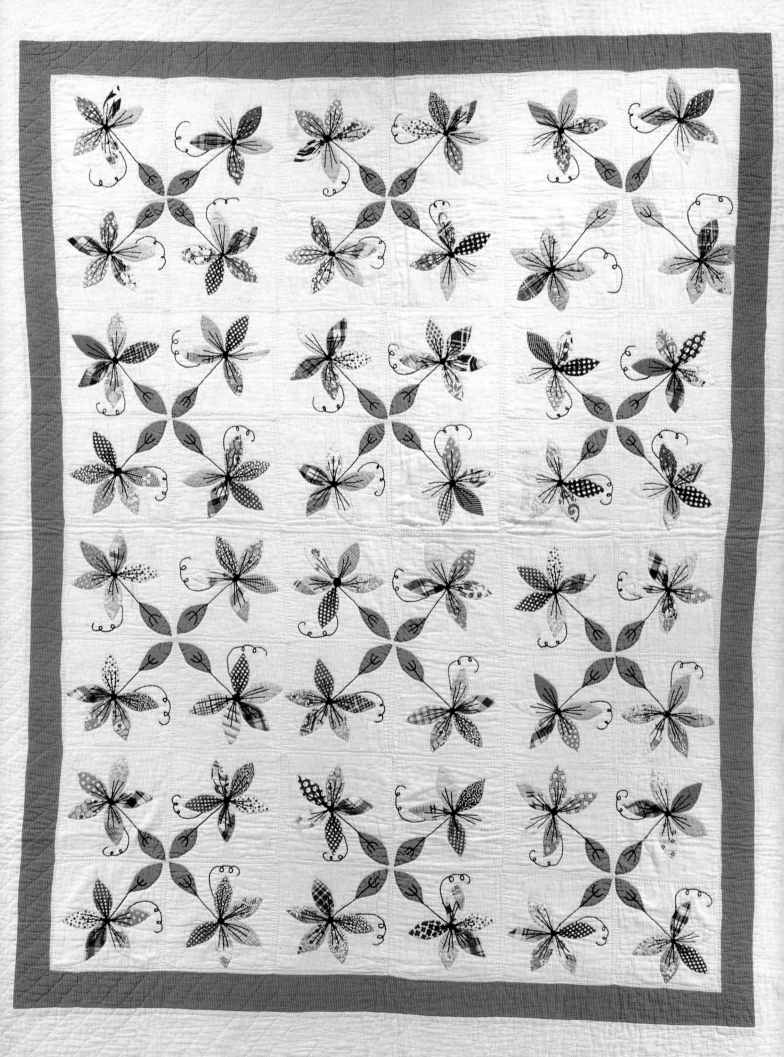

3 APPLIQUÉ TRADITIONS

Millie's Quilt c. 1920
Millie Chaput designed this charming floral quilt. A talented quilter who moved from Stone Lake, Wisconsin, to St. Paul, Minnesota, she created five-petaled flowers with one leaf in the opposite corner to balance the blocks and organized the blocks in sets of four. The petals are made from a varied assortment of bright pastel prints with a few solid colors, while the leaves are all cut from the same green.

Single lines of stem-stitch embroidery create tendrils, and stems that connect flower to leaf, and the petals are embellished with more embroidery. The quilting is simple: each block is outline-quilted and diagonal rows of quilting pull the pink inner and white outer borders into a whole.

HAND APPLIQUÉ

• The charming and popular traditional Sunbonnet Sue pattern is based on the work of Kate Greenaway (1846-1901), a British artist and writer, who is best known for her illustrations of children. In this version made in the 1930s, prints typical of the period have been used to make the dresses with coordinating or contrasting solids for the feet, arms, and hats, which are all embroidered with the same flower, ribbon, and trim on the brim. The pattern and its many variations, which go by other names such as Dutch Doll and Colonial Ladies, are a favorite with hand appliqué addicts. There is a boy version, called Overall Sam, and the owner of this quilt, quiltmaker and designer Patricia Cox, has created a variation she has named Sunbonnet Girl.

Appliqué is name of the decorative technique in which a shape or motif of one fabric is cut out and applied to a background made from a different fabric. It is a method of textile decoration that dates back as far as the history of cloth itself, and can be found on fabric items throughout the world. Though it is sometimes classed as an embroidery technique, it has long been associated with the making of quilts. There is a wide variety of kinds of appliqué, and each type creates a different effect.

The idea for decorative appliqué may have come from the patching of holes in worn garments and household textiles. We know that Mary Queen of Scots created appliqué

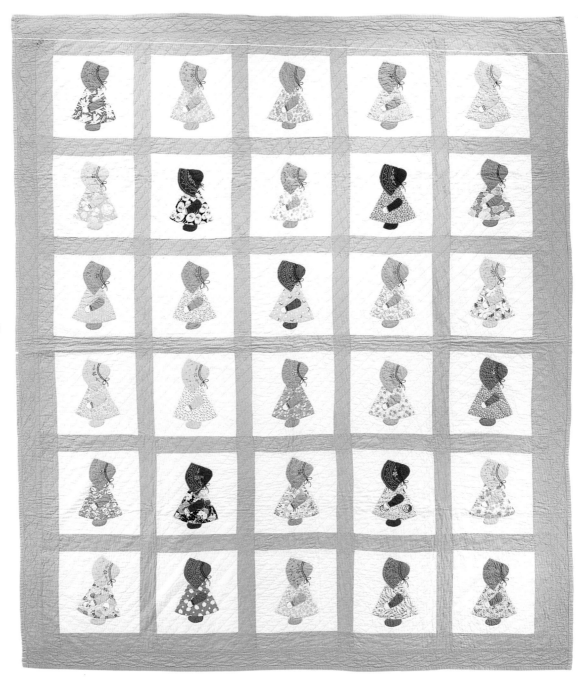

• This Ralli quilt from
the Sindh province in
Pakistan is made, in the
fashion characteristic of
the region, from cotton.
Colorful Nine-Patch
blocks are carefully
organized into twelve
diamonds made from
squares and alternated
with blocks of very fine
appliqué work on plain
backgrounds. Several
borders enliven the piece
further, with pieced
squares and sawtooth
edges that echo the
colors in the quilt blocks.
Sindh is the center of the
ralli quiltmaking region.
It lies along Pakistan's
border with India, where
ralli quilts are also made
in Rajasthan, Gujarat,
and the Punjab.
Courtesy Joss Graham
Oriental Textiles

works while she was imprisoned by her
cousin Queen Elizabeth I in sixteenth-century
England, and by the following century, the
technique was well established in Europe as a
prudent way to preserve clothing and other
textiles. Printed cotton fabrics from India
were produced in quantity and exported to
Europe where they were expensive, and their
value meant that they were preserved in any
way possible, appliqué being one of the most

popular. Motifs could be cut from an existing
piece and applied to a less costly background
fabric, and holes could be covered with
cutout motifs to give them new life.

In Britain, Indian "calicoes" were subjected
to import controls because they threatened
the local weaving and spinning industries. In
turn, as the American colonies were settled in
the eighteenth century, Britain placed tariffs
on fabric sent from its ports to the New

• This graphic modern-looking quilt was actually made between about 1840 and 1860. The snowflakes are examples of Scherenschnitte, or German papercuts, made from a small-scale red print fabric and hand appliquéd to the plain white background with great skill. The method of cutting geometric paper shapes was very popular in the second half of the nineteenth century.

• The paper-cut method was also used on this Cookie Cutter quilt, made by the mother-in-law of John E. Koemptgen in St. Paul, Minnesota, in the early twentieth century. The quilting motifs are also cookie-cutter shapes, including hearts, circles, diamonds, and the Star of David. The ruffled edging is a later addition. Minnesota Historical Society/John E. Koemptgen

World. In addition, looms and spinning wheels were forbidden in colonial homes, so cloth was a very valuable commodity, and even small scraps were hoarded to be reused. After the Revolutionary War, spinning and weaving, which had sometimes been carried out in secret to avoid the severe penalties that had been imposed, came into the open. As the United States grew in size and confidence in the early nineteenth century, a new textile industry, centered in New England, created domestic supplies that made less expensive fabric available to many seamstresses, but much fabric was still imported, and still expensive.

The main early use of appliqué for home furnishings was on bed hangings and draperies, both designed to keep out the cold and to cut down on drafts in rooms heated only with open fires. Bed quilts came later. By the late eighteenth and early nineteenth centuries, hand appliqué was widely practiced by quiltmakers, and as the price of fabric came down with wider availability, appliqué on quilts became more refined. Another factor in the widespread popularity of appliqué may have been, according to quilt historian Barbara Brackman, the mechanization of the pin-making industry, which meant that these tiny tools—essential to the technique—became more affordable to a wider number of seamstresses. Piecing and hand quilting developed alongside appliqué as quiltmaking became an artistic endeavor as well as a way of creating the warm bedcovers that were needed by every household.

Experts on the history of quiltmaking speculate that appliqué quilts tended to be kept out of everyday use, set aside for "best" or given as wedding presents to be treasured and looked after well. They were time-consuming to make, and many of the most beautiful survivors were created from fine material, so they were used less and have come down to us in pristine condition. Many of these quilts were made by young women as part of their dowry—their "bottom drawer" or "hope chest"—

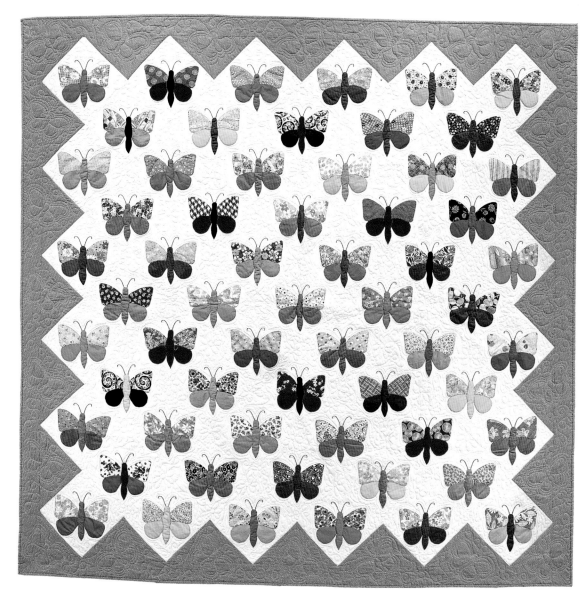

• The bright colors in the fabrics make this Butterfly quilt a very lively example of 1940s quiltmaking. The top wings are cut from typical 1940s prints with the bodies and lower wings made from coordinating solids. The border was added later, made from a reproduction print in keeping with the original look, and the quilting was done then.

and allowed them to show off their skills with needle and thread.

Appliqué lends itself to curved shapes that cannot be achieved with patchwork, and many appliqué quilts have intricate designs that cannot be made by other methods. It is widely used to create pictorial quilts and quilt blocks.

Many traditional appliqué quilts are designed using naturalistic forms, especially flowers and other plants. Animals, too, especially birds and insects, appear. Motifs from Tudor and Jacobean crewelwork embroideries were adapted in the seventeenth and eighteenth centuries and transferred to quilts as they became more widely used as bedcovers. As transatlantic traffic increased, the ideas and designs, as well as quilts

themselves, were taken to North America, and an exchange of ideas and patterns between Britain and the colonies developed. Interrupted by hostilities in 1776-1778 and again in the War of 1812, the flow diminished briefly and then resumed. In the nineteenth century American quiltmakers began to work more and more using the block method of construction, and traditional appliqué patterns were adapted and new ones devised to fit onto a square of background fabric. Once a block was completed, it could be stored away until the maker had finished enough blocks to assemble them into a quilt.

Wreath shapes could be fitted neatly into this new format, and flowers and leaves were often added to enhance the block. Many patterns were designed across the diagonal

• This kit quilt was designed in the 1930s, and the bright pastel shades of the flower fabrics are typical of the era. The blue grid, an unusual feature of appliqué kit quilts, allows scope for special quilting such as the large flower motifs in the boxes.

with the main motif repeated in each corner, while others have the main motif in the center with other design elements projecting into the corners. Designs range from highly stylized to realistic, and can be simple or intricate. Leaves are sometimes created in a realistic style, but are more often stylized into vines and garlands, many of which decorate a border or outline a specific area of the quilt.

Needle-turned appliqué

There are various ways of working appliqué. The traditional method of hand appliqué is referred to as "needle-turned," because you use the point of the needle to turn the raw edge of the fabric under as you stitch. Many stitchers will turn the seam allowance under and pin each of the pieces in place before they start to sew, removing the pins in turn as they work.

• This beautiful President's Wreath quilt was made in Virginia around 1840-1860. The pattern was a popular American Colonial design that was widely made, but few examples are as fine as this one with its excellent appliqué and quilting. The quilt was never used, and the red and green print fabrics are as bright today, more that 160 years later, as they ever were.

• Made by Prudence Macklin Luken in 1850, the Crown, or Oak Leaf and Reel, quilt opposite is made from traditional red and green fabrics appliquéd on a white background. The same fabrics have been used to make the pretty appliquéd swag border with rosebuds.
Minnesota Historical Society

The same look will be achieved using other methods that enhance accuracy but are more time-consuming. Turning under the raw edges and basting the shape, or basting the shape over plain paper in a similar way to English paper piecing (*see page 20*) give a good edge to each piece, and can be very useful to beginners. Some careful planning is required at the outset, since the paper must be removed once the stitching has been completed and before the piece is quilted. The back can be slit open, and then the edges whipstitched to close the gap, for example. A modern method involves ironing each shape to freezer paper—a food wrap made from a layer of paper fused to a shiny silicone-type layer—to the right side of the fabric. It sticks to the surface of the fabric but can be easily peeled off once the piece has been sewn in place.

Folk art appliqué

Many appliqué quilts contain folk-art shapes, often of great charm. The tradition of folk art came primarily from using familiar everyday objects, with simplified lines and stylized forms as inspiration for the design. Motifs are generally less intricate than those found on more formal appliqué work, and they lend themselves to use on baby quilts as well as larger pieces.

Folk-art quilts often show plant forms—flowers, leaves, and trees—as well as baskets and other containers. Animals from birds and insects to mammals are featured, along with hearts, which were generally used only on quilts intended for newlyweds. Plant motifs often have long straight or gently curved stems that are cut on the bias, and bias strips can be used to outline and divide sections or to create grids and patterns within patterns.

Appliqué is found on quilts made by members of the Mennonite community, but it is not a technique found on traditional Amish quilts. Nevertheless, in the mid-1970s, a group of quilters in the heart of Amish country, Lancaster County, Pennsylvania, designed a new appliqué pattern rooted firmly in the folk-art tradition. The new design, the group's contribution to the American Bicentennial celebrations, was called Lancaster Rose. Made in both traditional Amish solid colors and patterned fabrics not generally associated with Amish work, it has become popular enough to be made in Amish communities around the United States.

Album quilts

Also known as presentation quilts, friendship quilts, or autograph quilts, many album quilts were made as presents to family and friends who were moving away, or to commemorate an event. In many examples, especially in appliqué, each block is different and each may have been made by a different person. In some, particularly those made of patchwork, each block is the same, but made or at least signed by a different person. Many quilts of this type were made to give to those who were leaving an area, often to go west toward the American frontier, to remember loved ones who might never be seen again. Some were made in recognition of service, perhaps the minister of the church, while others were used as fund-raisers, with people paying to sign their name to a block, which was then sometimes embroidered to preserve it longer than the ink used in the signatures.

In Baltimore, Maryland, the 1840 and 1850s saw the development of a unique type of album quilt. Known today as Baltimore Album quilts, these beauties are among the most prized by collectors. They feature beautiful and incredibly elaborate designs based mainly on plants and flowers, and many also include baskets, birds, a wide range of animals, different types of buildings, and patriotic emblems. The best are works of art of the very highest standard, and many are signed and dated, unlike most quilts made before the late 1900s.

• Rose of Sharon was probably the most popular floral appliqué pattern of the nineteenth century, when many examples were made. Named for the love poem found in the Song of Solomon, the pattern has many variations, but most were made, according to quilt historian Ruth E. Finlay, as bridal quilts.

In this quilt, made in about 1880, the appliqué motifs were sewn as individual blocks and joined so that each one touches the ones next to it. The use of solid colors is typical, but here the middle rounds of petals are made from a small-scale double-red print. The seams have all been quilted superbly with a running feather, while the entire background, including the border, has been worked in a diagonal grid.

• Made by Martha
Chatfield Micou between
1835 and 1840 in the
south, probably Virginia
or South Carolina, this
splendid broderie perse
quilt is square. The design
is typical of its time, and
the chintz fabric was
almost certainly printed
specifically to be used for
this type of cut-out work.
The octagonal central
medallion contains sprays
of roses, which reappear
in various forms in the
surrounding appliquéd
motifs, three of which are
swags surmounted by a
bird. These chintz designs
were the descendants
of bedspreads called
palampores from
Palanpur in the province
of Gujarat in India, which
began to be imported into
Britain during the
sixteenth century.
American Folk Art
Museum, New York/Gift
of Mary W. Carter

A poignant modern group of friendship quilts
known as the Changi quilts were made by
women and children held in the notorious
Japanese prison camp of the same name
during World War II. Women stitched their
names and hand appliquéd or embroidered
pictorial messages on squares of sacking that
were then turned into quilts and given to
male inmates in the prison hospital as a way
of signaling to their menfolk that they were
still alive.

Broderie perse

One of the oldest forms of appliqué found
on quilts is called "broderie perse," or Persian
embroidery. In this technique motifs are cut
from patterned fabrics—especially the highly
popular Indian chintzes—and applied in a
new pattern to a plain background fabric.
Shapes are sewn in place with embroidery
stitches, usually buttonhole stitch, or the
edges are simply turned under and anchored
with invisible stitches. By arranging the motifs
in a different way, totally unrelated to the
original fabric design, an entirely new look
could be created.

The name broderie perse was not used until
the middle of the nineteenth century, when,
according to Mary Gostelow, it appeared
following the Great Exhibition of 1851 at the
Crystal Palace in London, but the method was
already widespread.

The chintz prints that were commonly
used for broderie perse in the nineteenth
century were based on the palampores from
the town of Palanpur in the Gujarat region of
India, or the bedspreads that came out of
India to England in the sixteenth century, and
then later to America. Various origins of the
word chintz have been suggested, from the
Hindu word *chitta*, which means spotted, or
"chint," which is said to mean variegated.
Whatever their origin, these palampores, and
the cloth based on their designs, utilized a
vast range of colors in complicated depictions
of exotic plants, flowers, and birds.

As broderie perse became popular, some
manufacturers began to print fabric with
designs specifically to be cut out and used in
this way. The quilt on this page was almost
centainly made from such fabric.

• This mola was purchased in Naples, Florida, in 1993. It was made around 1960 and is an exceptional example of the genre. All spaces are appliquéd on a mola, with designs expanded to fill the gap or abstract designs used as a filler.

• This quilt, called Pele and made in 1985 by Patricia Cox, has an appliquéd top made of tie-dyed fabric developed in conjunction with Marit Kucera. The halo of light that separates the two colors gives a special effect. Ethel Howey, who was born in Hawaii and who has made many Hawaiian-style quilts, saw the top at the 1985 Houston Quilt Festival and christened it "Pele" in honor of the goddess of volcanoes. She quilted authentically with thread matching the colors of each areas, to accentuate the sculptural effect of the quilting.

Hawaiian appliqué

Hawaiian appliqué is a general term that actually covers several types of intricate applied work. Nineteenth-century missionaries in the South Seas taught the women of several island groups, including Hawaii, the Cook Islands, and Tahiti, to work patterns that were based on Scherenschnitte, a folded-and-cut paper art form that was popular in Germany in the second half of the 1800s. Designs are created by folding a square of paper in half and then in half again, then folding the square along the diagonal to create a triangle. The design is then cut out in the manner of a four-sided snowflake. In quiltmaking the pattern is enlarged and cut from a single piece of fabric, which is then applied to a background fabric using a turned-edge appliqué method.

Scherenschnitte quilts were usually made from two solid colors, and Hawaiian quilts are traditionally the same. It has always been a point of pride that Hawaiian quilts are designed by the maker and that each one is unique. Designs are usually based on natural forms, but are highly stylized. Most patterns are complex, with many curved and pointed shapes that need skill to stitch properly. Hawaiian quilts are echo-quilted following the shape of the pattern, which represents waves lapping against the shore. Quilts from Tahiti were seldom quilted, but were hemmed and used like bedspreads.

Modern quilters have adopted the technique to create new designs similar in feel to the traditional ones, using a variety of fabrics, not just solids.

Reverse appliqué

In reverse appliqué two or more layers of fabric are basted together and the design is cut out of the top layer to reveal the fabric underneath before being stitched in place. A related form of appliqué is known as channel appliqué, in which the finished design is similar to a line drawing. Two fabrics are layered together and the design is basted on both sides of the line. The top fabric is cut

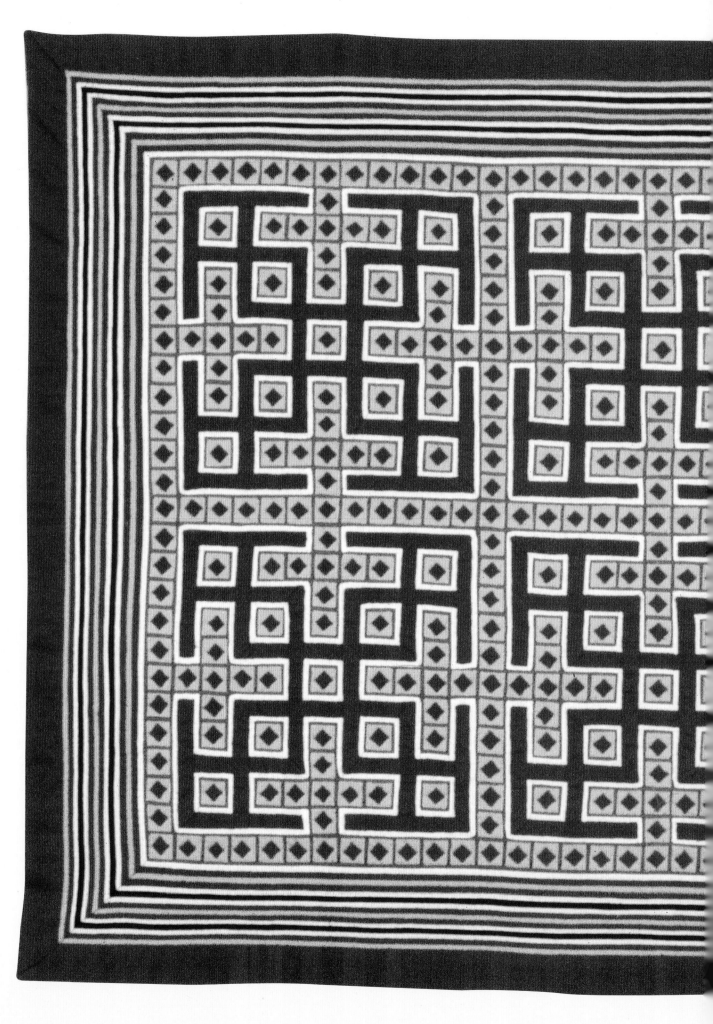

along the line and stitched down on both sides of the cut, maintaining the areas of top fabric but allowing the bottom fabric to show through as the "line drawing."

Two of the best-known types of reverse appliqué originated on opposite sides of the world. The Kuna, or Cuna, peoples who live in the San Blas province and islands off the Atlantic coast of Panama developed their version, the mola, which they used as parts of garments, especially women's blouses. The Kuna originally expressed themselves with body painting, but after traders brought cloth and sewing supplies in the nineteenth century, this was replaced by the reverse appliqué designs added to clothing. The colors predominantly used are red, black, and orange, with just about any other color being used in smaller amounts. When a color is only needed in a small area of the design, a small piece of cloth is inserted into the work, rather than using a whole layer of it. Designs are expanded to fill spaces and abstract designs are also used as a filler. Design inspirations come from village and jungle life.

The Hmong people, who originated in ancient China, are a group of mountain-dwelling farmers who settled small villages in Southeast Asia in Laos, Thailand, and northern Vietnam. After American troops were withdrawn from the area in 1975, groups of Hmong, many of whom had sided with the U.S. and had fled their homes, immigrated to the United States. They carried with them a tradition of fine needlework, especially the appliqué and reverse appliqué techniques used to create wonderful textiles called *paj ntaub* or *pa ndau*, "flower cloth."

Such fabrics are intricately worked pieces used for clothing, household textiles, accessories, and ceremonial items related to all phases of life, from birth and marriage to death. They share with molas the use of bright, highly contrasted primary colors and designs taken from nature, but paj ntaub work is generally geometric and abstract. Both are sometimes embellished with embroidery, and both have been adapted to make items to sell—molas to tourists who visit Panama and paj ntaub to American buyers at craft and art fairs and in museum stores.

• The *noob ncoos*, or funeral square, shown here was made by May Thao of Kansas City, Kansas, in 1984. This type of ceremonial cloth is usually made by daughters or daughters-in-law to honor parents. When a person dies, the cloth is placed under his or her head before burial. The design traditionally represents the property—house, other buildings, and land—owned by the departed, so that he can take his earthly goods into the next world with him. Worked in hand appliqué and the tuck-and-fold appliqué method that is a prominent feature of Green Hmong work, this cotton funeral square is highly geometric and brightly colored. The four sections of red paths delineated by yellow squares containing red diamonds are identical, and the extremely narrow borders of red, yellow, black, and white, with their meticulously mitered corners, echo the colors in the main design and frame the entire piece. Courtesy of John Michael Kohler Arts Center/ Photograph by Eric Dean

• British quiltmaker Mavis Haslam warmed to the designs of Charles Rennie Mackintosh, especially his stained glass, on visits to Glasgow, Scotland. Mackintosh was a local nineteenth-century architect and designer, leader of the Glasgow Arts and Crafts movement. In Glasgow Style, Haslam used hand-appliquéd bias binding for stems and to define individual petals. The quilt took second prize at the UK National Patchwork Championship in 1988.

• The mola opposite is from San Blas province and was made c. 1960. It is abstract in design, but superbly stitched, with smooth curves and sharp points. It was probably made for the tourist trade.

Bias-strip appliqué

Two types of appliqué work feature strips of bias-cut fabric. Celtic appliqué uses patterns based on the ancient spiral and interlaced designs associated with the culture of the Gaelic peoples of Ireland and Scotland. Stained glass appliqué uses bias strips like leading to outline shapes of different colors to create fabric pictures that resemble stained glass windows. There are several ways to make the strips, and the technique can be worked by hand or machine. Straight strips can sometimes be used instead, but they lack the flexibility of bias ones.

Project: HAND APPLIQUÉ

Needleturn appliqué/Bias strip appliqué

• Cockscomb and Tulips c. 1850. This quilt is a good example of borders being as important to the central design. Nine cockscomb blocks, set on point, are arranged in the middle of the quilt top. The style of the flowers and their size in comparison with the flowerpots creates a simple folk-art effect. An inner pieced sawtooth border crisply delineates the center, and a bold, graphic tulip vine twists around the outer border. The only deviation from all this meticulous sewing is the appliquéd outer sawtooth border where the corner triangles have been adjusted to fit the space available.

The traditional method of hand-appliqué involves cutting a shape, pinning it to the background fabric, and turning under a seam allowance using the point of a needle. Other methods that can be neater, quicker, and more accurate include turning under and basting the edges of a fabric shape, or basting shapes over paper, as in so-called English paper piecing, which creates a sharp edge to sew along.

One of the challenges when designing a border is how to tackle the movement of the pattern around the corners. This quilt has a sawtooth edge around the central area, which is repeated along the outside. Between the two is a gently curving vine with stylized tulips. Two of the opposite corners feature two flowers growing from the same stem. These double tulips have been stitched using needleturn appliqué with the shapes cut out using freezer paper. The stems are bias strips.

177

PART ONE: APPLIQUÉ TRADITIONS — HAND APPLIQUÉ

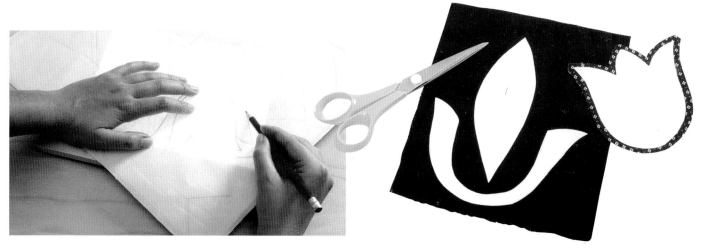

1 Cut a background square 14" x 16" (35.5 x 40 cm). Using a lightbox, trace the pattern on the right side of the fabric with a sharp pencil.

2 Cut the flower and leaf shapes from freezer paper and iron them to the right side of your flower fabrics—ours are red and black. Cut them out, leaving enough space all around for a ⅛" (3 mm) seam allowance.

3 Cut a 1" (2·5 cm) wide bias strip from black fabric. Fold lengthwise in half and press.

4 Place the cut edge of the bias strips against the pencil line on the background fabric. Pin and stitch in place by hand or machine about ⅛" (3 mm) from the cut edge. When in place, the folded edge of the long bias vine covers the cut edge of the stem. Pin and stitch as before, using matching threads.

5 Position the red flower shapes and remove the freezer paper. Pin the shapes in place and secure them with a line of basting (tacking) ¼" (5 mm) from the edge. Slipstitch the top edge of the petals and a little way down each side, turning under a ⅛" (3 mm) seam allowance and clipping where necessary. Do NOT stitch the lower edge.

6 Baste (tack), then slipstitch the black petals in place over the tulips. Next baste and sew the leaves in place. Remove all basting threads and press from the wrong side.

MACHINE APPLIQUÉ

• Sunbonnet Sue and her friend Overall Sam are most often worked by hand, especially on quilts like this one from the 1930s, but the unknown maker of the pink-sashed and bordered example on the right applied the shapes by machine. House of White Birches

• In this modern Sunbonnet Sue, the makers—Ethel Rice, Lydia Rice, and Elsie Cole from Davidson, Michigan—have made several variations of the design, including a gardening Sue and another sheltering under an umbrella. Or is it a parasol? The bright fabrics have been applied by machine, and the embellishments are embroidered.

While some antique quilts are machine appliquéd, the method is really a twentieth-century development. It is less time-consuming than hand appliqué, but gives quite different results. It is useful for pieces that will get hard wear or need to be washed frequently, like baby quilts, and it works well on clothing. Many quiltmakers prefer to use satin stitch to apply shapes; others sew with a straight stitch, or leave the edges raw. The technique is widely used in contemporary quiltmaking and art quilts.

Machine-stitched appliqué became popular with the invention of the zigzag stitch, which means that the raw edges of a single layer of fabric can be secured to keep them from fraying. It was made even easier when lightweight fusible webbing was developed, because it meant that pieces could be held in place without pins.

Webbing creates another layer in the work, however, and has a slight stiffness, so while it works well for wall hangings and cushion covers, it is not always the ideal solution for quilts. You can also pin or baste the shapes to be applied, or use fabric glue or basting spray, both of which wash out easily.

Satin stitch, or closed zigzag, is the most secure way to hold appliqué shapes in place, but there are other options. If the piece is fused, for example, the raw edges are protected by the webbing, and the piece can be blanket-stitched or secured with a wide buttonhole stitch. An open zigzag stitch can also be used, as well as blind stitch if you have the option on your sewing machine. Computerized machines have a selection of decorative stitches that can be used, too.

It is possible to use a machine straight stitch as well, turning the seam allowances

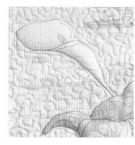

• Quiltmaker Janet Jones Worley of Huntsville, Alabama, has used the same design to make two very different wall hangings. In the version on the right, the calla lilies have been applied by machine to a printed background, and partial images have been appliquéd in the four corners. The main appliqué shapes have been heavily batted and the entire background has been machine-quilted in a meander pattern around them to make the lilies and their leaves stand out.

under and stitching just along the edge. This method is similar to topstitching, but must be worked very close to the turned edge, no more than ¹⁄₁₆" (1.5mm). Turning the edges under can be tricky, but there are modern tools to help. You can cut each shape from heat-resistant plastic and iron the edges flat, holding them in place with spray starch and removing the plastic shape when all the edges are turned. You can also use freezer paper to create a turned-under edge and remove it before stitching. Or you can baste the edges under in the traditional way. You can use open zigzag and blind stitch to secure turned-under edges, but both require practice to perfect.

Another method of applying shapes by machine is to mark the outline of each shape and cut the pieces out with a seam allowance. Anchor them on the background fabric by stitching along the marked outline with a straight stitch. Trim away the seam allowance as close to the stitching line as possible using sharp embroidery scissors.

• In the version on the left, Janet Worley has applied the lily-and-leaf image to a plain cream background and added a wide floral-print border which is bound with the same busy print. Both of these pieces were made in 2000.

Then satin stitch over the line of stitching with a stitch wide enough to cover the stitching outline and the raw edges.

Whatever stitch you use, begin on a straight or broadly curved edge and lift the presser foot but not the needle to pivot when you reach a point or corner. Work inner points first, then outer points. If you are using satin stitch, keep the stitches even and try to keep the edge of the shape in the center of the line of stitching. Rounded curves need to be handled carefully. Stop and pivot at regular intervals as you work around the shape. Keep the needle on the outside of outward curves and inside on inner ones. Miter inner points and corners by stitching to the end of the edge, then pivot with the needle on the inside, stitching over the previous stitches neatly. Grade the stitches at outer points and V shapes by reducing the stitch width as you approach the the point. Pivot with the needle outside the shape when you reach the point, then gradually increase the stitch width again

• Night Blooms, by Munni Srivastava, is three-dimensional machine appliqué work, with each double petal sewn separately. The centers of the flowers are double ruching; the background was quilted freehand in silver thread and large running stitches. The leaves are machine appliqué, and machine embroidery has been combined with hand stitching and tiny beads to add texture.

as you work along the next edge.

Raw-edge appliqué is a way of embellishing work, but is best used on pieces that will not need to be washed. Felted or closely woven fabrics that do not fray are best for raw-edge appliqué. If you are using a looser weave, you will need to be very careful if you want the piece to be applied to keep its shape while you work.

Tips

• use a lightweight stabilizer paper under the fabric while you work to keep the piece flat. Commercial tearaway stabilizers are available, or you can iron a piece of freezer paper to the back of the work.

• use a thin needle—size 60 is ideal—and change it often to prevent distortion in the work.

• use a strong, thin thread. Cotton machine embroidery thread is thinner than regular cotton thread.

• nylon thread can be used on top for an invisible stitch. Use cotton thread in the bobbin and adjust the tension, which will probably be necessary.

• silk dressmaker's pins are ideal for securing appliqué. They are both thin and very sharp.

• always test the stitch before starting work on the piece itself. Machine appliqué work is different from regular stitching.

• use an open appliqué or embroidery foot on the machine so you can see the work at all times. Remember that you cannot use a zigzag stitch with a quarter-inch foot.

• pull the bottom thread through to the top of the work to begin and stitch over it a few times with the needle on 0 to secure the end. The thread ends will be trimmed away when you have finished.

• sew all the edges of the same color, then change the thread and bobbin to sew all the edges of the next color.

• outlining shapes in dark-colored thread will give the appearance of the leading in stained glass windows.

• if you are using fusible webbing, make sure you trace shapes in reverse. This is especially important with letters and numbers, but most other shapes will be back to front if you do not reverse them.

• British quiltmaker Mary Mayne, inspired by the Victorian song "Daisy, Daisy, Give Me Your Answer, Do," has machine-appliquéd blossoms onto a subtle strip-pieced background. Its mottled shades of gray make the white flowers, with bright yellow centers, leap out from the cloth. The realistic placing of the blooms contributes to the overall effect. The quilt was the winner of the 2000 Sue Ridgewell Challenge Trophy awarded by the Quilters' Guild of the British Isles.

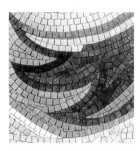

• "Waving, Not Drowning" was inspired by a design course taken by British quiltmaker Rose Epton-Peter in which she researched waves and circles to translate into fabric art. She basted the outline on a circle of black background fabric and filled in the shapes with small squares of hand-dyed fabrics applied to the surface with fusible webbing. Invisible thread was used to machine quilt in free motion to give the effect of an ancient mosaic.

• British textile artist and teacher Janice Gunner made "Carnival" in 2000 from colorful hand-dyed fabrics. Having learned a quick method of stitching curved shapes in a Ricky Tims workshop at the International Quilt Festival 1999 in Houston, she used the same machine-piecing technique to make the medallion-style background and machine-appliquéd raw-edged feather shapes and streamers. The appliqué shapes are outline quilted, while dense machine quilting covers the background.

Project: CAT BLOCK

Machine appliqué

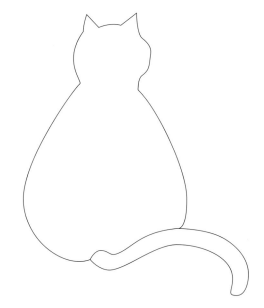

A sewing machine with a zigzag function is a useful tool in some types of appliquéd work. Several of the outline stitches on many modern machines can also be used to good effect.

There are several ways to hold pieces in place as you stitch around them. Pinning or basting are traditional, but are not always suitable for machine work. Basting spray, which allows pieces to be repositioned, and craft glue can secure fabrics while you work. Both can be washed out of the fabric easily when the piece is complete. If you have an open embroidery or appliqué foot on your machine, it will be much easier to see what is happening while you work.

The other way to hold fabric shapes in place is by using fusible webbing, an iron-on double-sided adhesive that is especially useful for working with small, thin, or awkwardly shaped pieces. When webbing has been fused in place with a hot iron, the bond is permanent and cannot be washed out. Both fusible webbing and basting spray have been used to make the cat block.

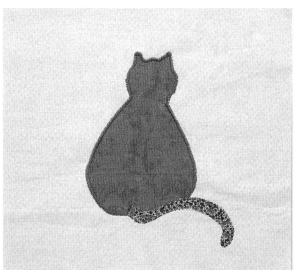

1 Trace each piece of the design. Machine-applied pieces do not need seam allowances.

2 Glue each tracing to cardboard or template plastic and cut it out.

3 Draw each piece on its chosen fabric. Make sure they are the right way up.

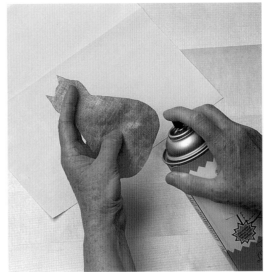

4 Spray the wrong side of the cat's body piece with basting spray and place it carefully in position on the background.

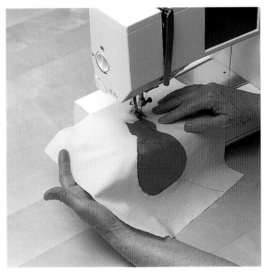

5 Stitch the body shape in position, beginning in a place that will be covered by another piece if at all possible.

6 Zigzag all around the body, working very carefully and slowly in tricky areas like sharp points.

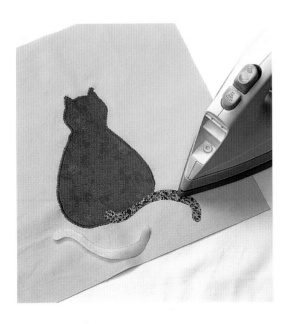

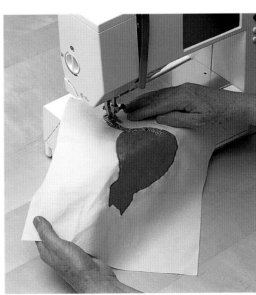

7 Iron the tail fabric to fusible webbing and cut out the tail. Peel off the paper backing and iron it in place on the body.

8 Stitch around the tail. We have used a more open, decorative stitch instead of zigsag.

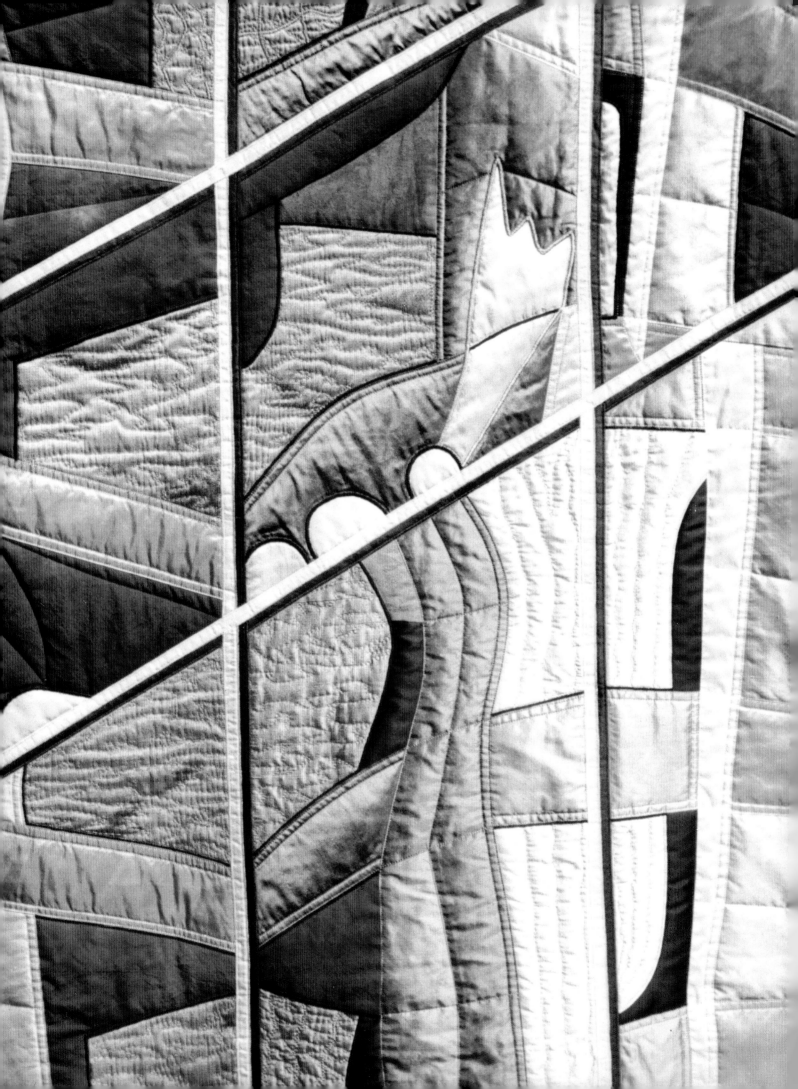

4 QUILTING TRADITIONS

Downtown Houston (2000)

This piece was made by British textile artist Janice Gunner who was the recipient of the Jewel Pearce Patterson Scholarship for International Quilt Teachers in 1999, and attended the International Quilt Market and Festival in Houston that year. As part of the scholarship, she attended workshops taught by leading quiltmakers at the Festival, and the following year returned to exhibit work made by her and her students to show how the experience had influenced her work.

She dedicated this quilt, of which a detail is shown, to her father Ken Hudson, who passed away while she was making it. "It was hard to concentrate," she says, "but I had to finish it—he was very proud of my work." Made from Thai silk and hand-dyed cottons, it interprets Gunner's view of the reflections of buildings in Houston's downtown. Like most of Gunner's work, it is machine-pieced and appliquéd, with machine quilting and embroidery.

HAND QUILTING

• The Windblown Tulips block was created by Marie D. Webster, the author of *Quilts: Their Story and How to Make Them*, the first published history of quilts written in 1915. She was also a well-known quilt designer and was responsible for a number of kit quilts. This whirling motif was a popular appliqué pattern, but the flowers on the right are not stitched. They are printed onto feedsacks that have been carefully joined and outline-quilted to make a very effective quilt. Many quilts from the era of the Great Depression in the 1930s were pieced from feedsack fabrics, and large sacks were often stitched together to make quilt backings, but this quilt is unusual in its use of whole feedsacks as blocks.

In the world of quiltmaking, quilting is the stitching that holds the layers—quilt top, batting, and backing—together. The quilt top can be patchwork or appliqué, or it can simply be a plain piece of cloth. The batting can range from a layer of fine silk to an old blanket, or even a worn-out quilt. The backing is usually a plain piece of fabric, but can be pieced. The three thicknesses must be stitched together to keep them from slipping around and to keep the batting from becoming a wadded-up mass in one corner. But quilting is also a decoration. It is said that quilting makes the quilt, and this is true in the literal sense as well as figuratively. Books have been written, and illustrated, to show what happens when the same quilt is quilted in a different way. The transformations can be quite astounding. Quilting stitches can be large or small. They can be neatly worked or uneven. They can be added randomly to the quilt—but most often they are carefully planned and worked, in which case they enhance a piece of fabric, pieced or plain, in a unique way.

Quilting has probably been used on fabric since humans first began to clothe themselves. Historical evidence has been found of quilted garments from almost opposite sides of the globe—ancient Egypt and ancient China—and fragments of quilted cloth dating from the Middle Ages in Europe still exist. Quilted armor was worn by medieval soldiers under their chain mail to make it rather more comfortable, as well as to provide both warmth and added protection against the arrows of their foes. By the seventeenth century, women of all classes in many areas across Europe wore very thick quilted petticoats for warmth, and fine quilted clothing, especially men's waistcoats, was extremely fashionable in most of Europe during both the seventeenth and eighteenth centuries.

The quilted bedcover.

The quilt as bedcover seems to have evolved at about this time, although there were already quilted bed hangings. These heavy curtains hung all around a bed to cut the cold that crept into every corner of drafty medieval buildings and to provide a measure of privacy to the bed's occupants in the communal living that characterized European life in the Middle Ages and beyond. The technical skills needed to create quilted items were familiar and widely practiced, and when colonists set out to escape poverty and religious persecution and begin life in the New World, they took the knowledge with them. Here, no doubt, both practices helped many settlers survive the harsh climate and general privations of life in an alien land.

By the end of the eighteenth century, quilted bedcovers were being produced on both sides of the Atlantic, and by the late nineteenth century quiltmaking was fully integrated into life in America and Europe. Frame, or medallion, quilts (*see pages 242-255*) were followed by strippy quilts (*see pages 256-263*) and blocks of all kinds, as well as intricate mosaic patterns (*see pages 96-109*) and appliqué (*see pages 156-187*).

These quilts were certainly quilted, but their main visual interest lay in the piecing of the tops. There are, however, quilts from the late nineteenth and early twentieth centuries that display the art of fine hand quilting as practiced by four particular groups of traditional quiltmakers.

Durham quilts and quilters

First were women and men from the north of England and the Scottish borders, particularly the northeastern counties of Durham and Northumberland, who from the early 1800s made quilts for a living. The cottage industry that developed around them lasted well into the twentieth century, and many of the quilts that survive have found their way into museums and private collections, attesting to both their importance in the history of quilts and their artistic value. Known collectively as Durham quilts, they are generally simple in design, ranging from wholecloth to star medallions and strippies, and decorated with quilting patterns of outstanding beauty worked in the finest of stitches.

The area is a center of coal mining, and many a miner's wife made extra money for the family by quilting. Clubs were formed in which a weekly subscription was agreed and the quilt delivered when the entire amount had been paid off. At this time as well, itinerant quilters, usually men, traveled from place to place, exchanging bed and board for the making of quilts, many of them works of great beauty. The most famous of them is Joseph Hedley, who is remembered more for his death at the hands of a murderer in 1826 than for his quilts, few of which survive. The crime, thought to be the work of robbers, remains unsolved to this day.

Other professional North Country quilters were known as stampers; they marked a quilt top with an appropriate pattern that was then quilted by the quilter—usually a woman—of the house. This trade developed in the area of Northumberland around Allendale and Weardale, and became an economic mainstay of the area from the late 1800s until World War I changed the world. The stampers, who actually drew the pattern on the quilt top with a blue pencil, worked in several ways.

• Fuchsias are among the favorite flowers of quiltmaker Maureen Baker, who designed and made this wonderful wholecloth in 2000. She calls it Fuchsiarama, and uses flowers in profusion. The balance between the elements—central motifs, elaborate border designs, and filler patterns—and the exquisite hand stitching led to its winning first prize in its category at Quilts UK 2001. Areas of trapunto add emphasis to the dramatic quality of the quilt.

• Thought to have been sewn by members of the Murray family of Allendale, Northumberland, this cotton wholecloth quilt dates from around 1850. The central flower basket is bordered by oval leaves and a hammock and daisy pattern, and all the quilting is of the very high standard that we might expect from the area. Bowes Museum

• The homespun wool in this hand-dyed quilt was probably mill-woven. It was made by a member of a Northumberland family named Keith sometime in the last quarter of the nineteenth century. Its quilting is unusual for a wholecloth—bands of strippy-type pattern run up and down the surface. Columns of wavy lines with a diagonal grid background alternate with diamond lattices interspersed with quilted flowers. Bowes Museum

A quiltmaker could send a quilt top to the company where it was marked for a nominal fee. Customers could order a particular quilt top, specifying fabric color, size, and even quilting pattern. And itinerant peddlers sometimes carried marked tops to be sold alongside his or her other wares. The two most famous stampers were George Gardiner, a draper (his shop sold fabric), and one of his apprentices, Elizabeth Sanderson. Both taught their marking skills to numerous apprentices, and the tradition continued well into the twentieth century. Because these tops were never signed by the stamper, few can be definitely attributed to either Gardiner or Sanderson, but they created a tradition that is instantly recognizable.

Hand quilting almost disappeared, both in Britain and the United States, as the twentieth century progressed. However, a small group of quilters, led in the North

Country by Amy Emms following in the footsteps of the Durham quilters, kept the tradition going long enough for late twentieth-century quilters to re-discover the skills and techniques.

Welsh quilts and quilters

Meanwhile, in another poor rural area of Great Britain, a similar skill bank of quilters had grown up. Welsh quilts from the late nineteenth and early twentieth century are similarly plain, but the patterns used are generally much more geometric than those from the North Country. There are also usually a series of borders around the edges of Welsh quilts that contain the large scale patterns. While North Country quilters had fairly easy access to the cotton fabrics produced in the nearby mills of Liverpool and Manchester, way out in the isolated mountains and valleys of Wales they had to

• The Lancaster Rose pattern was devised by a group of Amish quiltmakers for the Bicentennial celebrations in 1976. The original design had red roses with green leaves, echoing the colors of the historical emblem of the aristocratic English family of Lancaster, from whom Lancaster County, Pennsylvania, with its large Amish population, takes its name. This dramatic example, made in the 1990s, provides an interesting contrast between a modern appliqué pattern in decidedly non-traditional colors and a highly traditional dark blue border beautifully quilted with designs that are among the oldest used by Amish quilters.

depend on wool as their staple cloth. Woolen material is generally much thicker and heavier than cotton cloth, and much harder to work in any kind of fine detail. Many traditional Welsh quilts reflect this: the muted shades of thick fabric, usually tinted with a range of natural dyes, were generally cut into quite large pieces, while carded wool, old clothes, or even an old woolen blanket was used for the batting. The stitches used to quilt the layers of fabric together were usually much larger and farther apart than on cotton quilts. Needless to say, such quilts were usually extremely thick and heavy in weight, but the workmanship on many is still superb.

Amish quilts and quilters

Meanwhile, in several rural areas of Pennsylvania on the other side of the Atlantic, another group of quilters (as opposed to piecers or appliquérs) was creating an amazing body of work that was born of necessity, but which have become among the most famous quilts known today.

The Amish—the so-called Plain People who settled in self-sufficient communities, first in William Penn's colony established to provide a refuge to those suffering religious persecution and then in the American Midwest—are among the best-known of all quilters in the world. There is a certain irony

• This dramatic floral appliqué quilt was made, possibly in Indiana, around 1850-1860. The nine flower blocks are surrounded by an intricate border of floral vines, birds, and bunches of grapes, which is broken in the center of each side by an urn of roses and tulips. The exquisite hand quilting fills the background with more vines and leaves.

Another, almost identical, quilt is known to have been made in Ohio, so perhaps the pattern went west with a family of pioneers. University of Nebraska-Lincoln

in this fact, because the communities—devoutly religious and family-oriented—are among the most private and self-contained groups in the United States. Descended from a sect of Anabaptists who traveled from Germany to the New World in the 1720s, they eschew the modern world and all its time-saving conveniences, preferring to live on and off the land. It has always been their practice to use and re-use what they regard as essential and to ignore anything that they consider unnecessary or frivolous. Their homes are without electricity, powered instead by gas or kerosene. They work their fields—and most of them are farmers—without tractors, using horses, mules, and people-power, to plow and sow and winnow and reap. They build their homes and barns in community-wide efforts, without power tools or machinery. They have no cars—they travel on foot or in horse-drawn buggies. Their homes quite often have a sewing machine operated by hand or foot treadle that is used to piece the quilt tops and to make other household linens as well as clothing for both children and adults, but the quilting is always done by hand.

It was a natural progression to use fabric left over from sewing clothes for the family to make quilts. Since they wear no patterned fabrics, all their scraps were solid colors, and although shirts and some children's clothes are made from bright plain colors, trousers, jackets, and dresses are usually dark, either black, dark gray, or navy blue. Because most of the quilts are made from scraps, many of them quite small, there are very few wholecloth quilts in the Amish tradition.

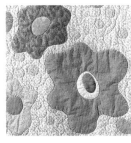

• Mary Mayne of Hertfordshire in England based this exuberant quilt on a greeting card designed by Esther Wragg, and, having obtained permission to reproduce it, named it Wragg Time in her honor. The nine background squares contain a variety of flower shapes that have been created using a number of techniques, from machine piecing to bonded appliqué and freezer-paper appliqué, while the punchy modern pieced border gives just the right edge to the piece. The elaborate hand quilting is different in each section.

Patterns adopted from their non-Amish neighbors—known to the Amish as the "English," no matter where in the world they may come from—were adapted over time to become characteristic of Amish work. The use of solid jewel colors glowing against somber dark fabrics, made in simple designs and beautifully quilted with great skill and precision, has made these quilts highly collectible. Most early examples, which date from the late nineteenth and early twentieth centuries, are now in museums and private collections, but the Amish quiltmaking tradition still continues, with beautiful quilts, many of them for sale, being made in the traditional way by hand in Amish settlements throughout the country.

Boutis and French quilts

France has, since the late eighteenth century, developed a tradition of hand quilting that is somewhat different from those across the English-speaking areas of the world. Most French quilts are wholecloth, and they are often thickly batted. Quilting patterns tend to be fairly simple in design, and worked in relatively large stitches. While solid-colored fabrics predominate, many examples are made from patterned material, often typical Provençal prints or a print in in a single color—usually red or blue—on cream or white, which is known as toile de Jouy.

The other common type of French quilts, which are known as boutis, are extra-thick and very heavy. Somewhat mysteriously they seem to have originated around the Marseilles area, where the mild winter climate and hot summer temperatures would seem to be at odds with their weight and bulk.

Choosing a quilting pattern

The patterns commonly used by the Durham quilters and the Amish have been copied and elaborated upon, and all kinds of variations abound. Designs were often exchanged by friends and relations across the oceans, and the metal or wooden templates that were used to mark them became treasured heirlooms or museum exhibits. There are thousands of books on the market with quilting patterns and motifs to choose from, and a selection of block, border and corner designs appear on pages 428-445 at the end of this book.

Patterns for quilting stitches should ideally relate to the design of the quilt top itself. A top with many seams across it will need no elaborate quilting—which would probably be totally lost in the pattern anyway—and it might be quilted just as effectively using a machine, rather than by careful hand-sewing. However, if a top has some plain open areas between the other design elements, these are often the perfect spaces on which to quilt rather more elaborate block or motif patterns. Curved blocks might be enhanced by using curving quilting patterns—but might look even better with straight lines emphasizing the curves of the top. It is equally true that quilting a sinuous curved pattern on tops that are based on straight-sided shapes can enhance the design. It is a matter of personal taste in many respects.

• Made in 2000, this astonishing hand-quilted patchwork quilt contains 6,400 individual pieces. Quiltmaker Toyoko Miyajima from Nagano, Japan, has created hydangea flowerheads that are amazingly lifelike, capturing the subtle pinks and blues that exist among the species, colors that can be altered by changing the composition of the soil in which the plant is grown.

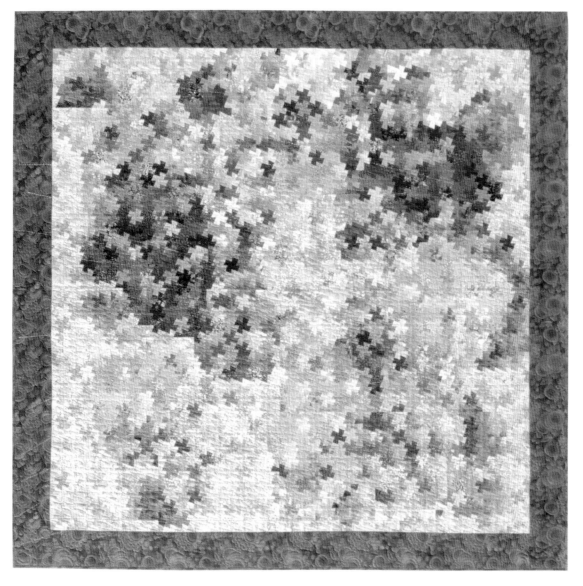

Hand quilting

For hand quilting, the layers must be secured together well first to prevent any puckers and tucks, and basting the entire top before you start is usually the best way to do this, especially if you use a hoop or frame when quilting. For smaller areas, it might be sufficient to use safety pins, instead of stitching. When hand quilting, most quilters prefer to use short, small needles called betweens, and most wear a thimble, or even two, to protect the fingers that are most involved in the method—one on the top hand, the other on the bottom.

Special quilting thread, which is thicker than ordinary sewing thread and which has been waxed to help prevent tangling and breaking, is recommended for hand quilting. If this is not available or you need a special color, it is possible to wax your own as long as you start with good-quality thread.

A technique known as rocking achieves the neatest stitch in a quilt. It is basically a small running stitch, but it is made by inserting the needle at a right angle to the fabric and bringing it back through at another right angle without pulling the thread through until you have taken several stitches onto the needle. If it sounds very difficult, that's because it is. It is a stitch that needs a great deal of practice to get right and to do with any kind of speed, but it is worth it to be able to make the small neat stitches that are the mark of a master quilter.

Beginning and ending the thread can be done in more than one way. For instance, the thread can be knotted at the end and the knot pulled through the first fabric layer and left in the batting, caught in the fibers. Alternatively, you can take a backstitch at the beginning and end of a row and again bury the thread in the batting. For neatness, it is essential that the thread ends are secure and do not come loose as the quilt is used. For quilts that will have heavy use, and may be laundered, it is wise to be extra sure that the ends will not pull free.

• This beautiful quilt pictures five bouquets of appliquéd flowers in urns, one in the center and one at each corner, and repeats the motifs in the plain white blocks using trapunto, or stuffed quilting (*see pages 204–211*). Several of the same shapes have been altered to create the border, and charming yellow birds have been added to the bottom and both sides. The stitching throughout is exquisite, from the fabulous padded areas that echo the appliqué, to the scalloped edges of the double blue border surrounding the border flowers. Each section is almost identical to the others, but the subtle variations in the motifs and patterns in each block are worth looking for carefully. The quilt is American, and is thought to have been made in Ohio around 1920–30. Milwaukee Art Museum/Gift of Julie Hayes and Thomas E. Sutherland

• The Rose of Sharon is a variation of the Whig Rose design (*page 166*). The name refers to the Song of Solomon, a love poem from the Old Testament. It was one of the most popular floral patterns throughout the nineteenth century and because of its religious inspiration was a favorite for quilts made for ministers or for fundraising. This quilt was made by an unknown quiltmaker around 1870, possibly in Pennsylvania. University of Nebraska-Lincoln

Project: HAND QUILTING

Transferring a design to fabric

Quilting by hand has been practiced for thousands of years in some form in almost every culture known to historians and anthropologists. What probably began as a way to hold layers of clothing together for warmth became a decorative art that has been used to embellish clothing and home furnishings in a tradition that continues today.

Quilting patterns can be transferred to the finished quilt top either before or after the layers are basted together. Straight-line designs, including grids of squares or diamonds, are the easiest patterns to stitch and to mark. They are useful for filling large background areas, and look good on borders. Straight lines can be drawn straight onto fabric using a ruler and a suitable marker. Narrow masking tape can be applied to the quilt after the piece has been basted to delineate straight lines. Stitch along one or both edges and then remove the tape. Some intricate designs, especially for corded quilting, are best transferred by basting a tissue paper tracing of the pattern to the fabric.

This Rose of Sharon appliqué is bold enough to translate well into a handquilting design. Extract the parts of the pattern that appeal to you and adapt them to suit. Here, the central flower design has concentric rows of quilting to fill the large space.

A lightbox may be used to trace the pattern, but an alternative is to photocopy the design and tape both it and the fabric to a window, preferably on a bright, sunny day. Another method is to trace the design on tissue paper and baste (tack) along the lines, then remove the paper carefully, leaving the pattern basted on the fabric.

Tracing the Design

1 Choose a design. For dark background fabrics, place the pattern on a lightbox. Lay the fabric on top and trace through using a marking pencil. If the fabric is pale, it may be possible to trace without additional light.

3 Cut a length of quilting thread no longer than 18" (45 cm) and start to quilt from the center. The central flower has the outline and center circle marked. Fill in the rest of the flower as you wish. Concentrate on using even stitches of equal size rather than the tiniest stitch possible! When you are stitching the stems and leaves, stitch from the center toward the end leaf. The intermediate leaves can then be stitched in order.

2 Layer the top fabric, batting (wadding) and backing fabric and pin. Baste (tack) starting with two lines crossing through the center and work toward the outsides. As these stitches will be removed later, keep the knots on the top of the fabric.

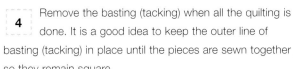

4 Remove the basting (tacking) when all the quilting is done. It is a good idea to keep the outer line of basting (tacking) in place until the pieces are sewn together so they remain square.

Tissue-paper Template

1 Trace your design on tissue paper and baste it to the fabric using small running stitches to mark the lines of the pattern.

2 When all the lines have been stitched, use the point of a needle to tear gently along the lines of thread to remove the paper without disturbing the lines of basting.

• This pieced cotton patchwork quilt was made in about 1850 by an unknown quiltmaker. Pieced blocks made in an unnamed pattern from *Godey's Lady's Book* alternate with white ones; the plain blocks feature trapunto quilting that includes grapes, feathers, and a selection of floral motifs. A double red sawtooth border encloses the quilt. Minnesota Historical Society

TRAPUNTO

The term trapunto, the Italian word for quilt, has become the overall phrase that is applied to all quilts that are decorated with padded areas stuffed from the back to raise either the motifs or channels above the flat surface of the piece. Trapunto work today covers a number of related but slightly different techniques—stuffed work, corded quilting, and padded appliqué work are all included under its umbrella.

The type of work called trapunto first appeared on bedcovers during the Middle Ages and is found on one of the oldest European quilts known. Thought to date from about 1395, the so-called Tristan quilt in the collection of the Victoria and Albert Museum in London, has been attributed to a Sicilian maker. It shows corded quilting, which may account for that technique's other name, Italian quilting. Skilled needleworkers from various parts of Italy, including Naples and Sicily, migrated to southern France, especially around the port of Marseilles, during the fifteenth century, and were probably the original practitioners of the beautiful work that developed into the lucrative textile trade in the area between the fifteenth and eighteenth centuries. Many of the most beautiful of the textiles produced were stuffed and corded quilts, a number of which survive today.

By the beginning of the eighteenth century the Marseilles trade was so widespread that quilted clothing, particularly men's waistcoats and ladies' petticoats, and even babies' caps and bibs, were known throughout Europe. Many of these garments were decorated with exquisite corded and stuffed work, and the techniques were also found on bedcovers of the time. Historical records show that thousands of women were employed in workshops in Provence, not just around Marseilles but in other cities in the area as well, including Avignon and Arles, during

the seventeenth and eighteenth centuries. Trapunto quilts made in Provence were found on beds all over Europe, and soon the covers, and the techniques used to make them, had traveled to the New World as well. Small, and sometimes even large, areas of stuffed quilting are found on both British and American trapunto quilts dating from the nineteenth century, as well as exquisite examples of corded quilting.

Decorative patterns

Textile historians give credit to the needlework designers in Provence for seeing and developing the potential for creating highly decorated and complex patterns using this painstaking and time-consuming technique. Earlier trapunto quilts from Italy tended to be pictorial in nature, with many of them, such as the Tristan quilt, telling stories to a largely illiterate population.

The Provencal designs began as simple grids worked in single or double lines, usually diagonal on the body of the quilt, but over time, beautiful stylized patterns, especially floral designs, were created and passed from one needlewoman to another. The thing that sets Provencal quilts apart from British and American ones is the thickness of the finished article. This is especially true of the quilts known as "boutis," which date from the nineteenth century when women in Provencal villages along the Mediterranean coast resurrected the old trapunto techniques to make heavy bedcovers as well as garments. Many of the patterns that occur on antique examples of boutis are taken from the original Marseilles motifs, but they are executed on a much bigger scale and the quilting stitches that hold the finished layers together are rather larger, since the thickness of the finished quilt prevented any attempt at delicacy. These quilts, like the earlier Marseilles examples, are always worked as wholecloth

• A collaboration between designer Eiko Okano and quiltmaker Hisae Machiaoka, this quilt, which they call Grape in Autumn, was made in Tokyo in 2000. A simple medallion quilt, the white inner border frames a beautifully quilted trellis basket of daisies, roses, cascading ferns, and leaves. The wide outer border features both appliquéd and stuffed trapunto grapevines.

• This variation of a Whig Rose was made around 1850, possibly in Ohio, by an unknown quilter. The appliquéd blocks are arranged in a diagonal trellis pattern, and the white spacer blocks feature sumptous hand quilting and trapunto motifs of roses and buds. The appliqué is in traditional red, pink, green and white, with the all same colors echoed in the border.
University of Nebraska-Lincoln

quilts, made from one single type of fabric. However, the cloth was not necessarily just one solid color as is common in wholecloth quilts from other areas, and traditional colorful Provençal prints based on small-scale wood block designs are found, as well as pieces made from various toile de Jouy fabrics. The materials used to make them consisted, as with almost other quilts, of two layers of fabric—a top and a backing piece—and a middle layer of thick batting. Unlike other quilting techniques, on many boutis quilts the batting has been pushed away from the lines of quilting stitches, which makes the areas between the stitching even fuller and more sculptural in feel.

Corded quilting

Corded quilting, which creates raised linear designs on the surface of the fabric, is used rather sparingly on bedcovers today, but it is ideal for trimming garments and makes very pretty pillow covers and other small household items. Although it is traditionally worked by hand, it is possible to stitch the channels by machine. A fairly fine fabric is needed for the top—cotton, silk, and lightweight linen are all suitable. A design of close-spaced parallel lines is marked on the top, which is then backed with a layer of loosely woven material basted to the wrong side of the fabric. The marked channels are stitched with small and evenly-spaced running

• Trapunto work has been combined with machine quilting on this exquisite floral medallion quilt. Its French maker, Christine Moulin from Soisy-sur-Seine, made it in 2002 while her daughter was working with a humanitarian aid organization in India. Its design is based on a motif at the Taj Mahal and words from the Koran: "Have no fear, remember the promised garden." The central flower, with other flowers arranged around it, is very similar to a compass with the main eight points marked, and it is enclosed in a hand-appliquéd ring like a sunburst. The beautiful areas surrounding the center are also floral, with hand-dyed fabrics used to make the appliqué work. Gold-thread embroidery has been used as embellishment, as well as dense machine quilting.

stitches or backstitch (or they can be worked on the machine if you prefer—*see pages 222-223*). When the entire design has been stitched, the basting is removed and the cording is inserted through the loose-weave backing along each channel using a blunt tapestry needle. Be sure to use a fully-washable cord or yarn if the item will need to be laundered at any time.

Stuffed quilting

Stuffed quilting, which is sometimes simply called trapunto, makes padded areas on the surface of a quilt. It is a high-relief technique that can add greatly to the sculptural quality of a piece of work. The stuffing needs to be completed before the quilt is batted and backed.

Two layers of fabric, wrong sides together, are needed to work trapunto. The top fabric should be firm but pliable, the back one thin but closely woven. The design is marked and the two layers basted together. The stitching, like corded quilting, can be small running stitches or backstitch, and is worked from the top. The backing fabric can be trimmed away around the design to reduce bulk if you prefer. The stuffing is done from the wrong side. Small slits are made in the backing fabric and stuffing is inserted into the pocket that has been created. Only a little stuffing at a time should be used, and each bit should be poked into a corner or edge before more stuffing is introduced to keep lumps from forming. When the area that can be reached by your stuffing tool—a blunt needle, bodkin, or crochet hook—is filled to your satisfaction, whipstitch the slit closed and move to the next area. When the stuffing is completed, the quilt can be batted and backed, and the regular quilting can be worked.

Appliquéd shapes can be stuffed in a similar way to add depth and interest to quilt tops.

Project: TRAPUNTO

Stuffed quilting/Machine appliqué

The petals of the flowers on this dramatic Mexican Rose quilt from about 1880 are stuffed, giving the quilt additional textural interest. The instructions here show how to apply the petals by machine and stuff them from behind. Yellow backgrounds appear frequently on Pennsylvania Dutch quilts, and the Mexican Rose block was popular around the time the quilt was made, in about 1880, by an unknown maker. The colors are also typical of the era, and the workmanship is superb. Appliqué blocks alternate with red spacer blocks, and the wide border features an appliquéd trailing rose border with flowers, buds, and leaves. Collection University of Nebraska-Lincoln

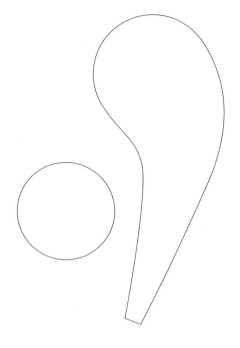

1 Trace the design on the right side of a square of background fabric with fine light pencil.

2 Fold under ¼" (5 mm) at each long side of the black fabric strip. Position one edge where the stem will lie, and stitch the folded edge down. Ease the other side of stem slightly closer to the first edge and stitch so a little fullness is left in the stem fabric.

3 Make a template for the petal shape. Trace around it on the wrong side of the petal fabric and before cutting it out, machine stitch just outside the marked line using matching thread. Cut the shapes out, trimming the outer edge to ¼" (5 mm) outside the stitched line. Clip the curves along the seam allowance, but do not cut through the stitching line.

4 Turn under the raw edge at the stitched line and baste (tack) to background. Set the machine to a shorter stitch length and width and machine appliqué the petals in place using a machine blindstitch.

5 Cut a 1¾" (4.5 cm) circle of orange fabric for the flower center. Stitch just inside the outer edge with running stitch. Pull up the threads to gather, stuff lightly, then pull closed. Slipstitch (blind stitch) in place by hand.

6 Turn the block to the wrong side and make a small hole behind a petal by separating the warp and weft threads. Lightly stuff the petal through the hole, using a wooden toothpick or small orangewood stick. Poke the batting (wadding) to all parts of the petal. Close the opening and repeat with other petals.

MACHINE QUILTING

• This brightly colored Amish-made Maple Leaf lap quilt was bought new at a fund-raising auction in Strasburg, Pennsylvania, in 1994. The pieced leaf blocks are set on point, and the white spacer blocks are filled to the edges with beautifully stitched roses. The triangular filler blocks inside the inner border are quilted with clamshells, echoing the curves of the interlocking hearts that decorate the border.

We tend to think of the sewing machine as a modern device, but the first example was patented in 1790 by an Englishman, Thomas Saint. Designed to stitch on leather, it was impractical and not a success, technically or commercially. Various inventors in several European countries continued Saint's work, and by the 1830's several other versions of machines that stitched fabric had been developed. Some of them had patents issued, but none was practical enough to see wide use.

The first practical machine to be marketed for home use was patented by its American maker, Elias Howe, in 1846. Shortly after Howe took out his patent, another American machinist named Isaac Merrit Singer came up with a similar device, although he knew nothing of Howe's machine. A patent battle

ensued, and Howe won the right to collect royalties on his machine. Singer, however, had patented a presser foot in 1851, and he continued to improve his machine, eventually turning his company into a synonym for home sewing machines. In 1889, the Singer Sewing Machine Company added an electric motor to its machines, and a new era in home sewing was born.

By the late nineteenth century, sewing machines were found in many homes, and numerous examples of antique quilts made on a machine still exist. Indeed, it became a status symbol to be able to quilt on a machine, since it proved that a family could afford to own one.

In spite of the refinements that have occurred over the past generation with zigzag and other attachments, as well as computer

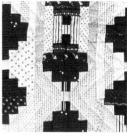

• This wonderfully graphic Courthouse Steps quilt was made around 1890 from a variety of fabrics. Both the reds and the whites are prints, including stripes and dots. The overall tone shows remarkable consistency for such a scrappy quilt, and the areas of striped fabric add visual texture and a lively feel. It was purchased as a top, new backing and binding were added, and simple machine quilting has been worked in a diamond pattern that outlines each red stepped area. Courthouse Steps is a familiar and popular variation of Log Cabin. Because the blocks are made from strips, the design is a good way to make inroads in a well-stocked scrap basket.

chips that provide special stitching at the touch of a button, most of today's home sewing machines are still based on Elias Howe's double-thread lockstitch invention. And in many areas of the world, people still depend on the foot-treadle and hand-cranked machines that would have been familiar to Singer and Howe.

Choosing how to quilt

Many quiltmakers face a dilemma when they are ready to quilt a piece of work. Should they quilt by hand or machine? Or combine the two techniques?

Hand quilting (*see pages 190-203*) is time-consuming and requires a certain expertise to work well. Machine quilting is quicker and requires a certain expertise to work at all. First, you must be entirely familiar with your machine. Manuevering three bulky layers of material can be difficult, so you need a good amount of physical space to machine-quilt a full-size bedcover. And as with hand quilting, you need to practice.

If you have made a quilt entirely by hand and see the piece as a future heirloom, most experts advise hand quilting, especially if the design has a number of open areas that will look effective with intricate motifs. Curved quilting patterns are usually easier to work by hand, especially on large pieces, unless you are an experienced machine quilter.

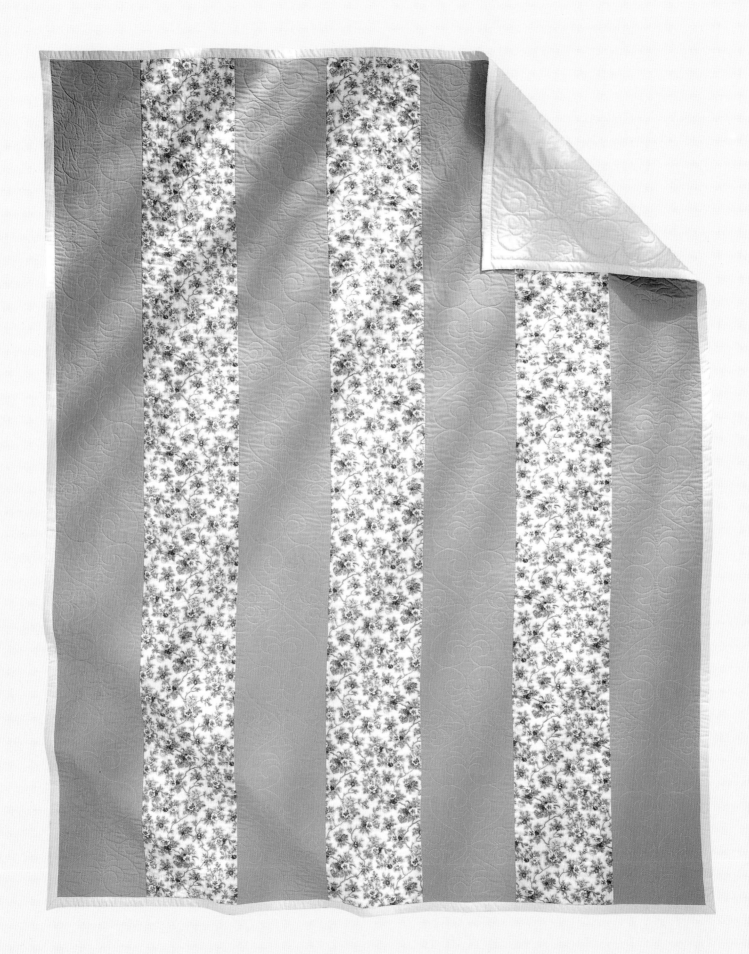

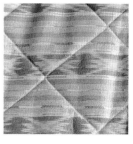

• This Thai silk quilt uses traditional ikat fabric in green and yellow, combined with wide stripes of plain yellow silk down the length of the quilt on either side. The machine quilting is a simple, large diagonal grid, to avoid taking attention away from the subtle patterning of the fabric itself.

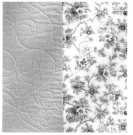

• The block-printed floral calico and peppermint-green cotton fabrics used to make this strippy quilt shown opposite evoke the color combinations of the 1930s. Designer/maker Miranda Innes has machine-quilted the plain strips with a sensuous curving motif, but has left the busy printed ones unquilted. The yellow backing fabric has been turned to the front to make a punchy binding.

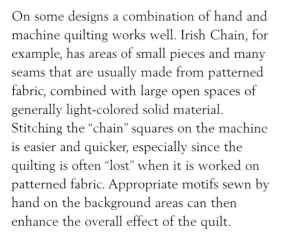

On some designs a combination of hand and machine quilting works well. Irish Chain, for example, has areas of small pieces and many seams that are usually made from patterned fabric, combined with large open spaces of generally light-colored solid material. Stitching the "chain" squares on the machine is easier and quicker, especially since the quilting is often "lost" when it is worked on patterned fabric. Appropriate motifs sewn by hand on the background areas can then enhance the overall effect of the quilt.

Quilting by machine

There are many reasons to quilt by machine. The pace of life today means that quiltmakers piece more by machine than by hand, and many of them machine quilt for the same reason: they lead busy lives, and working on the machine allows them to finish more quilts. If the fabrics used to make a quilt top are patterned or particularly small, the quilting will be the means to hold the layers together and will add texture to the piece, but the quilting pattern will not show up as a

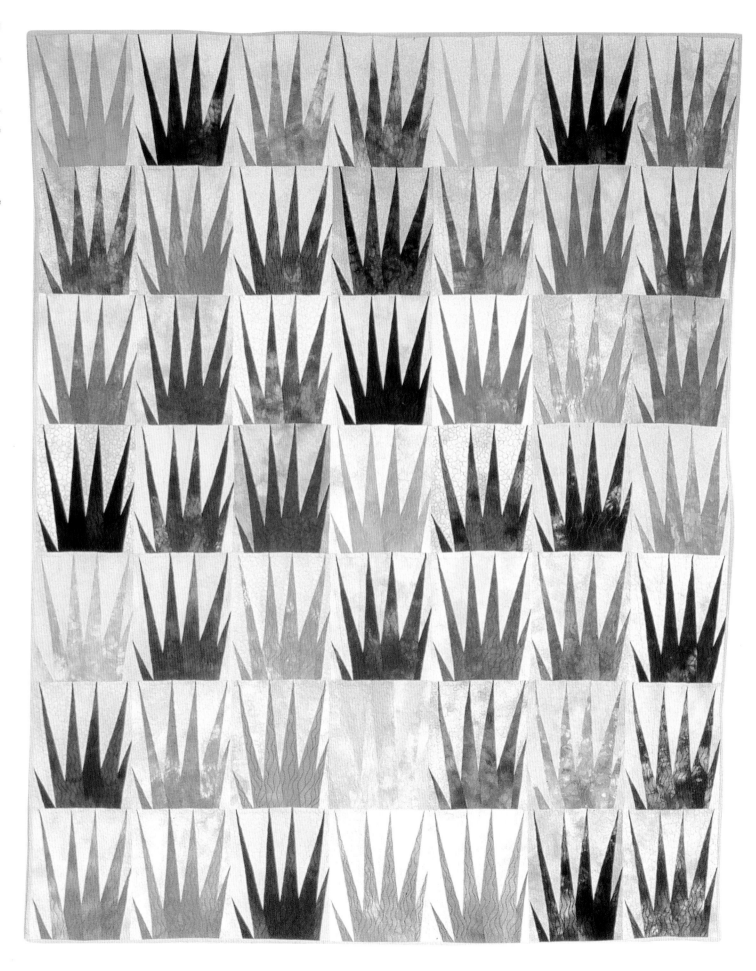

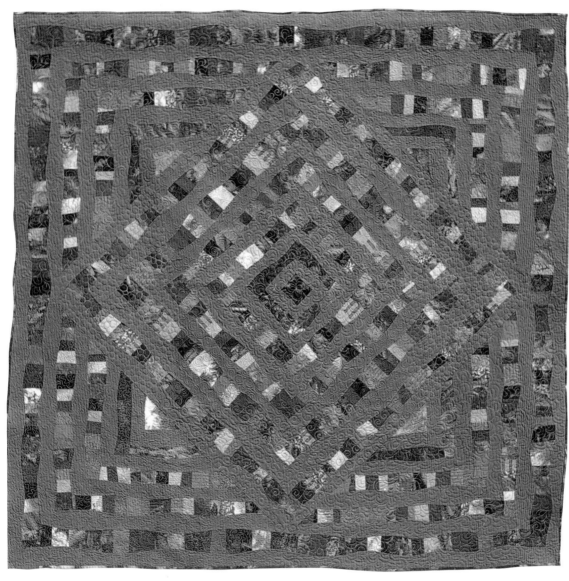

• Free-motion machine quilting worked in space-dyed cotton threads covers this lively quilt by Rose Epton-Peter. She learned the curved technique from Janice Gunner (*see pages 185, 188, and 408-409*) and used pink because it was "the only plain fabric I had a lot of at the time!" The pieced strips are made from cotton fabrics from her stash.

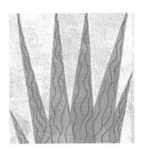

• Rose Epton-Peter made the opposite piece, the first in a series of Grass quilts, in 2004. Wanting a simple but effective design that could be colored in different ways, she created the block on the computer and printed it straight onto tracing paper. The hand dyed fabrics were machine-stitched directly onto the tracing paper, which was then torn off. The quilt is free machine-quilted using rayon thread.

feature in its own right. For quilts that are destined to receive heavy use and multiple launderings—those made for babies, children, or teenagers, for example—machine quilting is probably the best method to use.

Straight-line quilting is the easiest way to machine quilt. You can outline-quilt around individual shapes in the quilt top, or quilt in the ditch, which means working on top of the seams between pieces. Grid patterns are relatively straightforward to work and can run either up and down, or diagonally. They can also be square or diamond-shaped.

There are fewer motifs suitable for machine quilting than for hand work. Shapes must be large enough to work conveniently, and need some continuity of line so that stopping and starting are kept to a minimum and corners can be avoided wherever possible.

Free-motion quilting is a more advanced technique in which the feed dogs on the machine, which feed the fabric under the needle automatically, are disengaged to allow you to move the quilt along at your pace. It can be used to outline motifs in a similar way to machine embroidery, and for stipple, or drizzle, quilting, in which a continuous meandering line is used to fill background areas. Stippling is a wonderfully fast way to quilt a large area, but bear in mind that because the lines are worked close together, it flattens the areas of the quilt where it occurs. Used around a motif such as a flower, however, it creates extra lift in the unstitched motif itself that can enhance the texture of the piece. Remember that the ideal stipple quilting never crosses a previously stitched line.

• A contemporary version of a strippy quilt, made in tomato-red and deep lime. The machine quilting doodles over the whole surface of the quilt, irrespective of the strip seams. Two colors of thread have been used, so the stitching disappears and reappears, depending on which color strip they are in. The stitching designs include flower motifs, ferns and leaves. The quilt is called Daisy Doodle, and it was created by Ingrid Press, of East Sussex in England, in 2003.

Before you begin, you need to plan the best sequence for stitching the longest unbroken line possible. In general, it is best to start working in the center of the quilt, moving out to the edges. Quilt the inside areas before doing the borders. It can be useful to work in quarters, starting with the sashing and working out to the borders. If you are quilting straight lines and motifs in the same quilt, start by stitching the straight-line areas in the ditch or by outlining them. Then work the motifs. If you are filling in areas of background, with stippling for example, do those areas last.

Preparing to quilt by machine

Preparing a quilt sandwich with the top marked is the same for machine quilting or hand quilting, but basting with safety pins is not recommended for machine work since each pin must be removed as you come to it. Keep basting stitches fairly small so they don't get caught under the presser foot as you work.

If a piece is small—under 36 inches (90cm) square—you can lay it flat. Otherwise, you need to roll it. Working on a flat surface, roll or fold one edge toward the middle so that side will fit into the area between the needle and the motor of the machine. Rolling or folding helps to distribute the substantial weight of the quilt and to keep the layers taut as you work. You can roll two opposite sides toward each other if you prefer, but it is sometimes easier to work if the side outside the machine is left as flat as possible. Secure rolls or folds with bicycle clips or large safety pins to make them easier to handle. You may want to set up another table or an ironing board behind your machine table to help take the weight of a large quilt as you work.

Most machine quilters prefer to quilt with a special foot known as a walking foot, which feeds the layers through at the same pace. A regular presser foot feeds the three layers through unevenly, with the bottom layer going through faster than the top and batting, which

• A French quilt from Valbonne in Provence, of traditional toile de Jouy, but in a non-traditional colorway of yellow and white. The bands of plain white feature machine quilting in a design of curling feathers, while the body of the quilt is stitched in a small diagonal trellis design.

can cause wrinkles and puckers to appear. Use a medium-long stitch for quilting, and always test on a practice piece to make sure the tension is correct and to get a feel for the process.

Straight-line machine quilting

When you have the quilt positioned under the needle, take a single stitch and raise the needle and the presser foot. Pull the bobbin thread through to the surface, take a couple of stitches forward and then a couple back. Then you can begin a row of machine quilting. If you need to turn a corner, keep the needle in the fabric, lift the presser foot, and turn the quilt to the new direction. Lower the foot and continue. When you finish a row or area of stitching, take a couple

of backstitches to secure the thread. When you finish a rolled-up area, take the quilt off the machine and unroll a new area. Roll up the quilted area to compensate, and continue quilting.

Free-motion machine quilting

While practice is essential for all aspects of quiltmaking, free-motion quilting demands a concentrated effort to master successfully. It is a very challenging skill, and few people perfect the technique without a great deal of concentrated practice.

The best way to approach free-motion quilting is probably to work on small projects until you get the hang of moving the piece under the machine in a way that results in smooth lines and even stitches.

• This quilt is basically a wholecloth quilt with a single motif. Called English Daffodil, it was made in Hampshire, England, in 2001 and given as a wedding present to quiltmaker Jane Hill. The central design, which consists of eight interlocking daffodils, is based on an appliqué pattern by Edyth Henry called Hawaiian Daffodil. The background and border were meander-quilted on a long-arm machine, and the daffodil motif is trapunto work that helps to define the design.

Once you have prepared the quilt sandwich, you must disengage the feed dogs according to your machine's instructions. You will need a free-motion presser foot, either a darning, quilting, or appliqué version. All are open in the center; the ones that are split at the front make it easier to see the stitching as it happens as you move the fabric manually.

Start as for straight-line quilting by taking a stitch and bringing the bobbin thread to the top of the work. Take several stitches without moving the fabric to tie the threads. Then with one hand on each side of the foot, place your fingers on the fabric lightly and spread the area under the needle out slightly. Run the machine at a moderate, even speed, not too fast or slow, and move the fabric under your fingertips smoothly. Go back and forth or side to side, with the needle following the marked quilting design, or moving in a stippling pattern. Always leave the needle in the fabric when you stop stitching to prevent the work from slipping. When you have finished an area of quilting, tie the threads again by taking a few stitches without moving the piece.

Long-arm quilting

Among the recent advances in quilting technology is the long-arm quilter. These machines make quilting faster and the results can be very attractive, but they are highly specialized, require training and lots of practice, and they are expensive. Unless you do an enormous amount of machine quilting or work professionally, you will probably not need to know how to use one.

• The quilt shown here was made by Rose Epton-Peter in 2001 and is called From the Desert to the Sea. Epton-Peter had bought a range of fabrics with no particular project in mind, and they looked so good together, that she just added fabrics from her stash to make a simple, machine-pieced quilt that allowed the colours to speak for themselves. The machine quilting is an overall meander stitch, which adds texture to the piece without distracting from the vibrant colors and geometric design.

Project: MACHINE QUILTING

Machine quilting techniques

Quilting by machine was traditionally the ugly stepsister of the art, but the advent of sewing machines designed to cope with the layers—and especially the speed they made possible—have brought the skill into its own in recent years. Well-worked machine quilting is attractive and versatile, aided by the range of machine embroidery threads that are now available. Always test your stitching on a spare sample first.

Many quilts today are machine quilted on long-arm machines, which, although they are rather expensive, can give highly professional results if the user is thoroughly trained and experienced on the machine. In many places there is a thriving cottage industry of long-arm quilters, who will quilt other people's work on their machine.

Straight Lines

Straight lines can be marked on the fabric and stitched. You can simply mark one line at a time and then use the foot as a guide. A special walking foot is available that helps to keep the layers moving at the same speed.

Curved Lines

Curved lines can be marked on the fabric beforehand and stitched, or the curve can be followed using a special bar—found on many machines—that measures the distance from one line to the next as you work.

Meander Stitch

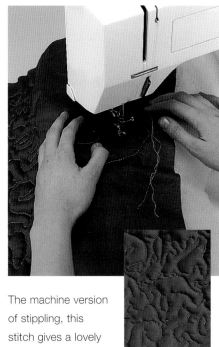

The machine version of stippling, this stitch gives a lovely close stitched texture as it wends its random way through the area to be quilted. This method works best if lines are not overstitched.

Quilt-as you-go

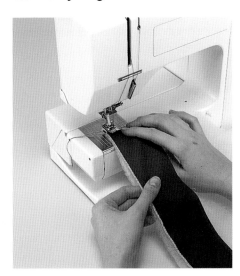

1 Cut fabric strips the desired width, and a piece of batting 2" (5 cm) bigger all around than the finished size of the block. Place two fabric strips right sides together and wrong side down on the batting. Stitch the right-hand edge of the strips through all the layers.

2 Fold back the top strip and place a third strip of fabric right side down on the second strip. Stitch in place along the right-hand edge. Repeat to cover the batting each time.

Rolling

A large quilt can be difficult to handle under the machine. Roll up the edges of the area to be stitched, to distribute the weight and make it much easier to move the piece around. Bicycle clips can be used to hold the roll in place.

• This crisp-looking Tailor's quilt is made from scraps of wool suiting material and tied in the corner of each triangle with red wool yarn. Each triangular block is pieced from two smaller triangles, half from lights, half from dark fabrics. These fabrics are used again in the two wide borders, including the middle one, which is pieced from random squares and rectangles of lights. The red of the yarn is picked up in the narrow inner border and the binding.

UTILITY QUILTING

Many cultures use different forms of utility quilting in their textile traditions, to hold layers of fabric and batting together. Sometimes also called big-stitch quilting, utility quilting is usually light years away from the tiny, neat, and evenly spaced stitches of the finest quilting found on more traditional quilts, but it is still very much a part of the wider art of quiltmaking.

Tying

Tying is the best-known form of utility quilting. It is probably the quickest way to quilt a piece of work, and gives a soft tufted finish. High-loft or firm batting is easier to tie than to quilt conventionally, but any type of batting can be used.

In the United States, tied quilts are associated with pioneer log cabins and slave quarters, and American tied quilts are often referred to as comforters. It is true that many of the best antique examples were made on the frontier, but the tradition of tying exists wherever quilts are made. Tying is a strong component of the African-American quiltmaking tradition and is still widely used today. Many Log Cabin and Crazy quilts from the late nineteenth and early twentieth century are tied. The many seams in each type make hand quilting them an arduous task, and tying was a quick way both to avoid the thickness created by the seams and to finish the piece.

To tie a quilt, take strong thread through all the layers, usually—but not always—from the top. The thread is brought back through close by, ideally secured with another stitch, and tied with a secure double knot before being repeated at intervals all over the quilt. Some quilters cut the ends with each tie; others prefer to take the thread to the next spot and then trim all the ends at the same time when the tying is completed.

Almost any strong thread can be used for tying, including yarn, string, pearl cotton or several strands of embroidery floss—and even thin ribbon. Yarn must, of course, be thin enough to go through the eye of the needle and the layers of fabric and batting,, and many quilters prefer synthetic yarn over natural fibers because it will stay tied much better. Strands of floss of different colors can also be combined for a wonderful effect. Ribbon and yarn can both be tied into bows on top of the securing knots, and buttons and beads can be added to the thread before the final tying to add a decorative if somewhat lumpy touch.

Sashiko

Japanese in origin and design, sashiko is an ancient and complex form of utility quilting that has become popular around the world in recent years as a decorative technique. Traditionally worked on dark blue fabric in white or sometimes red thread, it was originally used to hold several layers of worn fabric and interlining together to make warm clothing. Sashiko was widely used on garments worn by farmers, fishermen, and forestry workers for warmth, and by firefighters as protective clothing.

The stitch used for sashiko is always a running stitch, and the closer together the stitches were, the more long-lasting the garment was thought to be. The dense stitching found on some antique examples not only creates the intricate patterns, but sometimes actually appears to be the fabric itself. The patterns are highly geometric and traditional, with evenly sized stitches and spaces between. The stitches are longer than in the Western tradition, and the spaces where a number of stitches meet are crucial to the design. Each section of a pattern should have the same number of stitches in each repeat.

• The four traditional geometric sashiko designs in this sampler were stitched to be made into a bag. Pattern has evolved over hundreds of years, and most have evocative names: top left is Water Wells, or *igeta ni hakkaku tsunagi*; top right is Pampas Grass, or *nowaki*. The two bottom patterns are variations of Waves: *seigaiha* (*left*) and *hishi seigaiha* (*right*).

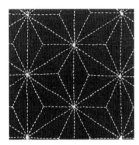

• The top left sample here is called Mountains and to its right is a variation of Arrow Feathers. The two bottom examples are traditional-looking adaptations of sashiko quilting. Stitches must be regular and are usually spaced about six to the inch. White cotton thread on indigo fabric is most common, but garments stitched in red, or made from red fabric and stitched in blue or white, are also found.

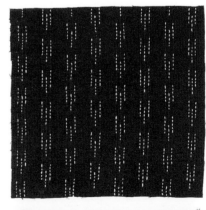

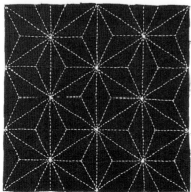

• The detail pictured on the right is a close-up of two beautifully geometric patterns on a twentieth-century backpack from Japan stitched in traditional white cotton thread on indigo-dyed cotton fabric. Sashiko was used by rural peasants to decorate garments and furnishings from the seventeenth to the nineteenth centuries.

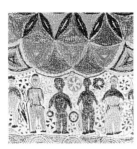

• This unfinished kantha quilt from Bengal made of cotton dates from the mid-twentieth century. The quilting on kantha work is achieved when several layers of thin, usually cotton fabric are stitched together, held in place by the dense embroidery that is characteristic of kantha. Here, embroidered motifs include flowers, animals, people, and geometric patterns that fill up the background areas. Courtesy Joss Graham Oriental Textiles

Kantha

On the other side of Asia, another utility quilting tradition is still widely practiced. Kantha work originated in the area of the Indian subcontinent that is now Bangladesh on the eastern side of India. It was first used to hold several layers of worn fabric such as sari cloth together, and was used mainly on household textiles to get more use from old clothing. It consists of tiny stitches worked in

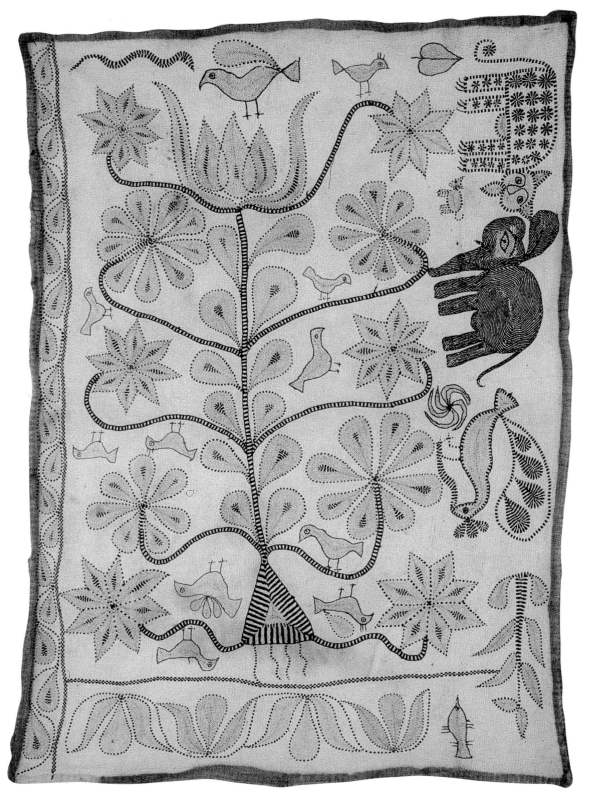

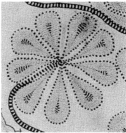

• Dating from around 1900, this small Tree of Life kantha has great naive charm. It features an elephant, a tiger, and several birds. The predominance of red and blue for the embroidery is typical of older kanthas. Courtesy Joss Graham Oriental Textiles

a variety of bright colors, usually on a light-colored background, with motifs consisting of fanciful animals, people, plants, and abstract or geometric designs. Many generations of stitchers have created kantha work, and making items of kantha has become a cottage industry that sustains a number of villages in one of the poorest countries on Earth. The women who practice the craft often create their own designs as they work, so there is a wide variety of motifs and patterns.

Sammi

The Saami are an itinerant community of religious mendicants, living in small groups along the canals and waterways of Sindh in

• Several fabrics in startlingly different colors have been pieced together to make the wide outer border of this ralli quilt. The large and decorative quilting stitches have been worked in white thread and arranged in concentric rectangles around a line stitched in the center of the piece. Courtesy Joss Graham Oriental Textiles

India. Their quilts, or ralli, are a unique textile tradition which, in their subconscious juxtaposition of color, invite appreciation as pieces of "contemporary art," while still remaining firmly based in the age-old tradition of both reusing and beautifully embellishing old cloth for use as an everyday household item.

Recycled and patched cloth, making the old and worn out into new and usable pieces, has a long association with the great religions of Hinduism, Buddhism and Islam. The quilts that are still made today continue to be very vital and exuberant in fabric, color and design and are often quite beautiful pieces of workmanship. The cloth is first patched, and then the base quilting is worked, starting from the outside and moving into the center in concentric rectangles, often with embroidered right-angle shapes set into the corners. A rather limited repertoire of embroidery stitches is used, but what makes the Saami ralli distinctive is the interplay of color in the running stitches which enlivens the overall field, and creates a classic example of optical color mixing.

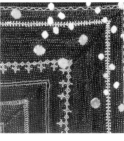

• This quilt was made in the Aami Fakir Community in Sindh province in Pakistan in about 1950. The community is located in the Indus delta, where traditional ralli quilts are widely made. The intricacy of the stitching is typical of the quilts of the region, the tie-dyed background cloth less so. A number of different embroidery stitches have been used here. Many ralli quilts have strongly geometric patterns that are very similar to many block designs used in patchwork quilts. Courtesy Joss Graham Oriental Textiles

Big-stitch quilting

The vogue for home decorating country-style has led to a rise in popularity of big-stitch or utility quilting, which was originally used to finish quilts in a hurry, particularly on the American frontier. Most of the traditional stitches used were based on embroidery stitches, including cross stitch, French knots, crow's foot, Mennonite tack, Methodist knot, and half buttonhole stitch. Most of these stitches can, just like tying, be worked in embroidery floss or narrow ribbon, as well as in yarn and quilting threads. Pictures and descriptions of the most common of the big-stitch quilting stitches are shown on the following pages.

Project: UTILITY QUILTING

Utility stitches

Utility quilting takes many forms, from tying to big-stitch quilting such as that found on many everyday African-American quilts to highly geometric embroidery-type stitches found on Japanese sashiko and Indus Valley rallis. Many individual embroidery stitches can also be adapted to use as quilting, giving interesting special effects to modern examples. Instructions for working most of these stitches can be found in embroidery books.

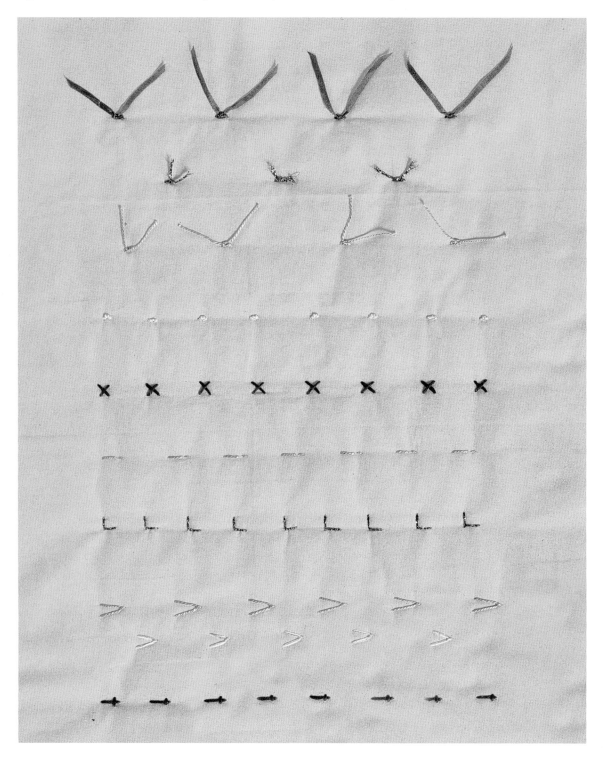

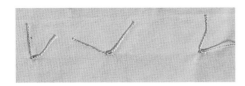

Tying

Quilts are usually tied with thick thread or embroidery floss. The needle is usually taken from the top to the back, brought back again very near the original entry point, and tied in a square knot. Taking a double stitch makes the tie more secure.

Decorative Tie

Decorative and novelty thread can also be used to tie quilts and wall hangings. The loose threads can be an interesting additional decoration. Some quilts are tied with the ends of the thread on the back instead of the front.

Ribbon Tie

Tied quilting is quick and easy to work. Ribbon or yarn can be used as long as they are narrow enough to go through the eye of the needle, which must be pointed, not blunt, to go through all the layers of fabric and the batting.

French Knot

Small knotted embroidery stitches known as French knots can be used to secure the layers of quilts together. The back of the quilt will be smooth, but French knots will create a small bump on the front.

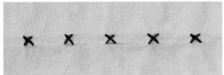

Cross Stitch

Embroidery stitches are a useful way to hold quilt layers together. Cross stitches can make very effective method of quilting, especially when certain decorative effects are desired.

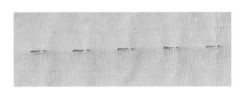

Methodist Knot

Methodist knot is another kind of embroidery stitch, which gives a dot-dash effect on the front side and can be placed to create very interesting patterns across the surface of the quilt.

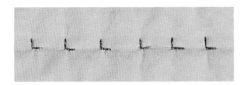

Half Buttonhole

Half buttonhole stitch makes an L-shaped stitch. Varying the size of individual stitches in any of the stitches shown here will create new patterns.

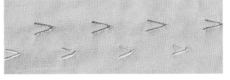

Crow's Foot

Crow's foot is another individual embroidery stitch. Based on Fly stitch, it can be used to make interesting bird tracks across the surface of a quilt, either straight rows or meandering trails.

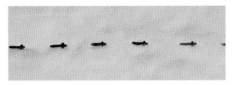

Mennonite Tack

Mennonite tacks make a spaced line of horizontal crosses that, like other individual embroidery stitches shown here, can be used to great effect.

PART TWO

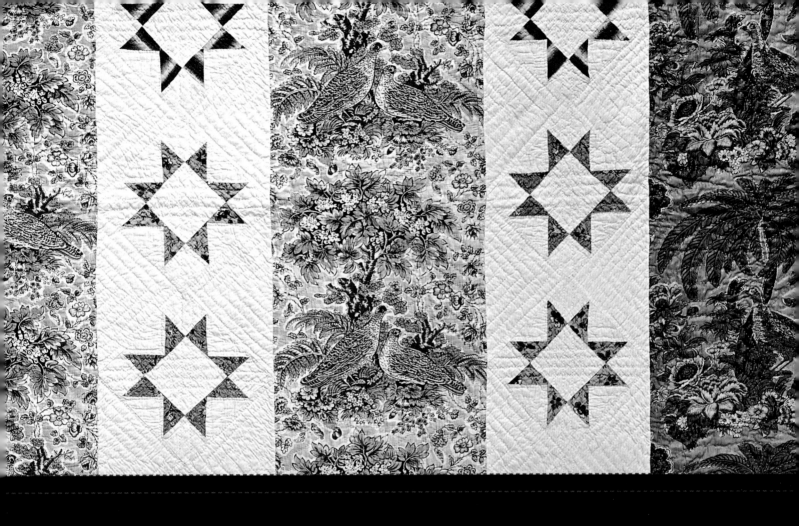

PICTURE GALLERY

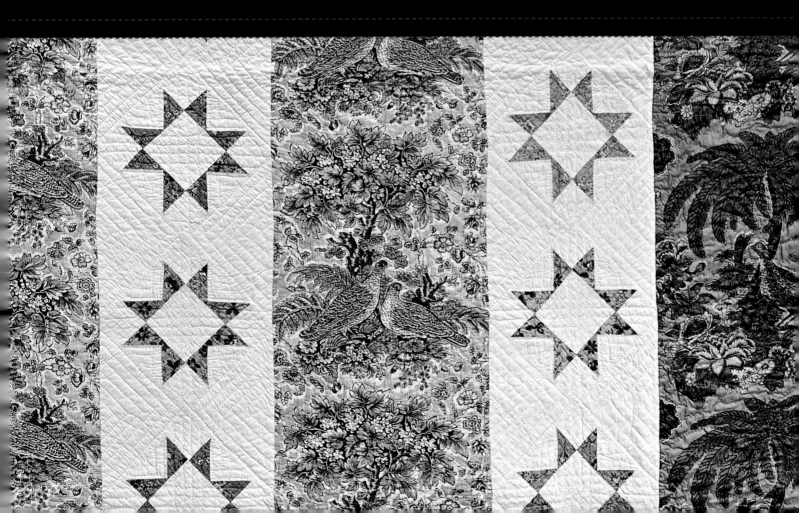

WHOLECLOTH

Satin Wholecloth (1935)

Hulda Semalia Forschen

Minnesota Historical Society

This yellow/white satin single-bed quilt has symmetrical plumes extending from the corners into the center, which is quilted with a diamond grid.

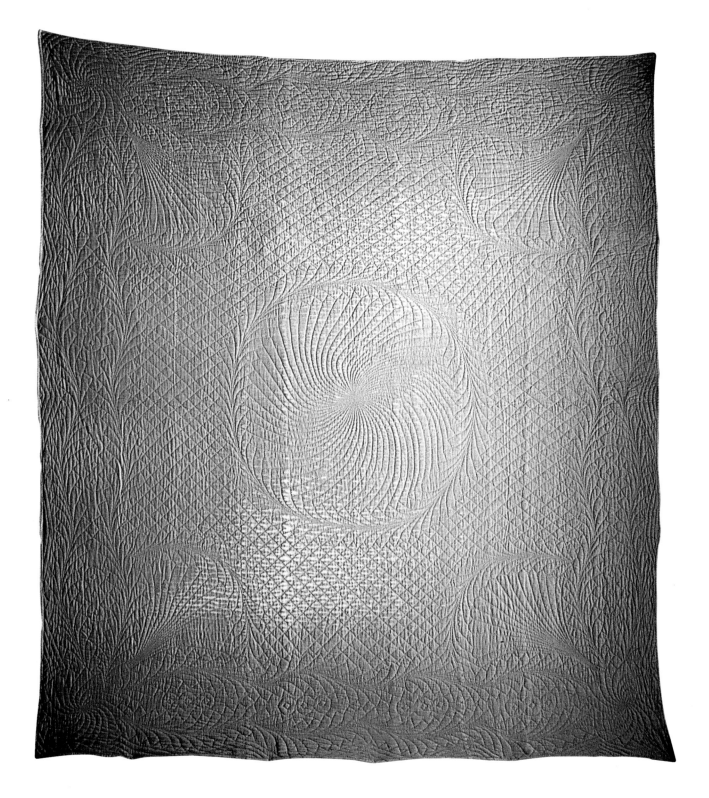

Sateen Wholecloth (c. 1940)

Mrs. Lowe

Beamish: North of England Open Air Museum

The family of the maker of this hand-quilted wholecloth came from Spennymore, County Durham in the north of England, and they had used this same design for generations. The central motif is a large single whorl, which is edged with a narrow feathered circle. Fans echoing the whorl decorate the corners and are connected by running feathers, with a diamond grid covering the background areas.

Wholecloth (1861)

Sarah C. Stern

This exquisite wholecloth quilt was made in Maryland. It is extraordinary both in its intricacy and beautiful workmanship. Trapunto quilting has been used to stuff many of the individual floral motifs, as well as in the corded zigzag frame dividing the center from the border motifs, which gives wonderful texture to the piece. The central motif features a large vase with a bouquet of flowers, surrounded by many floral designs.

Norwegian Wholecloth (c. 1765)

Maker unknown

Minnesota Historical Society/Gift of Marie G. Thomsen

The bottom corners of this true antique, made by the great grandmother of the donor and her two sisters, have been cut out to fit around the posts of a bed.

The intricate center—which contains rose, scroll, and shell motifs as well as a diagonal grid—extends into a square that is bounded by another square. The edges are equally elaborate with double spirals contained in zigzag lines. The top is plain apple green, the backing has small red print flowers with black leaf tracery.

Double-sided Chintz Wholecloth (c. 1830)

Maker unknown

Milwaukee Art Museum/Gift of Collectors Corner

This early American quilt is unusual —it has two fronts. Each side has been joined to make a large piece, one a polychrome chintz with quails and palm trees, the other from red-and-white toile that has a closely spaced design of stone castles, manor houses, and ruined battlements. The quilted parallel zigzag lines have been worked quite close together.

It was probably made in New York state, and was featured in the 1997 Quilt Engagement Calendar

compiled by quilt expert Cyril I. Nelson and published by Penguin Studio.

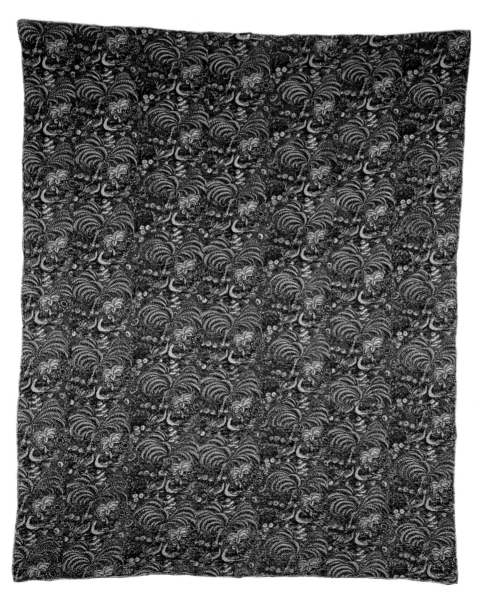

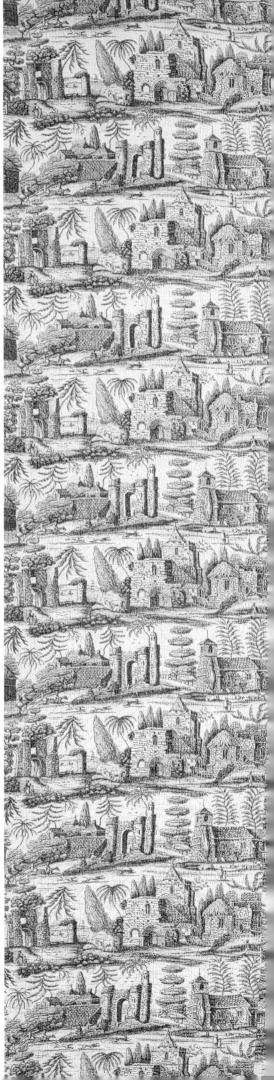

MEDALLION

Hollyhock Cottage (1930–40)

Maker unknown

American Folk Art Museum/Gift of Margaret Caviggo

Medallion quilts featuring a central panel surrounded by a series of borders are among the earliest of quilt designs. This pre-World War II variation is a charming twist on the tradition. The design is based around an appliquéd and embroidered central medallion and features straight-line quilting. The central element of this quilt is typical of the themes predominant in decorative arts, particularly textiles and ceramics, at the time, with the embroidered flowers encircling the cottage drawn from Jacobean crewel-work embroidery, and the blue and pink border flowers showing a Germanic influence. The combination of appliqué and embroidery, and the careful use of the open area around the center, quilted in straight closely spaced horizontal or vertical lines, creates a thoroughly charming piece.

Traditional medallion quilts have several separate borders, with a few of them almost always pieced. Here the borders have been applied to a wholecloth background quilted in a plain diamond grid to give the same effect. The rows of simple flowers face each other and are framed by a scalloped pink binding a shade deeper than the outer row of flowers.

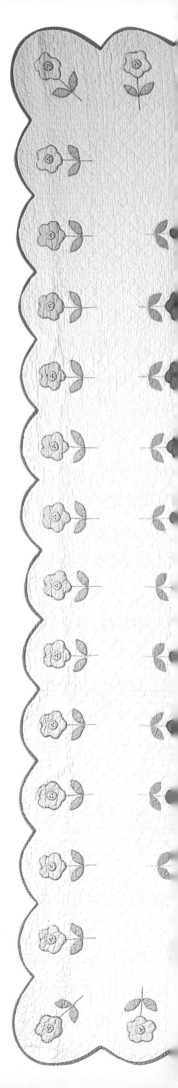

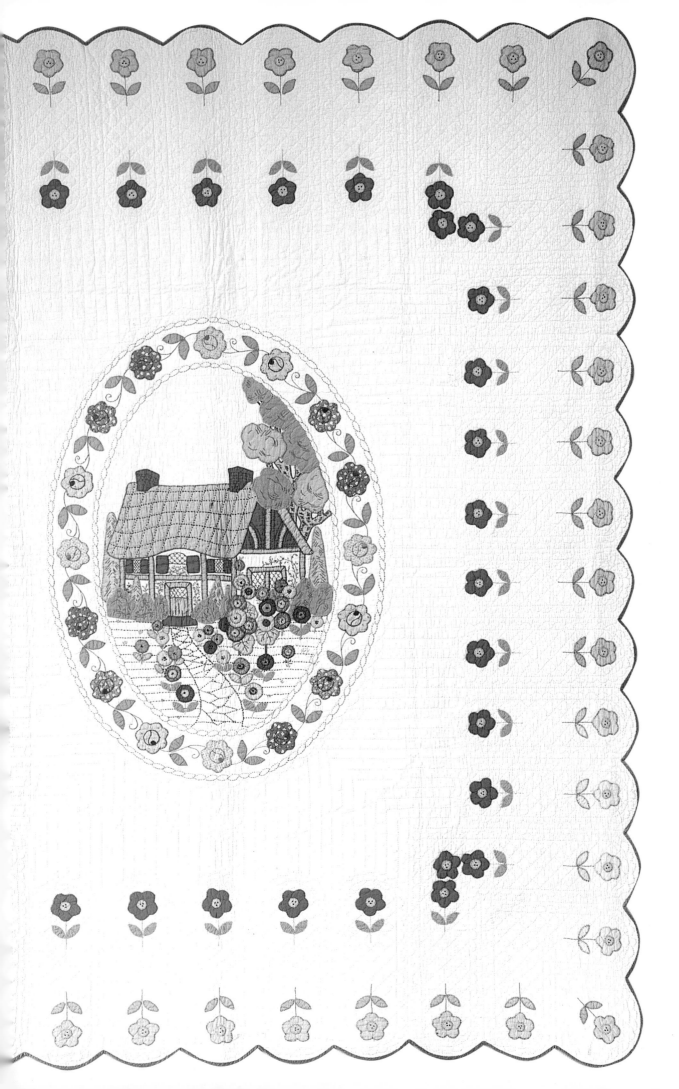

Patchwork Medallion Star (1900)

attributed to Elizabeth Sanderson

Beamish: The North of England Open Air Museum

Elizabeth Sanderson was one of the best known of the "Allenheads stampers"—professional quilters who worked in Northumberland in England, in the areas around Allendale and Weardale. They marked tops with an appropriate pattern, which could then be quilted by others—usually the lady of the house. Sanderson was an apprentice of the equally well-known George Gardiner, who also had a shop selling fabric. Like other stampers of the late 1800s Sanderson never signed any of her work, and she also taught many apprentices, so very few of the tops of this time can be definately attributed to her.

However, she often used this patchwork star pattern, and this particular quilt was most probably put together and marked either by her, or by one of her apprentices in around 1900.

In places, the marking is still visble. The intricate pattern in the stars is balanced by the simple crosshatched background of the center square.

Mennonite Diamond in the Square (1890-1900)

Maker unknown

One of the quintessential Amish quilt designs, Center Diamond, or Diamond in the Square, is a variation of the traditional medallion quilt form. This stunning version, made in Pennsylvania at the beginning of the twentieth century, features a decorative tulip appliqué in the center diamond. This motif sets it apart from its strict Amish antecedents, for the Plain People would never use such "fancies" on their work. They do, however, decorate the edges of the main shapes with the sawtooth motif, giving this group of quilts an unparalleled dramatic impact.

The color contrasts of red and dark blue on this quilt make the design even more impressive, and highlight the superb quality of the workmanship—both the piecing of many small sharp points and the quilting. The quilting itself is typically Amish, diagonal grid on the background of the center diamond and the square in which it sits, with a triple cable in the red border and a feathered cable, beautifully matched at the corners, along the outer border. Red binding finishes the edges in keeping with the rest of the quilt.

Squares within Squares (c. 1860–90)

Maker unknown

Bowes Museum

This medallion quilt is pieced mainly from squares of printed cotton. The center is a diamond of floral chintz in a square of striped fabric. The square itself is made from triangles around the four sides of the central diamond, three of which are cut to run the same way—with the fourth running in the opposite direction.

The first narrow border around the center is made from a dotted-pattern fabric that also appears in random places in one of the borders. It has corners cut from the same fabric as

the diamond center, and four of the other borders also show the same fabric in their corners. The next border is a double one, which is made from squares and outlined with a strip of narrow striped fabric with plain corners. Another double border is made in a diamond-and-hourglass pattern outlined with a single border of squares. The final border is the same width as the previous three, but is cut from a single piece of cotton cloth rather than pieced.

Made by a member of the family who lived at Snow Field Farm at Stanhope near Weardale in County Durham, a center for quilting in the Northeast of England, the quilt contains many striped fabrics, which adds greatly to the lively feel of the piece, and the dominant pink and brown tones are typical of the era in which the quilt was made. The maker has quilted each border strip separately, using a variety of patterns that were well known in the area around Weardale.

Diamond in the Square (1835-1850)

Maker unknown

Bowes Museum

This quilt was, like the one opposite, made by a member of the family at Snow Field Farm. The diamond at the center is a square of floral chintz with a spray of flowers, grasses, and leaves, and turned on point in a square cut from a floral printed calico. The first border is made from triangle squares cut from the same 1830s dress fabrics that have been used to make the entire quilt. The corners of this and the following border, and the squares set along each diagonal line out to the corners of the quilt, are all cut from the same chintz fabric. The second border is made up of squares set on point, with filler triangles to make straight edges. Beyond that is a background of squares on point divided diagonally by the floral corner squares.

The quilting is an allover design of Wavy Line, combined with Stars and Four-petal Flowers. Wineglass and Clamshell are used in the center area, and a Wave pattern appears on the outer edge.

Double-sided Rectangular Medallion (c. 1890)

Maker unknown

Bowes Museum

This subtly colored medallion quilt by an unknown maker is unusual because it is rectangular, not square like so many of its kind. Only three fabrics have been used—a solid blue cotton with two cotton prints, one pinkish stripes, the other a small-scale pink and blue print on a pale background. The central long triangles are surrounded by a series of borders in which the patchwork is minimal—only the corner triangle-squares that appear on four of the seven borders needed to be pieced. The two blue borders, both narrow, have no contrasting corner squares, but the borders made from the prints, save for the outer border, have corners made in each case from both prints.

The reverse side of the quilt is a strippy made in plain Turkey red strips alternated with printed cotton ones. The quilting has been planned and executed to match the piecing of the medallion top, with oval leaves in the center and Cable Twist, Feathered, Geometric, and Wavy Line with Fans along the borders. The planning of the quilting has been expertly done; the lines of stitching are balanced and beautifully worked.

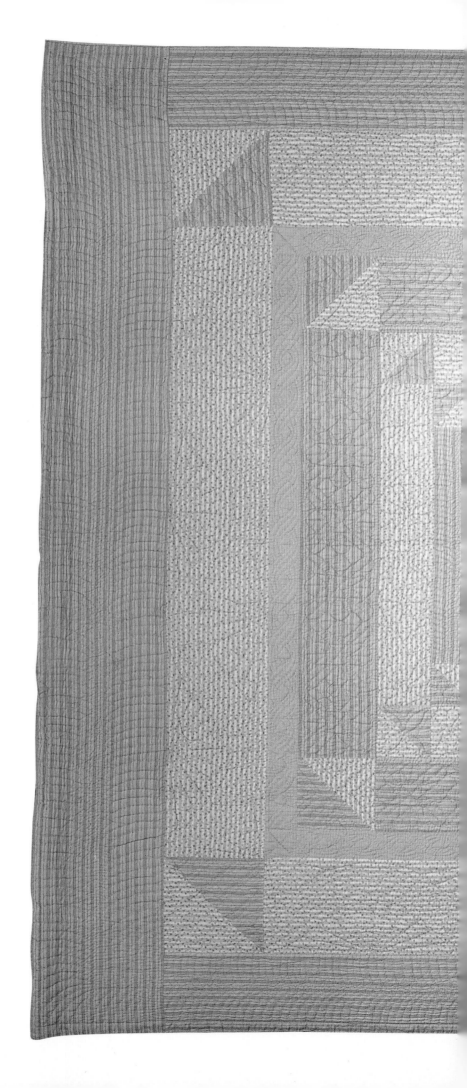

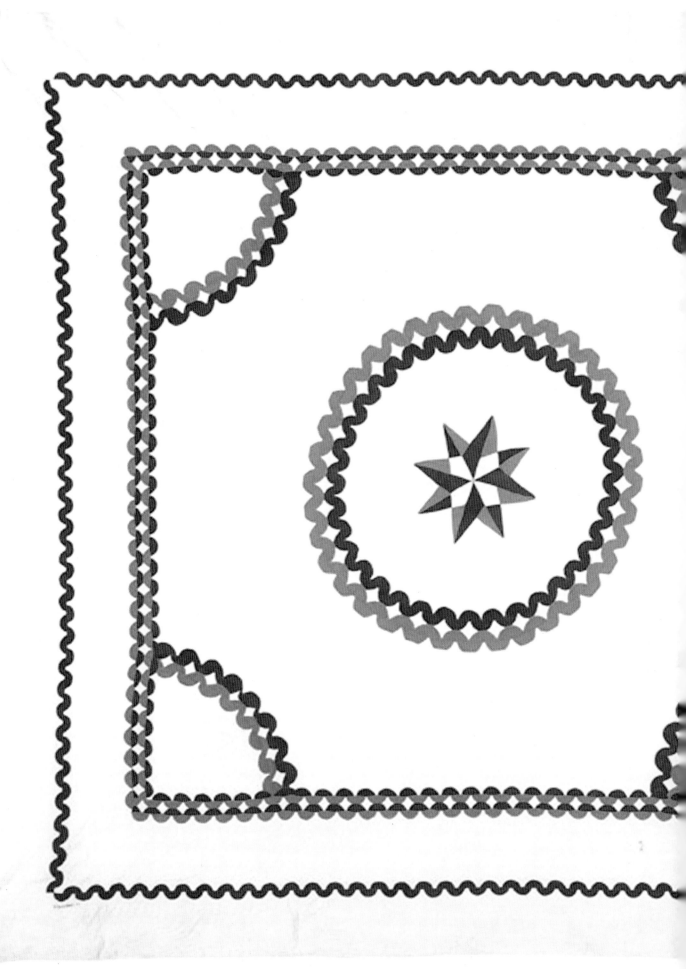

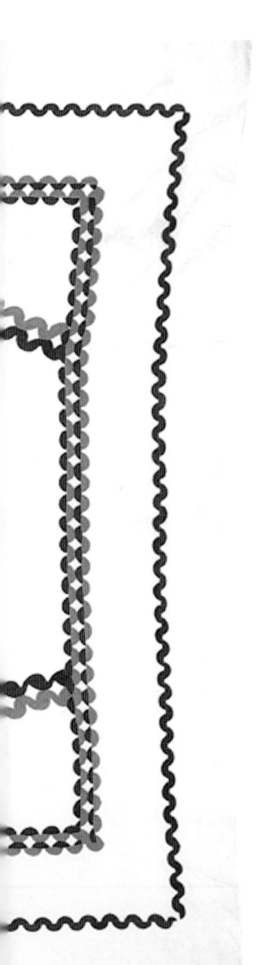

Medallion Quilt (1857)

Marie Ann Schoffstall Laudenschlager

Minnesota Historical Society/Part of the Joyce Aufderheide collection

This medallion-style quilt was made in 1857 by Marie Ann Schoffstall Laudenschlager (1804-1879), who signed it "M. Laudenschlager." The red, green, and white central star is an interesting and intricate variation of an eight-point star block inside a circle of red and green rickrack-style pattern. The same zigzag motif is used to make various border patterns that create the framing for the medallion. The white cotton background is quilted with grapes around the star. Mrs. Laudenschlager lived in Dauphin County, Pennsylvania, at the time that the quilt was made.

Provençal Quilt (1990s)

Miranda Innes

The French have a tradition of simple patchwork quilts that often combine prints and plaids, but the quintessential French quilt is probably the type made in Provence in the South of France, using the brightly colored cotton fabrics for which the area is well known. These fabrics, known locally as "les indiennes," are the descendants of cotton cloth imported into the region from India, beginning in the seventeenth century. The original materials were printed by hand with wood blocks in small geometric patterns and vivid hues, and became so associated with Provence that they are now known around the world as Provençal prints. Most of the designs available today are no longer printed by hand, but many of them still emulate the subtlety and brightness of the originals. The fabrics can be purchased in outdoor markets throughout the region, a delight for the traveling quiltmaker.

Provençal cottons have an extraordinary ability to blend well with one another, and this quilt is a good example of their capacity to coordinate together into a totally harmonious whole. Three different prints have been combined around a central rectangle made of a tiny geometric green and red patterned fabric: stripes of floral, a yellow and green print, and an outer border of the same material used for the center. The quilt is bound in a bright red that echoes the red found in each of the main fabrics and backed with a dark green solid fabric. The quilting is simple crosshatching in the center, with parallel straight lines in an outward sequence around all the borders.

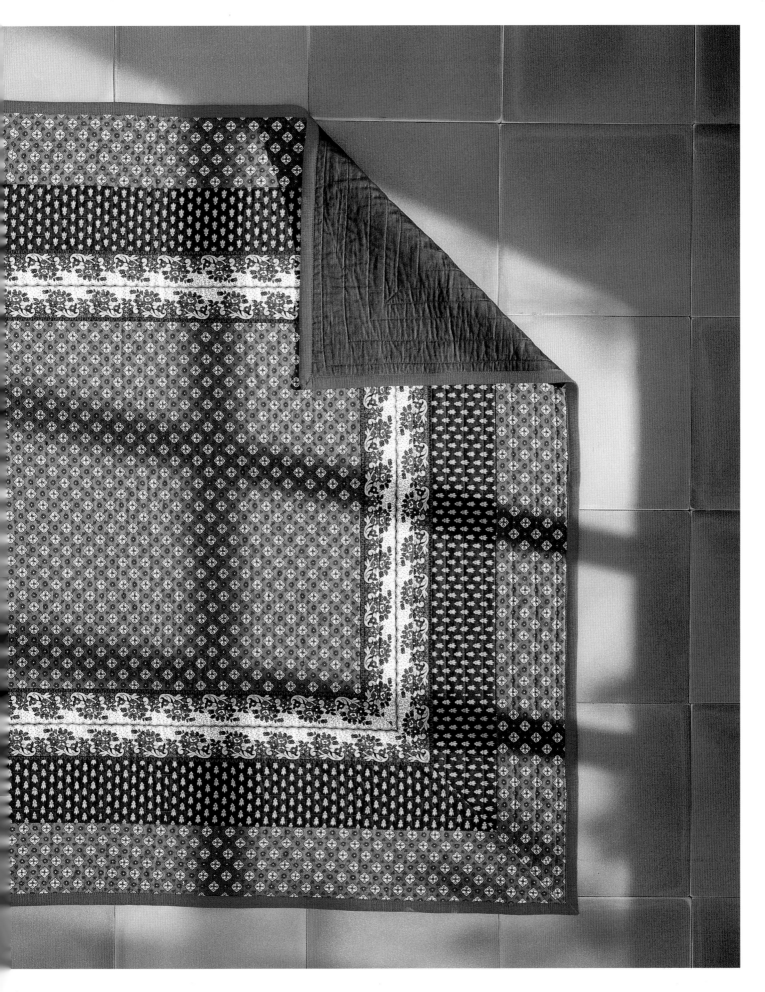

STRIPPY

Variable Star Strippy (c. 1825)

Maker unknown

This beautiful soft-colored quilt was made in America as a strippy in the traditional style that was widely practiced in the Northeast of England in the nineteenth century. Both of the two documented chintz patterns, one used to make the strips and the other as the border, feature birds, and they are printed in harmonizing colors. English quiltmaker Barbara Chainey saw the quilt for sale at the International Quilt Festival in Houston, Texas, and immediately summoned her friend Patricia Cox, an American collector and quiltmaker. As neither of them felt that they could afford it alone, they purchased it together, and since all the quilts in Barbara's collection are British and all of Pat's are American, it now lives in the Cox household in Minneapolis, Minnesota, and is looked after by Pat. It is the oldest quilt to be found in the Cox collection.

The design of this quilt is highly traditional, but a number of elements make it atypical. The Variable Star blocks are made from a selection of different fabrics in shades of brown on a cream background that are beautifully coordinated with the prints, which have been cut to emphasize the pattern. The superb workmanship is evident in the piecing of the bottom border to hide the seams as well as the quilting— straight-line grids on the star blocks and curves on the border.

Chintz was a highly prized commodity around the time that this quilt was made. When the American colonies were part of the far-flung British Empire, all fabric had to be imported from England under laws designed mainly to protect the cotton trade in Liverpool and Manchester. Spinning wheels and looms were outlawed, and fabric was heavily taxed. Hence, cloth was expensive, and recycling was a necessity for most households. After the War of 1812, however, cloth, including highly prized chintz, became more widely available. The price dropped, and quilters up and down the settled East Coast of the United States benefitted enormously. Quilts such as this one, with its carefully planned strips—indicating access to a good amount of the cloth—were one result.

Strippy quilts were widely made in the Northeast of England, particularly in County Durham and Northumberland, where generations of quilters passed on the patterns that were used. Generally, alternate strips in a quilt were stitched with a different design, and many of the traditional patterns have names that point out their origins, such as Weardale Chain and Weardale Wheel. The area is rich in coal, and many miners' wives and widows earned much-needed cash making quilts for more affluent households.

There were even quilting clubs, to which subscribers, usually around twenty, would pay a small weekly stipend, giving the quiltmaker a steady if small income, and each member in turn would receive a finished hand-quilted quilt. Records show that strippies were among the most common type made, especially after home sewing machines became available, with a typical quilt being completed in two to three weeks. The simplicity of the patterns may well have stemmed from this fast speed of working.

While historians feel that the form of the strippy originated in the North of England, it does also turn up in other quiltmaking traditions. The Amish in particular have adopted it to make their Bars quilts, in which strippies, which originally had no borders, are surrounded by beautifully quilted frames of contrasting fabric.

Stripes (c. 1975)

Annie Mae Young

Collection of the Tinwood Alliance

Annie Mae Young (born 1928) is one of an extraordinary group of African-American quiltmakers in Gee's Bend, Alabama. Arthritis has slowed her down, but she was prolific through most of her life, making quilts from the fabric on hand and turning them into works of color-field art.

The strips of corduroy used here were left over from an order for pillow shams placed by the Sears Roebuck catalog company with the Freedom Quilting Bee, a cooperative venture established in "The Bend" in the 1970s. Workers at the Bee were allowed to keep the offcuts, and a

number of fascinating quilts resulted. Since corduroy can only be cut on the straight grain (bias cuts fray to nothing), all these quilts are comprised of such strips, and by turning the strips so the nap runs in different directions, wonderful effects of light and shadow occur.

Durham Strippy (c. 1883)

Miss M. H. Graham

Beamish: North of England Open Air Museum

This very dramatic and graphic quilt was made in Wearhead, County Durham, in the Northeast of England. The use of wide and narrow strips together is quite unusual, but the choice of fabrics—Turkey red and cream cottons—and the beautifully worked quilting are both very typical of the area and of the time. Each cream strip has a running diamond quilted along its length, while the red ones have quilting in hammock and double hammock patterns.

Joseph's Coat (c. 1890)

Maker unknown

This stunning strippy quilt was made in Pennsylvania at the end of the nineteenth century by a Mennonite quiltmaker. Although it is in the tradition of Durham strippies, it has a number of distinct differences. The strips are much narrower than those in typical British versions, and where Durham strippies usually are made from only two or three fabrics, here there are seven different, vibrant colors, always arranged in the same order, even on the borders, which are cut at an angle to make the quilt even livelier. The exquisitely worked quilting patterns are also repeated: single feather chain facing one another in the burgundy and brown as well as the yellow and orange strips, double cables in the blue and green, and a running diamond in the red ones. The feather chain pattern has been used on all the border strips, facing in alternating directions on each strip.

Mustard and cream strippy (1899)

Isabella Calvert

Beamish: The North of England Open Air Museum

Mrs. Isabella Calvert of Thornley in County Durham, England, made this exquisitely textured strippy quilt as a wedding present for her sister Barbara. The mustard yellow and cream strips are made from Roman sateen, a fabric that was very popular with quiltmakers for both its wonderful sheen and the texture that was created when it was quilted. The back of this quilt is also made from sateen, in a dark pink color.

The cotton fabrics found in most nineteenth-century strippies from around County Durham and Northumberland were woven on looms that made cloth a yard wide. Bedcovers need at least two yards of width, and making strippies was probably a less expensive way to make these attractive and useful articles—one bed's length of expensive fabric could be cut into strips and alternated with less expensive material, often muslin (calico).

Most strippies are made from strips of two colors. Many are two solid-colored fabrics, while some have two or more prints side by side. Frequently a solid is combined with a patterned fabric. They are often arranged with an even number of plain, or light, strips—usually white or cream—alternated with an odd number of the darker fabric or a print. This means that the dark-colored or printed fabrics occur as the center strip of the quilt and on the frequently handled outside edges.

The quilting on most strippies usually follows the strips, but on this version, the fan, rose, and running diamond patterns appear confined inside their strips, while the crosshatching, feathered cables, and diamond infills overlap the seam in places. Most of the quilting on traditional strippies from the North of England is extremely finely worked.

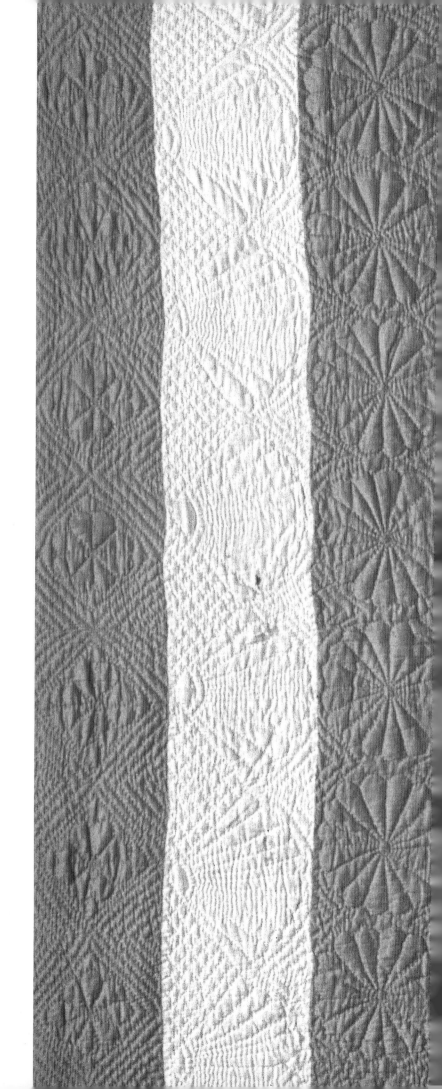

AMERICAN BLOCK

Iowa Sampler (c. 1930)

Maker unknown

Many quilts are made from a series of separate blocks of the same size. Because the technique of making quilts this way was widely practiced from the early days of the American colonies, these patterns have become known as American blocks, although many of them were carried to the New World by quiltmakers from Europe, especially from the British Isles.

Sampler quilts are made from blocks of different patterns that are combined to make a pleasing whole. In the quilting revival that has taken place and gained momentum during the past generation, sampler quilts are a very popular teaching tool that is used in workshops and classes to introduce participants to a variety of designs and techniques, as well as providing a showcase for different styles of patchwork and appliqué. Beginners can start by making simple blocks, and gradually move on to more difficult patterns, while more experienced quiltmakers may very well want to work with blocks of the same type—say, houses or baskets or stars, for instance—but which are all different designs.

Because they are usually diverse, the blocks in a sampler quilt are generally separated by sashing. They normally are made from the same selection of fabrics, or at the very least, they use the same color and tonal palette. The blocks can be pieced, appliquéd, or quilted, and the techniques can be mixed. A good blending of color and an effective balance between the elements are the most important criteria for a successful sampler quilt.

The example on the left is unusual, in that it was made in the 1930s, when sampler quilts were relatively rare. Its thirty blocks are worked in a variety of typical '30s prints and a big selection of solids. No single color dominates in the blocks, but the entire quilt is pulled together beautifully by the bright mint green sashing—also typical of its time— with the pink and green corner blocks at each intersection. On the whole, it shows considerable skill in balancing the blocks to create a very pleasing design. There is an interesting mixture of block styles and of patchwork techniques, and both the piecing and the quilting are of the highest quality.

The Trip Around the World block is a miniature quilt-in-a-quilt, constructed from 1/2" (10mm) squares that combine solid colors and printed fabrics very effectively. Just below it, the Dresden Plate block has dozens of blades that are equally tiny. The Clamshell block, with its diagonal rows of small scalloped shapes, has a purple edge along one side—perhaps an indication that the maker ran out of a crucial fabric, or maybe it is a "superstition" block. All of the blocks in the quilt are examples or sometimes variations of traditional patterns.

The quilting is admirably simple, and does not distract attention from the design. Each block is worked in a diamond grid, and triple running cables curve along the sashing.

Blue and White Broken Dishes (1875-1900)

Maker unknown

The spiky, complex-looking block known as Broken Dishes has a number of versions. It is often made as a scrap quilt from numerous different fabrics, which makes its name, meant to convey a pile of broken china, rather more understandable, and more often than not, at least three colors are used. Working with just two colors, as has been done in this quilt, is somewhat more unusual.

There are both Four-Patch and Nine-Patch variations, and the block here is made using a square-within-a-square technique. A blue square is edged with white triangles, and the resulting square is then edged with larger blue triangles. Strips made from squares and triangle squares are then used to border the square-in-a-square to finish the block.

The tiny-scale dark blue print fabric used for the background—the plain spacer blocks and the borders—is the same throughout, but the blocks are made from a surprisingly large variety of different fabrics. They are all blue prints with a tiny white motif, but they display an amazing consistency of tone. Indeed, from a distance they all appear to be the same fabric.

The quilt is well executed but simple. The pieced blocks are outline-quilted very close to the seamlines—almost stitched in the ditch. A closely spaced grid has been used on the spacer blocks, with three straight rows on the border.

Baby Bunting (1930-1940)
Maker unknown

Baby Bunting, and its variation Mohawk Trail, are among the most complicated block patterns. Both curves and sharp-pointed isosceles triangles can be tricky to piece, and this design combines the two into a wonderfully lively quilt. Two different blocks are needed to make the pattern. The main block is a background square with a curved fan shape in each corner. The fan is topped by a curved strip, which is in turn topped by a series of triangles pointing into the center. The connector blocks have two of the same spiked fan shapes set side by side on two opposite sides of the block. Hundreds of small scraps, from geometrics—including stripes, checks, gingham, and dots—to small-scale prints typical of the 1930s, and a few solids, are held in a cohesive design by the plain white background. The placement of the colors seems to be completely random.

There are an almost unimaginable number of seams in the finished top, and the quilting has been cleverly planned. The white background areas are heavily stitched with a double wineglass motif that echoes the shape of the patchwork in the blocks and adds wonderful texture to the entire piece. The accuracy and skill displayed on the quilt point to a highly experienced quiltmaker.

Single Wedding Ring (c. 1915)

Maker unknown

Single Wedding Ring is sometimes called Indian Wedding Ring. This version is a Five-Patch block based on a central square surrounded by an octagon and outlined with small light and dark triangle squares. Its curved shapes are purely optical; the entire quilt consists of straight lines. When you look at a single block in isolation, this fact becomes obvious, but looking at the quilt as a whole tricks the eye into believing that the shapes are curved.

Sashing, made of the same cream fabric that has been used for the background of the blocks, separates each unit. The cream fabric also makes the border outside the blue triangles that outline the quilt, which are the same size as the triangle squares in the blocks. None of these triangles match at the corners of the border, and three of them finish with a parallelogram, a shape that doesn't occur anywhere else on the quilt. The blue fabrics are all solid colors, but several different shades have been used, and two of the blocks have at least two different blues within them.

The entire quilt is quilted with a simple and effective diamond grid that is perfectly in scale with the size of the blocks.

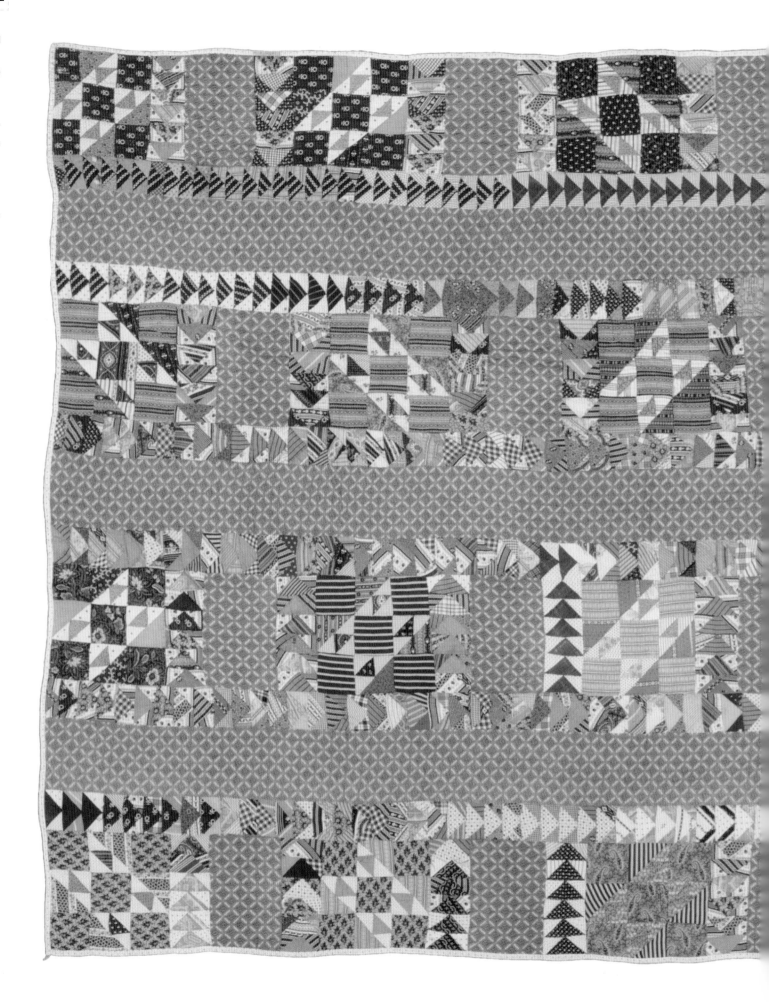

Hovering Hawks (c. 1864)

Huldah Mae Mitchell Horton

Minnesota Historical Society/Part of the Joyce Aufderheide collection

The maker of this typically mid-nineteenth-century scrap quilt, Huldah Mae Horton (1839-1927), lived in McLeod County, Minnesota. She has used a good variety of cotton scraps, including quite a number of solids as well as prints and geometrics—stripes and checks in particular—with a printed background fabric, a small-scale pattern in two tones of brown/beige. Hovering Hawk is one of a group of patterns, including Jacob's Ladder, Railroad, and Rocky Road to California, that are made from squares and triangle squares divided along one diagonal. Mrs. Horton has joined strips of Flying Geese, also made from scraps and with a seemingly random color placement, into rows of Wild Goose Chase that have then been stitched to two sides of each block. These are then combined with alternating pieces of the same fabric, which ultimately becomes the background, to make four long strips. She has then added a long strip of Wild Goose Chase to each side and alternated these new strips with three strips of the background fabric to make the top.

The quilt was quilted at a quilting bee in a log cabin farmhouse sometime near the end of the Civil War. It is now part of the Joyce Aufderheide collection at the Minnesota Historical Society.

Basket and Blossom (1930)

Addie Lee Cope Butler Daniel

Courtesy of Merikay Waldvogel

Baskets have always been very popular American blocks. They appear in many different forms, and are almost always set on point, as in this charming quilt. Addie Lee Cope was a widow at just 21, when her husband of sixteen months, George Butler, died of typhoid fever. She then went back to live with her parents in Henry County, Tennessee, and—taught by her mother and her grandmother—became like them expert in many needlecrafts, especially quiltmaking. She was married again in 1938 to Jack Daniel,

and their daughter Emily Daniel Cox now owns this quilt, which was made before she was born.

Mrs. Daniel and her mother and grandmother collected the patterns that were published in papers and magazines, and made their own templates. They also collected fabric by the bolt and stored it on shelves in the sitting room.

The pattern for this cotton quilt was probably from a design that appeared in a newspaper. Each of the twenty baskets is pieced from squares and triangles in two colors on a

cream background and contains a different flower. The blooms and leaves are all cut from bright-colored solid fabrics and appliquéd with blanket stitch in the baskets, which are topped with a handle, all of which are made from the same material and machine-appliquéd in place. Blue spacer blocks make a bright, unifying background. The binding is pink. The quilting is a simple crosshatch grid that covers the entire quilt except for the top half of the baskets where the flowers and handles are.

Blue and White Crib Quilt (c. 1910)

Maker unknown

Minnesota Historical Society

Crib quilts have a charm all their own. They are usually large enough to allow the maker a fair amount of creativity, and small enough to keep the task of making one from becoming too daunting. And there is usually a period of several months in which the work can be completed. While crib quilts can be made in any style that appeals to the quiltmaker, many are made from blocks.

This cotton crib quilt from Minnesota has a very fresh look in spite of its 100 years. The blocks are quite a good size for a crib quilt—about 4½" (11.4 cm). The diamond blocks are simply made in blue and white, which is repeated in the inch-wide sashing and its corner squares. The outer sashing forms a border, and the blocks are quilted in a crosshatch grid with a single running diamond in the sashing that crosses each corner square diagonally.

The quilt is now owned by Mrs. Charles Sheppard.

IRISH CHAIN

Postage-stamp Triple Irish Chain (c. 1875)

Maker unknown

The Triple Irish Chain pattern is traditionally—and most easily—pieced from two different Five-Patch blocks using two or three colors. However, if the center of the plain block is pieced as a standard Five-Patch block, it has so many seams that it becomes very difficult to quilt, so various methods are used to add pieced border strips to plain squares to leave an open area in which to add decorative stitching.

Before it came to Patricia Cox, who is a noted quilter and collector of quilts, this particular piece had been displayed nailed up over an open fireplace. Though incredibly greasy, sticky and grimy because of this treatment, it proved to clean up very beautifully and it is now one of the most prized items in her collection.

This is a pure scrap quilt—an assortment of prints and geometrics have been mixed with solids in a gloriously random assortment. The squares in the chain are a mere ½" (12mm) and the larger plain squares only 2½" (6cm) each. The quilting is utilitarian at best—the diagonal lines are anything but straight.

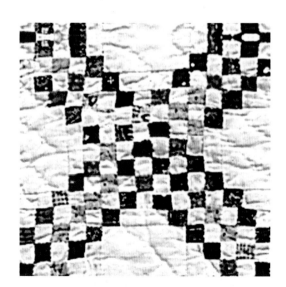

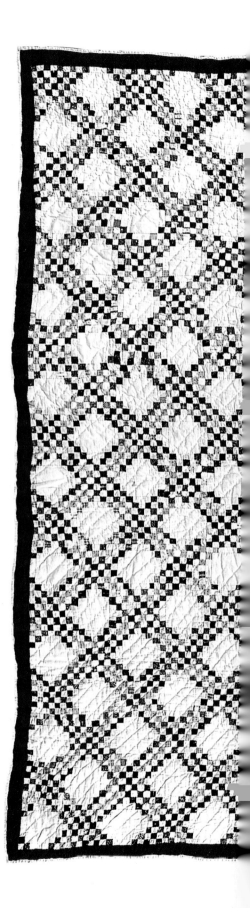

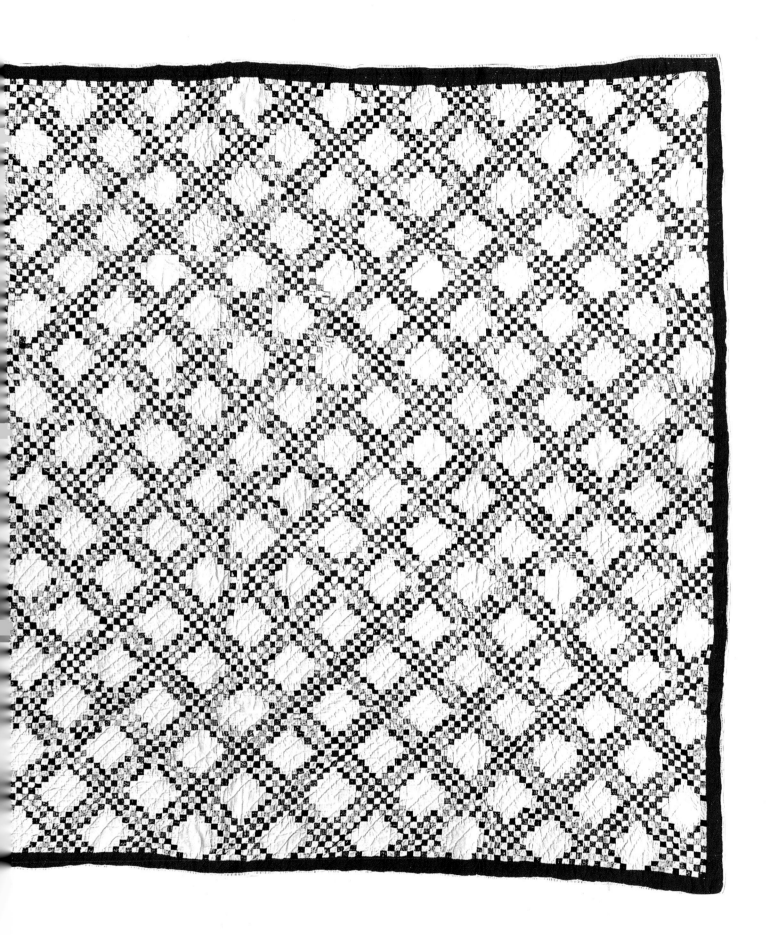

Red and White Double Irish Chain (c. 1920)

Maker unknown

Red and white quilts are among the most dramatic of all the color combinations, and nowhere more so than in this beautiful example of a Double Irish Chain. The same two fabrics are used throughout the entire quilt, indicating that the maker bought them specifically for this piece, rather than using scraps.

Like most Irish Chain quilts, this one is deceptively simple. The diagonal chain effect is made by alternating two different pieced blocks. The first is a checkerboard Seven-Patch block made mainly from squares of the alternating colors. The second is a plain white square with side strips that have contrasting squares in each corner the same size as the squares in the first block. The design is assembled from strips of the two fabrics which are sewn into sets and then cut and reassembled to make the blocks. The superb workmanship extends to the quilting, which is a simple crosshatch grid that makes the quilt looks as though it is composed of hundreds of small squares. It extends out to include the borders, which contain the quilt with some exuberance. The narrow strip of red binding outlines the edges of piece superbly.

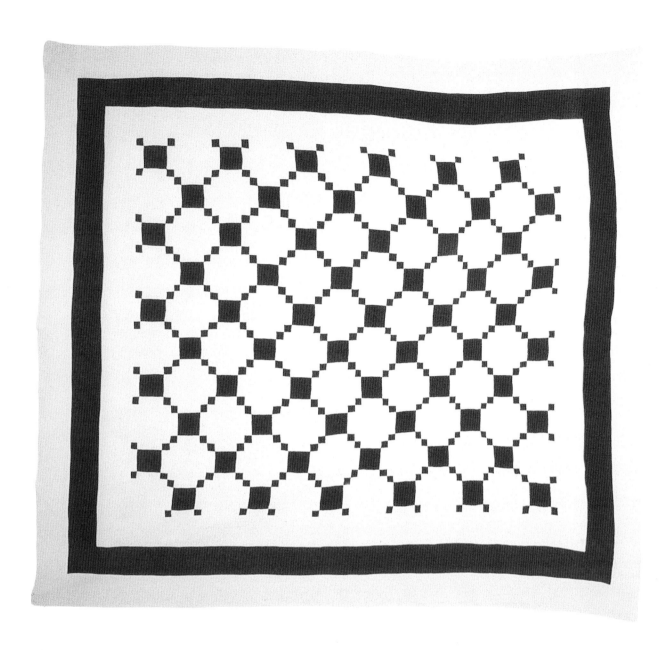

Single Irish Chain (c. 1870)

Maker unknown

Beamish: The North of England Open Air Museum

More subtle than the quilt on the left but equally appealing, this Single Irish Chain quilt was made in Northumberland. It is an unusual variation of the Irish Chain design: it uses two blocks and two sizes of square to create the diagonal chain effect. The pieced block is a Nine-Patch variation in which the center square is three times the size of the corners, so it is constructed by sewing white strips with small red corners to the sides of a large red center square. The setting squares are plain white, the same dimensions as the pieced square, so the quilt is put together in rows alternating pieced blocks with plain ones. The triple border, in which each border is the same width, provides a good background for the well-executed quilting.

Single Irish Chain is often used in workshops and classes to teach the basics of patchwork and quilting to beginners, since the pieced block is a simple Nine-Patch. More complicated versions of the pattern abound for more experienced quiltmakers to tackle, and the design works well as a scrap quilt.

Red, White, and Blue
Double Irish Chain (c. 1900)

Maker unknown

The background of this Double Irish Chain quilt is unusual in that it is made from a tiny black-on-white cotton print, which is also used on the outer border. The inner border is cut from its reverse, a dark fabric with white dots. The blue and red chain squares are probably scraps—a number of different tiny checks and prints have been used on the red, sometimes almost pink, centers and several blues, mostly navy with small-scale white patterns printed on them.

The quilt is, like the one on page 280, made from two different blocks, a Seven-Patch and an almost plain one. If you look closely at the pieced block, you will see a square in the center of each side that is the palest of pinks, but which our eyes see as part of the white background. The chain squares are outline-quilted, the large spacer blocks have a traditional rose motif, and the outer border has, appropriately enough, a double chain pattern.

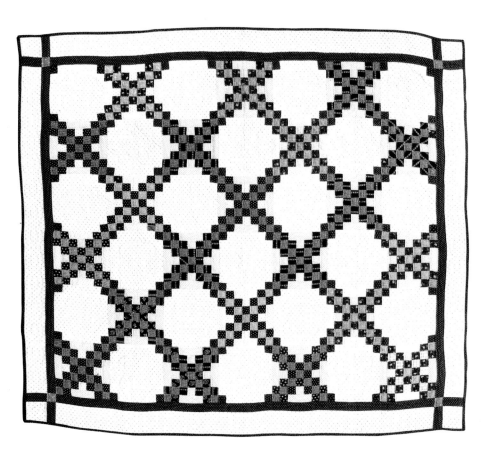

Single Irish Chain
(1875–1900)

Maker unknown

The tiny 1" (2.5cm) squares of the
chain on this beautiful quilt are
made from countless scraps of what
appears to be shirting fabric in
mainly checks, stripes, and plaids
with a few prints. The quilt is
actually a Nine-Patch chain, with
blocks made as Double Nine-Patch
from five light-and-dark and four
plain white Nine-Patch blocks, and
joined by sashing of plain white
strips with a single Nine-Patch block
at each corner. The color placement
appears to be completely random,
which adds greatly to the overall
feeling of exuberance. There are
three narrow borders: the plain inner
one delineates the main part of the
quilt, then comes a pieced one made
from the same tiny squares that have
been used to make the Nine-Patch
blocks, while the outer one is the
same width as the others and cut
from a plaid fabric.

The beautifully planned and
executed quilting consists of double
diamond shapes that link the
elements by crossing the squares of
the chain diagonally and meeting in
the white areas as chevrons with tiny
rows of quilting in each large
diamond shape.

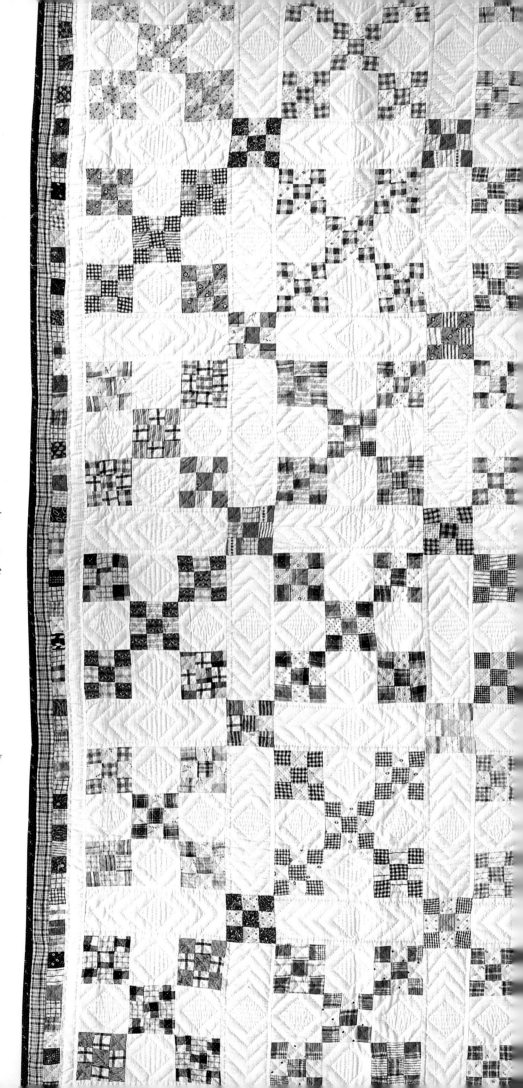

MILITARY QUILTS

Uniform quilt (1866-1872)

Joseph Rawdon

Courtesy The Quilter's Guild of the British Isles

In the years between about 1840 and 1910, many quilts were made by British military personnel. These patchworks almost invariably consisted of myriad geometric pieces cut from the wool fabrics used to make uniforms. Unlike today's olive drab and camouflage materials, service issue was brightly colored. Indeed, as every schoolchild knows, many uniforms had red coats, but yellow, green, blue, and white were also used. Some of the uniforms were worn in the field, others were the dress uniforms of various regiments.

This group of quilts has several names: military or uniform quilts; Crimean quilts, so called because the earliest examples appear to have been made during the Crimean War (1853-1856); and soldier's (or sailor's) quilts, although there are many fewer documented naval examples. Similar quilts made during the period—by men from wool, usually Melton, a heavyweight suiting fabric—cannot be authenticated as military quilts, and are known as tailor's quilts. There are known examples made by prisoners, presumably both to while away idle hours and provide some warmth and padding to their hard sleeping places.

The quilt shown opposite was made in India over a six-year period by Joseph Rawdon, thought to be a native of York in England, for Mr. Bootland from nearby Bradford. In a letter kept with the quilt, Rawdon makes it clear that some of the fabric came from uniforms worn by fallen comrades in arms. Its black and red pinwheels, complemented in the main part of the quilt by the circular compass motifs, occur again inside circles in the inner border, with the whole piece framed by the yellow and black sawtooth outer border.

The bearded stitcher pictured below is Samuel Attwood, a tailor in the British Army. He was stationed in India in the 1850s, one of many such personnel who would have been needed to keep the army—far from home—clothed and supplied with textile necessities. He is shown in civilian dress working on a huge quilt, which has not been traced.

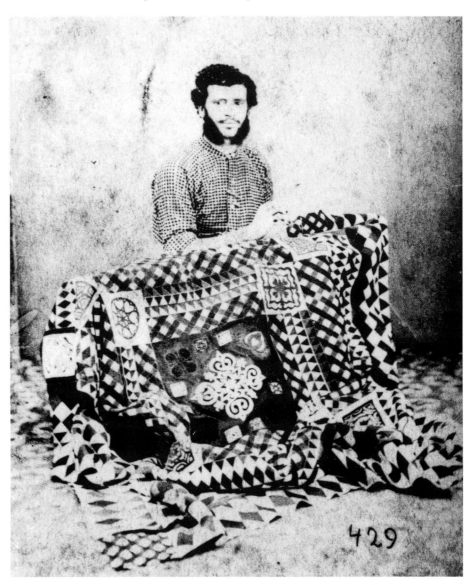

Hexagon Star Center Medallion (c. 1860)

Maker unknown

Courtesy The Quilter's Guild of the British Isles

This beautifully designed and executed quilt has been in the same family in Chester, in western England, for three generations, but the current family members do not have a record of the maker's name. Known by them simply as "the Crimean quilt," its central area is a subtle hexagon shape surrounded by a six-pointed star made from red, green, and white diamond tumbling blocks, which also appear again in each of the corners of the squared-up center medallion.

The five surrounding borders, all of which are the same width, have been meticulously planned and lead the eye out to the final, and slightly wider, simple red and black one. Each of the seams is beautifully embellished—as are a number of existing uniform quilts—with embroidered herringbone stitch worked in white silk thread.

Variable Star (1850-1860)

Maker unknown

Courtesy The Quilter's Guild of the British Isles

This small quilt, which is fringed on all four sides, is small enough at 44" (112cm) square to have been used as a horse blanket by one of its previous owners. Rescued from her surviving family by its current owner, it is thought to date from around the time of the Crimean War. It can be assumed that the maker—or perhaps the recipient—was from the county of Yorkshire, in England, since the fabrics are the same as those used at the time by various regiments from Yorkshire, and the White Rose of York has been very beautifully embroidered in the middle of each of the five center stars.

In addition, the center of each of the four Nine-Patch blocks that surround the central star contains a different embroidered motif.

Patchwork Table Cover (1895-1905)

Made by Lt.-Col. Hall-Dempster's orderly

Courtesy The Quilter's Guild of the British Isles

Military quilts made in India, like this table cover, were generally brighter and more colorful than the earlier Crimean quilts, in keeping with the bright hues found in the textiles of this more southerly land that comprised a great portion of the widespread British Empire. Made from square and diamond shapes, it contains various motifs that probably had regimental or personal significance to the Lieutenant-Colonel of the South Lancashire Regiment, for whom it was made and given as a present. The maker, Hall-Dempster's orderly between 1895 and 1905, used fabrics from dress uniforms worn locally by regiments stationed in the area. Note the three Prince of Wales feathers in the lower right-hand corner.

Mariner's Compass Center Medallion (Late 1800s)

Maker unknown

Courtesy The Quilter's Guild of the British Isles

One of the challenges thought to have appealed to the makers of many military quilts was using, and counting, the various materials in their work. This quilt was made in India by a convalescing soldier, who kept a record of his achievement: he used 7,000 pieces of fabric—red, yellow, white, and black—and sewed them together with 168,000 stitches. In addition, it is trimmed with 48,000" (1,230 meters) of the thin military braid that outlines each separate element.

Like all of the quilts in this section, and most of the known examples of military quilts, it has neither batting nor quilting. The embellishment along the seams of most of these quilts added strength to help stabilize the tiny individual pieces, which when joined made extremely heavy blankets and covers.

AMISH/MENNONITE

Chinese Coins (c. 1970)

Maker unknown

Since the work of Amish and Mennonite quiltmakers was "discovered" in the last quarter of the twentieth century, the distinctive quilts made by these groups have become familiar to a wider public. With their bright solid colors often set against dark background, traditional Amish quilts are among the most widely recognized type of quilt.

This stunning Chinese Coins variation is both typical of Amish quiltmaking and extraordinary in its beauty and workmanship. It is pure scrap quilt—the multicolored bars have been assembled from a variety of bright solid-colored fabrics in random sizes and contrast dramatically with the black bars and narrow inner border that throw the colors into sharp focus. Corner squares on the innermost border link the pieced border to the bars in the center, and a wide outer border, again in black, frames the entire quilt. The quilting on the black areas consists of variations of cable patterns, while the colored strips are simply outline-quilted.

The Amish and the Mennonites are descended from a group of Swiss and Dutch Anabaptists who arrived in the New World in the 1720s and settled first in Pennsylvania. From there, over the following 250 years, they have moved into other areas, with settlements in Indiana, Iowa, Ohio, Illinois, New York, Wisconsin, Minnesota, Kentucky, and Oklahoma, among other states. The Amish are the stricter of the two groups, but the religious beliefs and the overriding sense of family loyalty and community closeness are fundamental to the lives and lifestyles of both (*see pages 196-198*).

One manifestation of the differences between them is the Mennonite use of printed fabrics and decoration in their quilts. The Amish wear only plain colors, befitting their image as the Plain People in the eyes of the outside world, which means that the scraps they use to make quilts are never patterned. Nor do they add decorative touches such as appliqué. Mennonite clothing is sometimes made from print fabrics, and occasional decorative touches of embroidery or appliqué appear on their quilts. Some Amish quilters now make quilts for sale using new printed fabrics, but in the main quilts for their own use are still made from plain fabric scraps.

Variable Star (1905)

Maker unknown

This beautiful wool quilt was made in Ohio and is unusual in that it is dated. The habit of either signing or dating quilts was not widespread, with a few notable exceptions such as Victorian crazy quilts and a number of Baltimore Album quilts, until the late twentieth-century revival of quiltmaking, and even where a maker's name is known, dates cannot be assigned to the vast majority of Amish quilts.

Variable Star is most usually pieced as a Nine-Patch block with the tips of the star pointing toward the edges, but here the star is turned so that the tips point toward each of the corners. However, when the blocks of pink stars are set they are turned on point, so the star is upright. Plain dark green spacer blocks alternate with the star blocks, and the pieced inner border echoes all of the colors used in the stars.

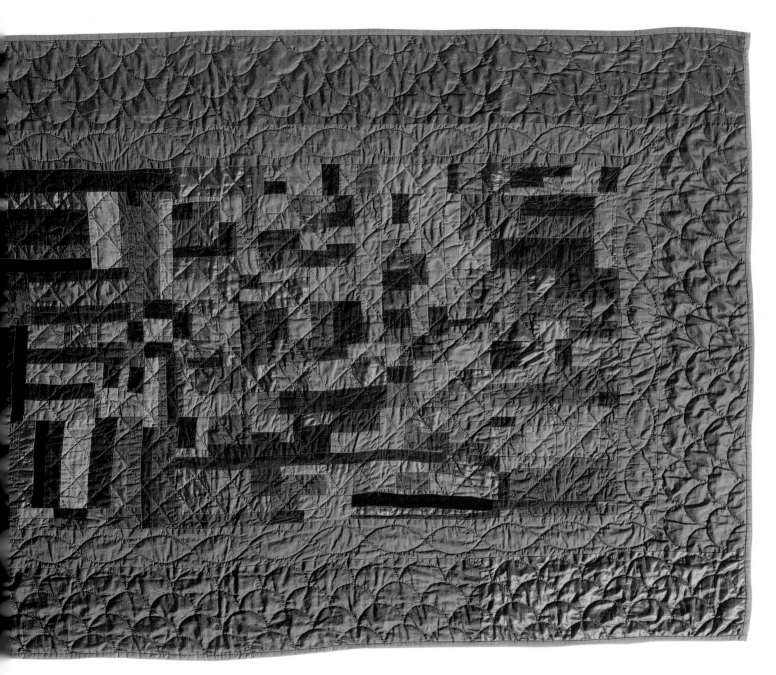

Scrap Quilt (c. 1980)

Maker unknown

This quilt, made from a true patchwork of scraps, was most probably meant to be purely functional. The dark overall tone is relieved by the bright blue, orange, and beige scattered throughout the piece, and in spite of the totally random nature of the piecing and color placement, it is a thoroughly pleasing work.

A simple diagonal grid has been used to quilt the center, with a cable in the rust-colored inner border and clamshells in the dark green outer part.

Split Bars (1925-1930)

Maker unknown

Together with Center Diamond and Sunshine and Shadow, the Bars pattern is a quintessential Amish quilt design.

Standard bars in an Amish quilt are usually strips of two or three colors, each cut the same width and alternated within the quilt, which is always bordered, usually by both a narrow and a wide border. When thin lengthwise strips are used to divide some of the bars, as in the quilt shown on the left, the pattern is called Split Bars. Other well-known Bars variations include Chinese Coins (*see pages 292-293*), Flying Geese Bars, and Blocks and Bars (*see page 300*).

The Split Bars variation shown here is strikingly modern and graphic, yet typically Amish. The cool blue-gray strips that outline the yellow tone down the red bars and wide, bright pink border, and the red used to make the wide bars, is repeated in the corners of the inner border and on the binding. The traditional quilting consists of crosshatching on the bars and curved feathers on the outer border. The inner border has a grapevine with grapes, with larger bunches stitched on the corner squares. Making the strips for the inner border the same as those that are used for the split bars is an unusual but effective feature.

Sunshine and Shadow (1997)

Maker unknown

Sunshine and Shadow has been part of Amish quiltmaking tradition since the early twentieth century. It is a one-patch mosaic pattern made entirely of small squares of carefully placed color, starting from the center and working out in concentric rows turned on the diagonal. In "English" culture—the Amish term for all outsiders—the pattern is usually called Trip Around the World, but as the Amish rarely venture far from their own homes and farms, they changed the name. Reminiscent of the light and shade in a field or garden, the name symbolizes many aspects of Amish life.

Jan Jefferson, a Lancaster County native, quilt collector, and social historian specializing in the Amish and their way of life, has written that the design is "a symbol for what it is to be Amish. The scraps symbolize plainness and frugality .... the wide borders .... their strong religious beliefs. The name also exemplifies the Amish attitude to life: along with light, there is darkness, with joy, sorrow."

This modern quilt uses thirteen different colors shading from a dark center to bands of almost white and back again to dark, and encloses the center in a narrow purple inner border and a wide dark green one. A simple diagonal grid has been quilted on the pattern, with a small cable and a wider double cable on the borders.

Shoofly (c. 1900)

Maker unknown

American Folk Art Museum/Gift of David Pottinger

Another popular Amish pattern, Shoofly is a Nine-Patch variation that works well when made up in just two colors, in combinations of several colors with the same background, or as here, as a true scrap quilt. The subtle colors in this quilt are entirely typical of Amish quiltmaking around the turn of the last century, and the way in which the fabrics have been combined point to its having been made strictly using available leftovers from the maker's scrap basket. The configuration of the lights and darks in three of the blocks makes them look quite different from the others, although they are all made the same way. The blocks have been set on point and tobacco-brown spacer blocks have been used between each one. A tan inner border and binding outline the outer border made from the same fabric as the spacer blocks, which is wider at the top and bottom of the quilt than along the sides. A quadruple cable pattern used to quilt both borders overlaps and unites them.

Blocks and Bars (c. 1910)

Maker unknown

This Bars variation was made in Mifflin County, Pennsylvania, before World War I. It is a typical Amish scrap quilt of the time—random blocks of color, square shapes alternating with strips—have been joined into bars and alternated with narrower strips that pick up the colors in the blocks. The colors range from bright blue and red to dark green, navy blue, and somber brown,

with a blue border to tie the design together. At first glance the entire border seems to be made from the same fabric, but a closer look shows frugal piecing that is obscured by the fan quilting. A diagonal grid has been quilted over the pieced center area.

Like the Strippy quilts (*see pages 256-263*) made in the Northeast of England in the generation before this quilt was created, the Bars design was

simple to make and the quilt would have been an important household item in the harsh winters of the areas where the Amish settled. Bars was a very quick and economical pattern that could be completed quickly, which helps to account for its popularity among the Amish, who nevertheless made countless variations on the basic theme, using what they had on hand.

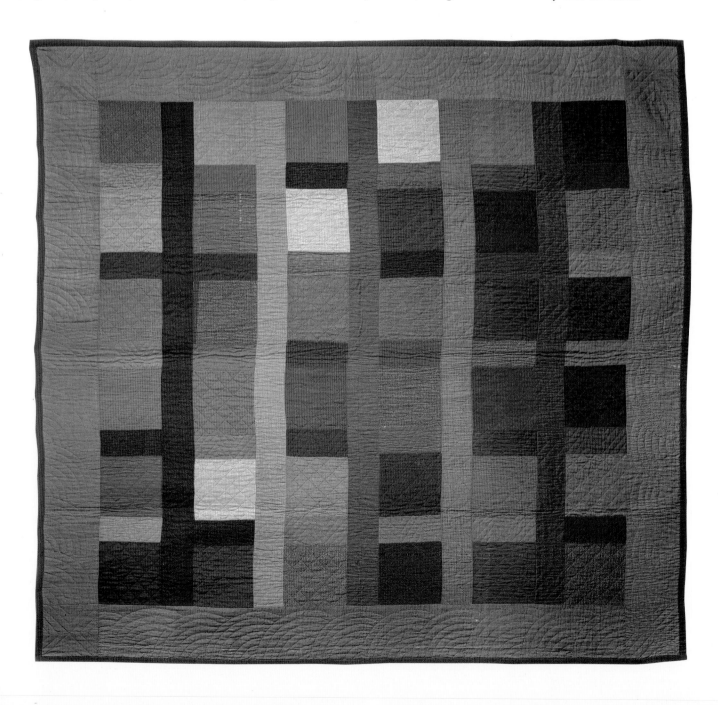

Schoolhouse (1920-1920)

Maker unknown

American Folk Art Museum/Gift of David Pottinger

The Schoolhouse pattern was widely used by American quiltmakers in the late nineteenth century, and it was probably passed on to Amish quilters around that time. Unlike most Amish patterns it is representational, not abstract. Few Amish patterns show recognizable objects, the other exceptions being baskets and a few flower forms. The reduction of the schoolhouse to its most basic form, almost like a child's drawing, gives the building an old-fashioned rural, one-room feel, and the block may

have retained its popularity among the Amish because it is much like many of the Amish schools that still exist today.

Because the Amish do not have cars, but travel by horse and buggy, it is important that schools are located near where the children live, and most settlements have their own, church-led school not unlike the little red version in the schoolhouse block.

This quilt is not red, however. The houses are blue with red-orange roofs on a white background. The inner

border is pieced from blue and white triangles on the long sides and white along all four. The black outer border echoes the sashing strips, which have blue and white checkerboard corners. The positioning of the blocks is not unusual for the time, with a center row running down the middle and the two outer rows facing outward so that when the quilt was seen on the bed, the buildings were all the right way up. The quilt was made from cotton and sateen, in the Midwestern United States.

Four Patch in Triangles (1910-1920)

Barbara Zook Peachey

American Folk Art Museum/Gift of Mr. & Mrs. William B. Wigton

In the 1790s, shortly after the first Amish settlers arrived in Pennsylvania, several families moved from Lancaster County to new land in Mifflin County. This stunning quilt was made by Barbara Zook Peachey (1848-1930) for her granddaughter Katie M. Peachey, descendants of the original members of the Byler Church, or Yellow Topper Amish.

Though the pieces are small, this is not a typical scrap quilt. There are two different blocks, one a pink and blue checkerboard, the other a striking orange and black square made from two right-angle triangles.

They are alternated in diagonal rows throughout the quilt, and the pink and blue four-patch blocks are all turned the same way, except for one in the bottom left-hand corner, which could be a "superstition" block or simply a mistake. The triangle squares are alternated with black facing in one direction and orange in the other to make a visually exciting pattern. The blue border is made from the same fabric as the small blue squares, and the entire piece is quilted in a diagonal grid that takes no account of the diagonal lines of the blocks.

Mennonite Irish Chain (c.1900)

Maker unknown

This fabulous Mennonite-made Irish Chain quilt has blocks of alternating red and green stripes as the "blank" areas between the yellow and red double chains, and a very beautifully pieced chain border. Each square of the chains is quilted with a diagonal line in each direction, and the entire background is stitched in concentric circles radiating out from every intersection. The design and the use of color make a very lively piece.

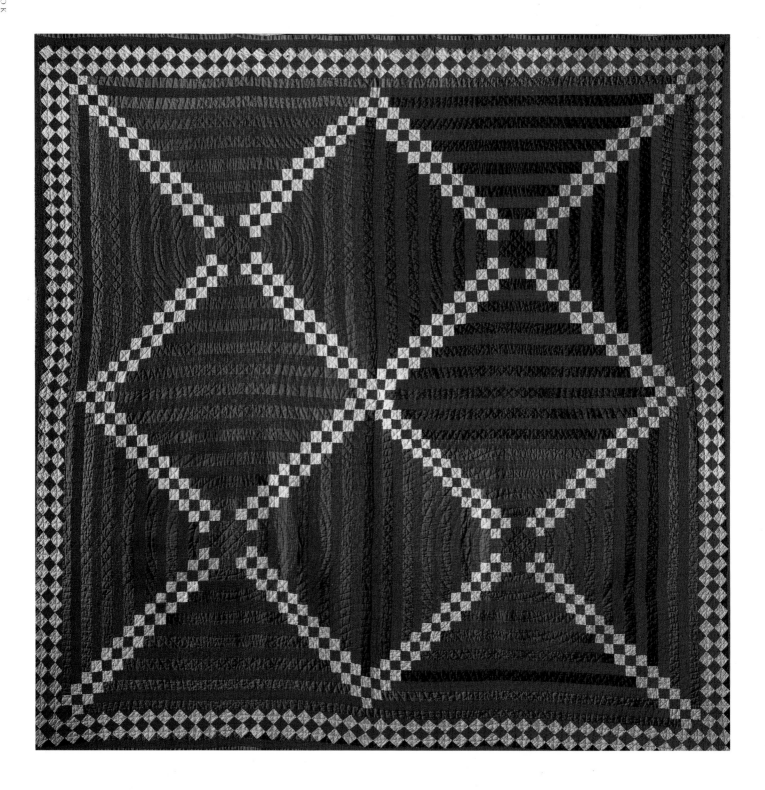

Ocean Waves (20th century)

Maker unknown

This Amish version of the pattern called Ocean Waves is another good way to make use of scraps. The bright colors on the black background make a dramatic statement, and the exquisite quilting, crosshatch in the black diamond shapes and partial cables on the wide black outer border, gives the piece extraordinary textural appeal.

Although it was made in Holmes County, Ohio, the color palette is more often found in quilts made in Lancaster County and other areas of Pennsylvania than on those of the Midwestern Amish, who tend to use warmer colors like orange and yellow. The cooler blues and pinks, along with a bit of red and darker green, are normally associated with the eastern communities.

AFRICAN/
AMERICAN

Housetop Half-Log
Cabin variation (c. 1965)

Lillie Mae Pettway

Collection of the Tinwood Alliance

In the Alabama community of Gee's Bend, a remarkable group of quiltmakers have over the past century created a body of work that has been recognized by a traveling exhibition in which this quilt appeared. Made by Lillie Mae Pettway (1927-1990), it is a variation of a Log Cabin pattern, which are known locally as "housetop" quilts. The bright solids are combined with a variety of prints, checks, and plaids, and the half-log blocks are divided by bars of heavy cotton olive-drab fabric, printed with serial numbers and letters. The straight lines of big-stitch quilting flow into each other in rows, and the binding is pieced, and rather wider than is usual.

Housetop is a popular pattern in the region, and the versions found among the Gee's Bend quilts are quite remarkable in their variety.

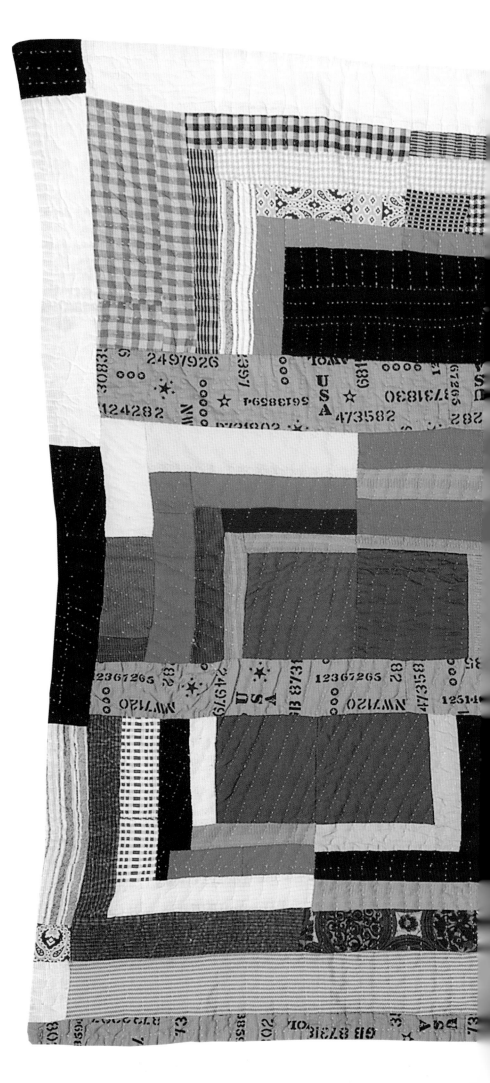

Checkerboard (c. 1955)

Polly Bennett

Collection of the Tinwood Alliance

Polly Bennett was born in Gee's Bend, Alabama, in 1922, and not surprisingly she first starting making quilts at the very early age of 8 or 9. She has lived just down the road in Rehoboth for many years, and still creates what she calls her "get-together" quilts—for which she works improvisationally using whatever comes to hand. A selection of fabrics of any size or color just get put together, until the final quilt is the size she wants it to be.

The quilt below demonstrates another side of her quiltmaking talents—as an expert in intricate patterns. It is carefully planned and constructed as four-patch blocks to make a perfect X of colors, with tones consistent throughout, even when the fabrics are different. The startling red cross that divides the piece horizontally and vertically has obviously been planned into the design—note the red squares on each side at the end of the strips.

Birds in the Air (1981)

Lucy T. Pettway

Collection of the Tinwood Alliance

Another remarkable quilt from Gee's Bend, this example is perhaps more traditional to the eye than some, but its flamboyant use of color and the variations in the sizes of the triangles make it unique. Lucy T. Pettway (1921-2004), known as Lunky, was one of the few quiltmakers in "The Bend" who was interested in making quilts using traditional block patterns, and she has collected block designs for years. The refinement of her work is shown here in the use of the soft-colored blue, yellow, and white striped border that echoes the yellow of the quilt, and the bright red binding.

Many of the families in the area have lived there since their ancestors were plantation slaves, and after the Civil War, when the emancipated men and women needed to take surnames, many of them took the name of the plantation owner, Pettway. The original Pettway family had left the land by the beginning of the twentieth century, but the descendants of the slaves are there yet. Many of them are still called Pettway, but they are not related to one another except by the bonds of community—and sometimes by marriage.

Schoolhouse (c. 1920)

Sarah Moore

Courtesy of Quilts of Tennessee

Sarah Moore was descended from slaves. She lived in Meigs County, Tennessee, and worked for the family of J. Howard Hornsby, whose members donated this quilt to the McMinn County Living Heritage Museum in Athens, Tennessee. According to the family, she made a number of quilts during her lifetime.

This cotton Schoolhouse quilt is rather more somber than most of its little red cousins, but the bright mustard yellow buildings, with their gray roofs and orange chimneys and footings on a pale background, still have great charm.

Each schoolhouse is framed in thin strips of either gray or medium brown, which creates rectangular blocks. The sixteen blocks have been sashed in dark brown with yellow corner squares and the same format has been used for the inner border. The printed fabric of the outer border softens the edge and ties all the colors together. The cotton flannel backing has been turned to the front to make the binding, and the quilt is tied at fairly close intervals with dark blue cotton thread, an unusual feature on Schoolhouse quilts.

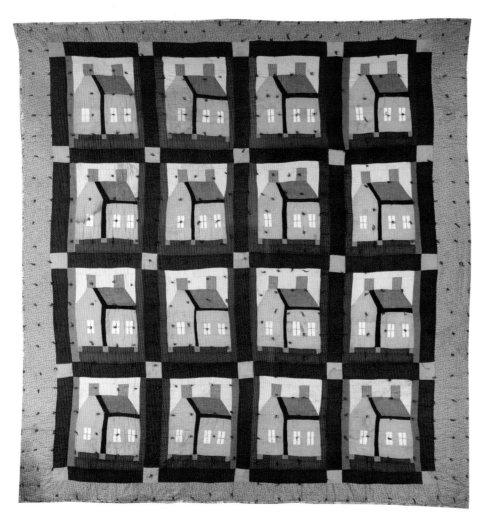

Courthouse Steps (c. 1970)

Loretta Pettway

Collection of the Tinwood Alliance

Loretta Pettway (born 1942) is another Gee's Bend, Alabama, resident, who has been less prolific than some of her quiltmaking neighbors, but is no less a natural-born color-field artist. She says she doesn't like to sew, but made quilts to keep herself and her close family warm. Her life seems to have been hard, even by the standards of The Bend, where many families still live in circumstances that border on poverty, but her quilts are remarkable testaments to a creative spirit.

Courthouse Steps is a variation of Log Cabin in which darks and lights are placed to create a stepped diagonal line throughout the block. Like Log Cabin, which is called Housetop in Gee's Bend, Courthouse Steps has a local name—Bricklayer. Pettway has used the design to make a single-block quilt of great drama. Made from strips of the "good" bits of old workclothes, it has a remarkable depth of field. In places, a light-colored selvage edge has been left to show as a thin line against the dark blue denim, creating the perspective that draws the eye into the quilt.

The quilting consists mainly of fairly equally spaced lines, that curve across the quilt on a slight diagonal, but straight lines occur all along one dark edge and can be found in places along the other. Quiltmakers from Gee's Bend say that they usually stitch a set of quilted lines for as far as they can reach across the quilt frame, then move themselves or the quilt and resume in the most convenient direction. The texture created on this quilt is certainly lively, whether the quilting was planned or not.

Rolling Star (c. 1930)

Estella Thompson Lillard

Courtesy of Quilts of Tennessee

Mrs. Lillard was a dressmaker who was renowned for her skills with fabric. She lived in Nashville, Tennessee, where she was in great demand making clothes for women in the African-American community. A tall, graceful woman, she served as a good advertisement for her work.

Her mother was a quiltmaker and taught Estella, who "enjoyed going to her (mother's) house whenever there was a quilting group gathered," according to her stepdaughter, Anna Lillard Donelson, the current owner of this stunning quilt. Its beautiful piecing and typically African-American quilting in an allover shell pattern attest to her technical expertise and love of fabric. The quilt is cotton, with sixteen star blocks in red, two shades of green, and white to make the Rolling Star pattern with its many points and inset seams. Red and white pieced strips, some made from different reds, create both sashing and borders at the top and bottom of the quilt. There is a corner square at each intersection in the sashing made from the same light green used to make the star blocks.

The backing is muslin (calico) which has been turned to the front to create a narrow binding. The flowing lines of quilting add to the texture and the sense of movement in the design.

NATIVE AMERICAN

The Late Great John Beargrease Marvel Mail Musher (1987/8)

Amy Cordova

Minnesota Historical Society

Across the frozen landscape, a Native American dressed in a fur-lined parka drives his dogsled team of three hard-working huskies to deliver the mail. In the background two horses wait patiently beside a sled carrying mailbags. Small animals and birds watch as the intrepid North Country mail carrier mushes his dogs, whip in hand.

When artist Amy Cordova made this evocative piece, she appliquéd the name around the side and bottom borders, and added the date to the hanging sleeve on the back. The snow is made from white satin, and all the details—fir trees, mountains, and forest creatures—have been applied with great skill.

The buttons on John Beargrease's coat are made from bone, and there are small brass bells on the dogs' harnesses and along the top and bottom edges of the quilt.

Although outsiders do not usually associate quiltmaking with the other arts and crafts of the various Native American cultures, quilts have been made in many communities for generations. Historians assume that the skills were learned via contact with European settlers, and a number of distinctive styles developed, from the brightly colored geometric bands of the Seminole in Florida (*see pages 322-325*) to the two-color appliqué beauties of Hawaii (*see pages 326-331*). Many of the quilts made by

Native American quilters are undistinguishable from those found in mainstream American quiltmaking, from the use of traditional block forms to the choice of fabric and color, and the technical skills are of the highest quality.

Art quilts, including the one pictured here, are being made by Native American fiber artists across the country. As the art quilt movement has grown during the past twenty years, Native American textile artists have explored many themes, including their own cultural roots and identities.

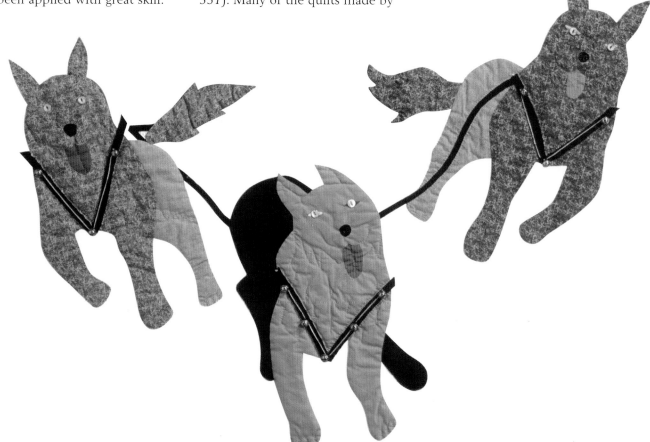

Reservation Quilt (c. 1915)

Rebecca Blackwater

The Sioux maker of this appliqué block quilt lived at the time, according to historian Marsha L. MacDowell, writing in *To Honor and Comfort: Native Quilting Traditions* (1997), either in Santee, Nebraska, or Rosebud, South Dakota. She was one of several women who worked for the wife of the superintendent of her reservation, Mrs. Ella Burton, in the mornings and spent the afternoons being taught to sew and quilt by her. The wonderfully evocative quilt shown here was made by Rebecca Blackwater and given to Ella Burton as a Christmas present by her husband Charles.

The quilt, filled with images of daily life on the reservation, also tells of conflict between the Natives and the white men. A number of the blocks are repeated, and some of the images are shown in reverse. In two places, a brave is shown near clumps of grass with his bow and arrow aimed at a flock of four birds, perhaps geese. The same brave, facing the other way, aims at an eagle, seen falling from the sky. Other braves carry guns, while two groups of three dance with tomahawks and others, seated, make music. Teepees are repeated, some facing one way, some the other. Two squaws tend a cooking pot, two others approach a table with baskets. The chief in a full feathered headdress sits astride his horse, with a squaw on horseback above and below him. Nearby two images are repeated: braves—one with feathers and one without—lead horses pulling a travois made of sticks with the family's possessions on it. Unusually, the squaw is on horseback. Charles Burton Thomsen, grandson of the Burtons and owner of a quilt made by Blackwater, relates that his grandmother asked Rebecca why she had reversed normal tribal practice, in which the men rode while the women walked. She replied that it was one of the few customs among whites that she approved of, so she made the quilt that way.

In two opposite corners of the quilt are a peace pipe crossed with a tomahawk. The images in the other two corners are more droll. In the top right, a bird lands on a branch that holds a nest with two eggs. In the bottom left, the same bird feeds two white chicks. The black background sets off the limited palette of colors that have been used. The three primary colors—red, blue, and yellow—are combined with white and light brown to make a coherent, visually pleasing, and highly interesting piece of work.

Eagle Star Quilt (c. 1999)

Rita Corbiere

Michigan State University Museum

Both the eagle and the star are among the most powerful of symbols for Native Americans, and Ojibwa quiltmaker Rita Corbiere has combined them in a masterful diamond design in this stunning work. A halo of yellow, red, and orange surrounds the dramatic central bird figure, sharply delineated in black with white wing and tail feathers. A black border outlines the star and is used again for the narrow border that enclose the entire quilt. Four smaller eight-point stars—bright plain red with multicolored tips and centers—are placed in the four corners signifying either the four winds, or the four main points of the compass. A triangle-printed multicolored fabric has been used to back the quilt.

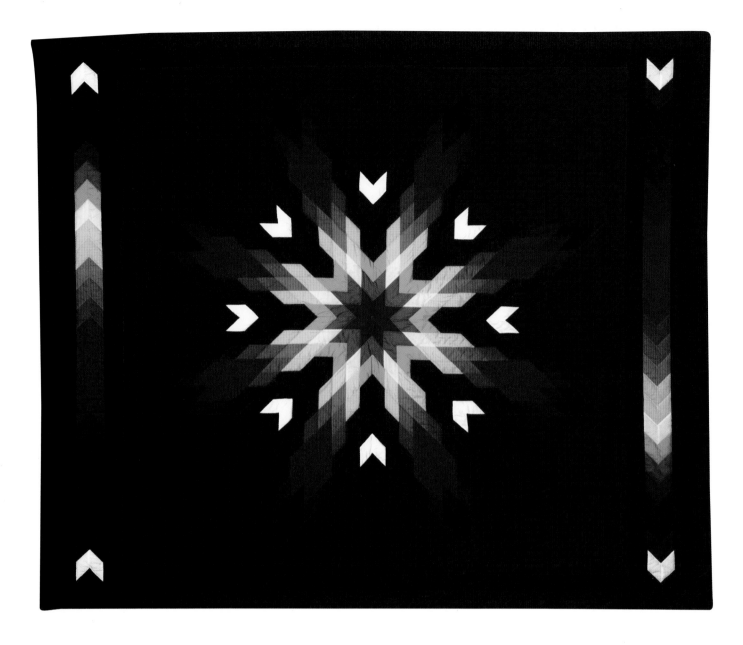

Bright Star Quilt (1996)

Paula White

Michigan State University Museum

Paula White is a member of the Ojibwa tribe who lives on Leech Lake Reservation at Bena, Minnesota. Her Star quilts are usually set on black backgrounds, unlike those of many other Native American quiltmakers, who consider the color unlucky. White has said that she began using black when her grandparents both died, because the color was a symbol of a very sad time for her and helped her in the grieving process. But the brilliant rainbow of colors used in this piece offset the somber qualities that might occur on such a background. Two bands of double diamonds on the sides of the border repeat the color sequence in the carefully planned and executed star, and lines of quilting radiate out from the white double diamonds in the corners of the star.

Star quilts are very much a part of the quiltmaking tradition of Native Americans, especially among the Plains Indian tribes. Eight-point Lone Star-type patterns are most often seen, but there are many examples of six-point star and Broken Star, and variations of them all. The star can be found on many Native artefacts, from warbonnet headdresses to buffalo-hide robes, as well as quilts.

SEMINOLE

Seminole Band Quilt (c. 1930)

Maker unknown

Courtesy of Chase Manhattan Arts Program

This lovely geometric quilt is unusual in several ways. Seminole work, of which this is a stunning example, is more often found on clothing than on bedcovers. And the colors here are not typical. They are softer and lean more toward pastels than the normally bright hues used by Seminole quiltmakers.

Three patterned bands are repeated in the quilt, alternating with strips of solid-colored fabrics of varying widths. The darker plain bands of black, dark blue, and brick-red add depth and body to the light pink, blue, terracotta, and creamy yellow, while the occasional band of white and the bands of red that match the border add zing.

Women on Seminole reservations in Florida have been strip-piecing patchwork since the early twentieth century. They were probably introduced to patchwork by missionaries after the reservations were established, and they were possibly given sewing machines about the same time, which would have made the piecing much faster than working by hand. Originally, they tore their fabrics to make sure the grain was straight, unlike today's quilters with their rotary cutters and rulers, but the end result was the same. Strips of solid-colored fabrics, torn or cut in varying widths, were stitched together and then cut apart, often at a sharp angle, before being joined again into bands of pattern that were incorporated into clothing such as blouses, skirts, and jackets, as well as bags and, occasionally, quilts. The same technique is used on Seminole reservations today to make many items, often on a commercial scale, and the clothing is still worn by many of the women as their tribal costume.

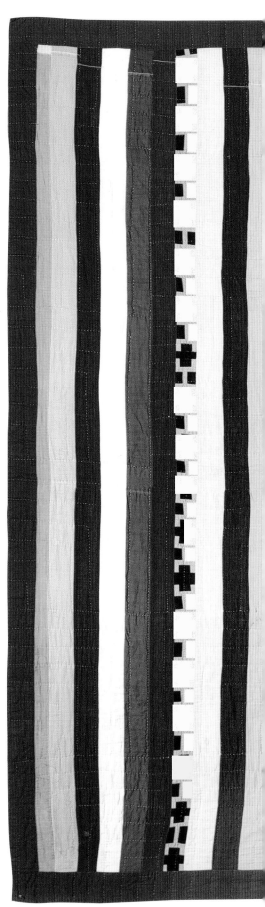

Evenings in the Garden (2000)

Rose Epton-Peter

Rose Epton-Peter dyed all the cotton
fabrics in this subtle but intricate
quilt. Using a random Log Cabin
method, she has used strips of
Seminole patchwork to construct the
thirty-six blocks, which are sashed
with shaded strips to take the viewer
on a visual tour of Stourhead Garden
in England on a spring evening.

Flower Garden (1995)

Karen Neary

This lovely Seminole-style wall hanging was made by Karen Neary of Amherst in Nova Scotia, Canada. She has used various strip-pieced patterns to create bands of color depicting flowers and fences, and separated by strips of plain fabrics.

She has varied the bright primary colors used in traditional Seminole work—yellow, red, blue, and green combined with black and white—with bright pink and a dark, almost olive green. The solid-colored bands are quilted with patterns that coordinate with the design of the nearby strips, including a chevron that echoes the green zigzag at the bottom of the piece, single rows of triangles in the dark green bands above and below the pink and red tulips, and the white borders of the yellow diamonds along the top. Straight lines of quilting have been used on the pink strips that are placed above and below the small pink and red double flowers, near the bottom of the hanging.

HAWAIIAN

Hawaiian Blocks (1991)

Maker unknown

The woman shown right was demonstrating the art of Hawaiian quilting in Poipu, Hawaii. The techniques were taught to women on the islands by missionaries—most of German lineage—in the nineteenth century, who were reportedly shocked by islanders' traditional clothing, which consisted of skirts made of long strands of grass and little else. The earliest quilts made on the island were done in the style of those made in New England at the time, but before long the island seamstresses seem to have blended the making of quilts with the patterns created by another skill taught to them by the white missionaries, that of scherenschnitte, or German paper-cutting, which is similar to cutting paper snowflakes or chains of paper dolls. These intricate patterns are made by folding a single piece of paper several times and cutting a design into it along the folded edges. Paper dolls are made from accordion-folded strips, while snowflakes are folded to make a six-sided design. Hawaiian patterns, like traditional scherenschnitte, use a square of paper folded in half twice, once in each direction, and then folded again along the diagonal. A pattern is then cut into the eight

layers, which when it is unfolded gives an intricate square design.

Nature's bounty surrounds everything on the islands, and the motifs are almost always based on natural forms like flowers, trees, leaf patterns, or fruit and vegetables. We don't know where the original idea to make the pattern into a one-piece full-size quilt top came from, but that is the form of the quilt style now known as Hawaiian. Originally a quilter made and named her own patterns, and no one else would then use that design. Thus every quilt is slightly different, but most share common characteristics. Hawaiian quilts are usually two colors, generally a light background and a darker motif, which is appliquéd to the background using a needle-turned technique to work by hand around the elaborate curves and sharp points of the pattern. The method for working such patterns, including smaller blocks of scherenschnitte, is now called by the name Hawaiian appliqué. The quilting is also standard for these designs, consisting of lines of echo quilting around the motif, which are said to represent the ocean waves lapping gently against the shore of the islands.

Kukui O Kahuku (c. 1880)

Maker unknown

This spectacular Hawaiian quilt is an interpretation of the kukui flower that grows on the island of Oahu. It was owned by a family named Wilcox who lived in the village of Kahuku on Oahu, hence the name Kukui O Kahuku. This piece is made all the more stunning by the outer pattern, made from the same mulberry fabric as the floral motif in the center. The two pieces are completely separate, but the designs echo and complement each other, attesting to the design skills of the quiltmaker as well as her prowess with a needle and thread. The echo quilting on both the background and the pattern areas is superb.

Paper Cuts (c. 1950)

Maker unknown

The 1950s was a time of unparalleled prosperity in the United States. World War II was over, and the majority of the women who had rushed to join the workforce, which was seriously depleted by the number of men who had been sent to the various theaters of combat, went back to their more traditional role as keepers of the home fires. A lack of time and shortage of materials had led to a decline in quiltmaking during the war, but some of the returning women began to sew again, more for pleasure than from necessity this time. However, as women became more and more inclined to work outside the home, and 1960s' feminism and sexual freedom gathered force, quiltmaking was relegated to the status of an old-fashioned, time-consuming craft made unnecessary by the easily available and inexpensive bedding of the time. Why spend months making a quilt when you could buy a comforter or duvet that would keep you warm the same night?

The joy of quiltmaking was rediscovered just in time, before its skills and traditional techniques were lost forever, in the past generation. Before the skill began to wane, an unknown maker created this scherenschitte quilt in bright blue and white. The paper-cut technique had been popular with nineteenth-century quiltmakers, and this version is in the traditional mode, but the pattern is somehow more starkly modern and less elaborate. The sawtooth inner border contrasts sharply with the plain white outer one, with its sinuous quilted vine adding curving texture.

Breadfruit (1915-1925)

Maker unknown

This stunningly intricate quilt is highly traditional in both design and execution. The design is based on the breadfruit tree which grows abundantly in the Hawaiian islands and was one of the basic foodstuffs of the islanders. The colors of red on white used by the unknown quiltmaker are the combination most often used in Hawaiian pieces, and the traditional echo quilting is quite superb. The complex pattern with its spiky leaves alternating with stems of fruit fills the background almost to the edge, and the central cross motif has a number of difficult aspects, from the sharp points to the deep cuts between them. The maker's skills are plainly visible, both in terms of the concept and the stitching.

AUTOGRAPH/ FRIENDSHIP

Schoolhouse Top (1897-1898)

Presbyterian Ladies of Oak Ridge, Missouri

American Folk Art Museum/Gift of Beverly Walker Reitz
in memory of Vest Walker

The Schoolhouse block was a popular choice in the nineteenth century for so-called album quilts, which were also known as friendship quilts. Quilts were often made as group projects, and took several forms. Some were made to raise funds for a particular cause by one person or a small group, and people paid money to sign, or autograph, the quilt, which was then given to the recipient together with the cash, or auctioned off to add to the total raised. Sometimes the participants in the project each made a block to be assembled into a quilt to be presented, perhaps as a gift to mark a special occasion.

We do not know why the Presbyterian ladies of Oak Ridge made this cotton top nor why it was never finished, but it carries many signatures. The windows and angled spaces between the walls and the roof, as well as the sky area, has signatures embroidered in red cotton floss the same color as the houses, and there are also numerous signatures, this time in white, in various places on the red houses. The sashing is somewhat wider than is typical, but these areas are unsigned. The simplicity of the block and the careful way in which they have been signed add to the overall consistency of the work.

The Schoolhouse pattern had a revival of popularity in the twentieth century, and appears on many quilts (*see pages 144-145*). It remains a well-loved and frequently made design today.

Red and White Friendship Quilt (c. 1898)

Maker unknown

This quilt belongs to Patricia Cox, a collector, designer, and quiltmaker, whose collection contains a selection of red-and-white quilts from various time periods. The block used in this particular quilt is called Album, perhaps because it gave enough open spaces to take a good number of signatures. Made of strips and squares, it consists of a colored X in the center surrounded by steps of another color, and finishes with triangles the same color as the center X along all four edges. Here, the signatures consist both of full names and initials, all embroidered in red floss on the white parts of the blocks. The red areas have not been embellished. The quilting is an all-over wineglass pattern.

Before the quilt came into Pat's collection, it belonged to Lydia Schuette of Dixon, Illinois. It was made for her stepmother, the wife of her father, the Reverend Schuette, who was a minister in Dubuque, Iowa. It is likely to have been made to raise money, either to supplement church funds or to help meet expenses within the Reverend's family. Whatever the reason for making it, it carries a large number of signatures, so it was hopefully a successful venture. In some cases, people paid less to initial a block than to sign it with a full signature.

Oak Leaf Autograph Quilt (1848/1849)

The Ladies of Clifton, Ohio

Minnesota Historical Society

This lovely and effective quilt, which is described as a "Remembrance" quilt, was presented to the Reverend and Mrs. Moses Russell by "The Ladies of Clifton, Ohio," on New Year's Day of 1849.

The appliqué block pattern is Oak Leaf and Reel, made in very typical colors of the period. The leaves are a rich mid-green, while the central motifs are made from a red and yellow cotton print, applied to a plain white background. The blocks are joined edge-to-edge, without any sashing between them. The backing of the quilt is also plain white. Names have been inscribed in between the design.

As is frequently the case with autograph quilts, we do not know why the gift was made to Reverend and Mrs. Russell. Sometimes such quilts were given as gifts for special occasions, and based on the authenticated date, this one may have been presented as part of the Christmas celebration.

Autograph Quilt (1866)

"Female Friends of John Roberts"

Minnesota Historical Society

This lovely album block is called Chicago Pavements and is constructed using squares and filler triangles, which creates a large cross shape in the center that gives a good area for signatures. The block just below the center of the quilt is different—it is a six-pointed compass star pattern which bears the inscription "Presented to John Roberts by his female friends, Dec. 8th, 1866." The blocks are pieced from a typical selection of red printed and plain white fabrics, with a few other colors including yellow used to make the squares that surround the central one in several blocks. In the center of each block are individual autographs and good wishes from the women who participated in the making of the piece. Gray sashing with white corner squares separate the blocks, which are set on point.

Many of these autograph quilts were given to friends or relatives who were moving away, many of them heading into newly opened territories on the other side of the country. Because of the long distances involved, and the difficulty of travel in general before the network of railroads and then highways was built, the participants and the recipients would almost certainly never see each other again, and a friendship quilt was a way to keep memories fresh in new and sometimes uncharted places.

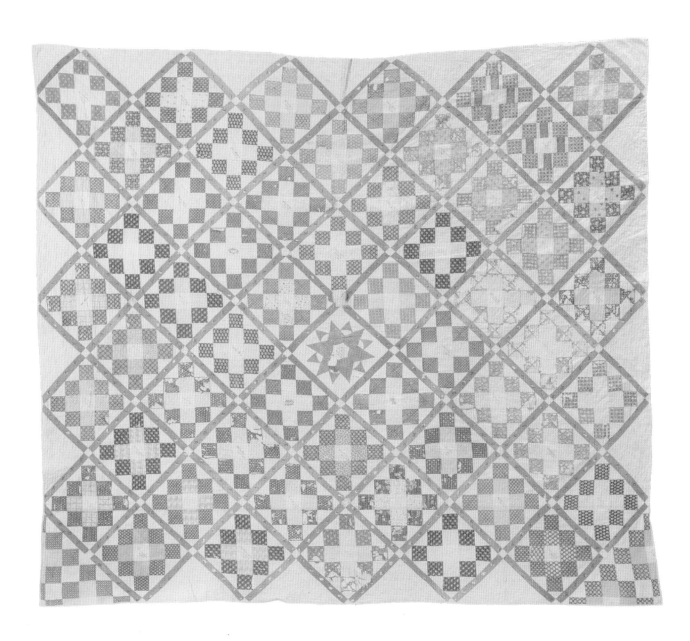

BALTIMORE

Baltimore Album Quilt (1843)

Several makers in Reisterstown, Maryland

Baltimore Album quilts were made, not surprisingly, in and around that city in Maryland, mainly between 1840 and 1860. Some historians believe that many of the blocks were designed by a small number of needlewomen who sold them to others to be made. Certainly the execution of the stitching on existing examples varies markedly from average to highly skilled. They were elaborate, with intricate appliqué patterns, some in blocks and others applied directly to the background, which was almost always white or cream. Typical motifs included floral designs—flowers, leaves, trees, fruit (especially the pineapple, a universal symbol of welcome) and the occasional vegetable; animals, especially birds and butterflies but sometimes mammals and other insects; buildings both public and private; landscapes and seascapes, plus other views; modes of transportations of the day, from carriages to trains and ships; and symbols of patriotism, especially eagles and flags. Baskets of flowers abound, most designed to test the maker's skill to the utmost. Traditional appliqué blocks are found on many Baltimore Album quilts, adapted to suit the quilt being made.

The quilt on the right is in the collection of Patricia Cox, a well-known quiltmaker and collector of American quilts from Minneapolis, Minnesota. Baltimore Album quilts have been a particular interest of

hers for many years, and she designs appliqué patterns based on images found in antique examples. This quilt is the only Baltimore Album in her collection, an early example with folk art-type motifs that are less sophisticated than many of the later quilts. Made in Reisterstown, a community northwest of Baltimore, it is dated 1843 and signed by several different makers. Four of the women are named Baker: in the dated block the name is Margareth, while Elizabeth has signed the center basket block. W. A. Baker's signature is in the block to the left of the dated wreath with a blue jay perched on a branch, and Mary A. E. has put her name in the pink carnation block in the top row, second from the right. M. A. E. Baker, presumably also Mary, has signed the clover block on the right of the center basket. Two blocks have only initials, and not all the blocks have signatures. Of the ones that are signed, some are stitched, while others are stamped with ink. A variety of typical prints of the time, mainly red and green with some pink and yellow but almost no blue, have been used, and the blocks are separated by a red and yellow small-scale print with pieced stars made from the same fabric on a white background in each corner. The sawtooth border has been constructed from the same red print and white fabrics, and an overall diagonal grid forms the quilting, including the border.

Baltimore Album Quilt (c. 1840)

Sarah and Mary J. Pool

This colorful example of a Baltimore quilt was made by Sarah Pool and Mary J. Pool, who each signed a floral block in cross stitch, Sarah in the tulip square second from the bottom on the left, and Mary in the flower and bud wreath on the opposite side of the quilt. The fabrics are brighter than on some examples, and there are more buildings and patriotic images than are normally seen. The workmanship on the highly elaborate twenty-five blocks is of an extremely high standard.

There is a wide variety in the flower motifs that fill the large number of baskets, vases, urns, and cornucopia, and more than the usual number of musical instruments, including a Greek lyre topped by a bird in flight, a motif that occurs quite often on quilts of this type. A head of steam has been embroidered spewing from the funnel of the little train in the bottom left-hand corner, and a pair of pink and blue gloves appear in the corners of the block with a fountain surrounded by cornucopia that is diagonally above the train block.

The blocks are set edge to edge without sashing, and the border continues the elaborate quality with its scallops on both sides and the well-planned but not concise zigzag vine with flowers at regular intervals.

Baltimore Album Quilt (c. 1850)

Attributed to Mary Simmons

The blocks in this beautiful quilt are somewhat unusually set on point, whereas most examples of Baltimore Albums are set square. They are not sashed, but the whole quilt is enclosed by a wonderful floral vine, beautifully planned and executed, with a red and green bunch of strawberries, or perhaps leaves, in each corner. There are birds, insects, and a squirrel, but all of the other motifs are floral, and the piece is wonderfully balanced. Even the triangular blocks that appear around the edges and at the corners to fill the spaces left when the blocks are turned on point are filled with a wide variety of superbly executed floral patterns.

This quilt is attributed to Mary Simmons, a leading maker of Baltimore Album quilts, and it was made for Eleanor Gorsuch, whose family then owned much of what is today the city of Baltimore.

The fabrics used on these quilts was generally of an extremely high quality. High-grade cotton was most often selected, but silk, and any kind of lightweight wool that could be applied easily are also found in some pieces. The colors used, as seen on this quilt, were generally rather bright primaries—red, green, yellow, and blue—with pinks and browns also often appearing in the form of flowers, birds, butterflies, and a selection of animals.

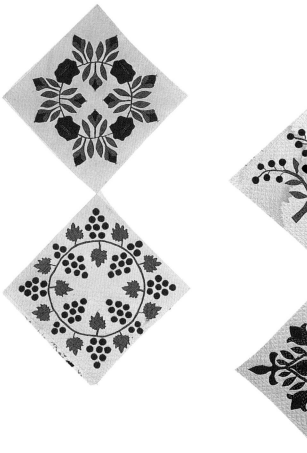

FOLK ART

Folk Art Quilt (c. 1840)

Maker unknown

Folk art is based on designs that are generally naturalistic, and most examples have a charming naive quality. They tend to be highly stylized and lack sophistication, but the simple forms of the folk-art tradition were widely made in the past, and continue to be worked today. Shapes tend to be simplified into gentle curves and straight lines, which are easier to cut and stitch than more intricate shapes. Appliqué is found more often than patchwork on folk-art quilts.

The charm of folk art quilts is undeniable, and this example, made in New York state in about 1840, is quite wonderful. The maker has used a variety of motifs that repeat in a regular pattern around the quilt, making a feature of the vagaries of scale and the general naivety of the design as a whole. The four white horses with their tack, the most realistic forms by far, are far smaller than the yellow cats, while the fish swim happily in a sea of vastly over-scaled flowers. Birds sit atop flowers that have stems like tree trunks and the scissors would be hard to use to cut out doilies the size of the red ones nearby. The four-leaf clover with double arrows are similar to patterns found in design throughout the world. The motifs in the center of the top and bottom could be Masonic devices.

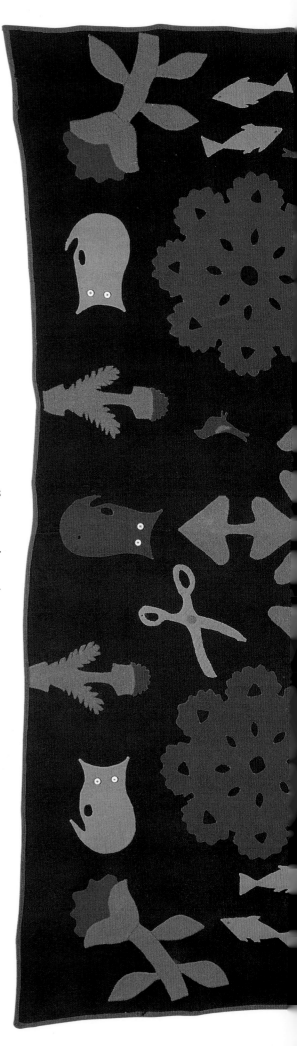

Part Two: Picture Gallery – Folk Art

Cross River Album Quilt (1861)

Eldad Miller and others

American Folk Art Museum/Gift of Dr. Stanley and Jacqueline Schneider

This charming quilt has clearly been influenced by the Baltimore Albums, but it was made in New York in 1861. Mrs. Eldad Miller (1805–1874) with others made it in Cross River, New York, at the beginning of the Civil War, and the inclusion of the stars and stripes in one square may be an indication of the makers' support for the Union. Except for the blue in the flag, the colors of the cotton and silk fabrics have been limited to red, yellow, and green on a white background. The motifs are mainly floral, more folk art than Baltimore, and there is a wide range of technical ability shown by the blocks. This is not surprising when we know that the ages of the contributors to the quilt ranged from fifteen to fifty-five, according to research conducted by Paula Laverty at the American Folk Art Museum. Ms. Laverty has also found out that they all lived within a few miles of one another.

The blocks are outline-quilted and there are individual leaf-and-bud motifs along the two side borders. The top and bottom borders are appliquéd with a grapevine and bunches of grapes, with two traditional leaf-square blocks in the bottom corners cutting the grapevine short on the left. A single block with grapes and leaves worked on a smaller scale than the border vine is also included to the left of the right-hand leaf square, truncating the bottom vine even more on that side of the quilt.

Farmyard Animals (1865-1875)

Maker unknown

The multicolored farm animals on this quilt are somewhat more realistic than the ones on the quilt shown on pages 344-345, but they are still wonderfully out of scale with each other. Dogs, ducks, cows, and horses all fill their own blocks, each standing on a piece of fabric—sometimes green or pink, and sometimes cut as one piece with the animal shape itself. The house in the very center of the quilt has a lawn, flowers at the front, and two rather vinelike trees. Each block is bordered with pink, and all are sashed with strips of white that have pink strips at each junction, forming a series of Xs that give a diagonal line to the otherwise very squared-up look of the quilt.

Mennonite Floral Folk-Art Quilt (1865-1875)

Maker unknown

This Mennonite quilt was made in Pennsylvania. It is a unique example of differences between Mennonite work and that of the orthodox Amish, but it is also very different from most quilts made in the Mennonite tradition. It is made in solid colors, but it is much more decorative and "fancy" than most work done by quilters from either community. Religious beliefs compel both the Amish and the less strict Mennonite to eschew worldliness in their lives, and the creating of elaborate, highly decorated possessions is generally outside the culture. While the fabrics used to work the appliqué motifs may have been left over from dressmaking, they all match, and are clearly not scraps in the usual sense. The folk-art theme is almost never found in the work of either sect, and appliqué work is virtually unheard of among the Amish of this period. The quilting, however, is typically beautiful and of the highest quality.

Flowerpot Crib Quilt (c. 1870)

Maker unknown

A vase full of highly stylized flowers covers this delightful crib quilt. The theme and execution are typically folk art: the scale of the long stems in relation to the flowerpot itself are all quite wrong, but they look completely right on the quilt and perfectly balanced to make a thoroughly pleasing overall design.

Only three fabrics have been used— red for the flowers, yellow for the flower centers, and green for the stems and vase. The daintiness of the charming design matches the size of the piece, and the appliqué is extremely beautifully worked.

The edges of the piece have been quilted in straight lines up to the appliquéd area, and then the quilting has been worked in diagonal lines over the top of the straight ones, to give the appearance of a separate border. Two individual flowers cross stems just below the vase, extending right into the "border" area and creating just the right symmetry in the overall layout.

Scenes from Childhood (c. 1880)

Maker unknown

While the execution of this charming crib quilt is more pictorial than folk art, the themes and the scale are certainly in the folk tradition. The use of a limited number of fabrics gives the piece a wonderfully even overall feel, and the delightful images of children at play have been carefully executed. At the top a toddler plays with a ball. Below a doting Victorian father carries another small child piggyback while riding on a rocking horse, his coattails pulled by an older girl. At the bottom a girl and a boy in a top hat greet a seated woman holding a baby. Or perhaps it's a doll and they are all children playing house. The faces and hair on all are beautifully drawn and realistic, including that of the doll/baby, and the appliqué is worked with great skill. They all stand on floors of acid green and yellow print fabric, the same that has been used to make the grass under the feet of the animals on either side—a cow, a cat twice her size, and two dogs of different breeds. The corner motifs are stylized cornucopia, each with two buds on stems, which are made from a different acid green and yellow print, which is also used to make the inner border.

The workmanship is superb, especially the quilting, which is used to outline each motif. Individual motifs are scattered over the white background and the outer border has simple diagonal lines.

Folk Art Daisy (c. 1865)

Maker unknown

Powerhouse Museum

This charming woolen quilt is in the collection of an Australian museum, but is thought to have been made in the United States, possibly by slaves in Texas freed just after the Civil War ended in 1865. There are 101 patches, and they vary substantially in both size and quality, leading to the assumption that the piece had a number of makers. Most of the appliquéd motifs are daisylike flowers, while a few have treelike shapes. The appliqué shapes are cut from hat felt and applied to the wool squares with blanket stitch, and decorative stitching outlines each block. The strange long-legged shapes in five of the blocks look similar to a letter M ... perhaps the initial of a maker?

KIT QUILTS

Red Poppies (c. 1920)

Maker unknown

The vogue for kit quilts reached its height after World War I during the 1920s and '30s, and this lovely lightweight cotton coverlet is a magnificent example. It has no batting (wadding) and was probably used as a summer bedspread. Made in Minnetonka, Minnesota, the original quilting was worked in red yarn, which the present owner found garish and, she felt, detracted from the beautifully executed appliqué, so she removed it. A well-known designer of appliqué and quilting patterns, she chose a curving pattern typical of the time and quilted the layers again with white quilting thread. The subtle colors of the leaves and stems contrast wonderfully with the bright reds and oranges of the flowers and buds. The flower centers are yellow with a narrow green outer ring that has been embroidered in each bloom with black floss to look realistic, like the distinctive stamens of the poppy.

Pink Poppies (c. 1933)

Nora, Winnie, and Euretha Irwin and Bonnie Carden

Courtesy Merikay Waldvogel

The makers of this charming kit quilt were from Andersonville, Tennessee, and probably bought it by mail order after it was featured in the Good Housekeeping magazine of July 1932. Designed by Anne Orr, a well-known quiltmaker and designer of the day, it cost fifty cents for an iron-on transfer pattern with directions for working the appliqué for the quilt and a matching rug.

The background they chose is plain white cotton sheeting. The leaves and stems are all made of the same green fabric, while the flowers and buds are in two different shades of bright pink. The divider strips that frame the central motif and create corners for individual blooms are cut from the lighter shade of pink.

The border area contains curvaceous stems of single flowers that touch each other to make a continuous vine of poppies, beautifully planned and executed. The quilting is also superb: a tiny ½" (125mm) diagonal grid in all the background areas, with rows of scallops edging the inside of the divider strips. All the quilting is worked in white thread except on the leaves, in which veins are stitched in green to match the fabric.

Pansies (c. 1930)

Maker unknown

This quilt pattern is catalog number 1365 from Paragon, one of the major makers of kits. Its owner is Patricia Cox, whose mother began a quilt from the same design in the 1930s but never finished it. When Pat saw this quilt for sale, she decided to add it to her collection to show what her mother's quilt might have looked like if it had been completed.

Flower Spray (c. 1940)

Maker unknown

By the late 1800s, kit quilts were being sold in large numbers containing a background fabric, with the appliqué and quilting designs already printed in place by recently invented machines that could stamp transfers onto fabric and paper. Sometimes kits included preprinted fabric for the motifs; in some kits the appliqué patterns were paper transfers and the quilter chose her own fabrics. Although kit quilts peaked in popularity before World War II, kits continued to be bought and made through the 1950s. In fact, they are still being made today, but most are patchwork, and appliqué tends to be offered as paper patterns. They offer the beginner, now as then, a chance to make a well-designed quilt and learn techniques in a seemingly simple way.

The majority of kits sold in the 1920s and '30s were floral appliqué patterns, and because they were advertised and sold nationally, similar examples can be found across the United States, and duplicates are also found in Britain, though fewer were sold there. The patterns appear in several distinctive formats, and motifs are repeated on most quilts.

The quilt on the right has the same simple spray of flowers repeated in staggered rows, with half-sprays in the correct alignment along the edges. Though charming, what makes this quilt special is the outstanding fan quilting that surrounds and enhances the motifs.

PICTORIAL

Butterflies (c. 1930)

Maker unknown

Minnesota Historical Society

Most quilts that are truly pictorial are worked as appliqué, which allows the maker to create more realistic images than can ever be possible with patchwork. Even when the designs are stylized, they feel more lifelike than the geometric forms generally achieved through piecing, and although much of the inspiration for all kinds of design elements are drawn from nature, fabric pictures, especially of the kind being created in the late twentieth century, are relatively new. Folk-art quilts (*see pages 344-353*) with stylized, out-of-scale images date mainly from the nineteenth century, and landscapes, or scenics, are an innovation from about the 1920s. Patriotic images appear on quilts from the early 1800s, and the realism found on Baltimore Album quilts (*see pages 338-343*) was executed between about 1840 and 1860. African-American story quilts, of which a number of beautiful and moving examples stil exist, were made both during slave days and until well into emancipation.

This quilt top, believed to have been made by a Swedish immigrant in Coon Rapids, Minnesota, features rows of stylized but entirely recognizable appliquéd butterflies in cotton prints typical of the 1930s when it was made. The blocks are muslin (calico) squares with each butterfly made of a different fabric and blanket-stitched in place with black embroidery floss. The pale sashing is very thin, and each vertical row has the butterflies facing in opposite directions.

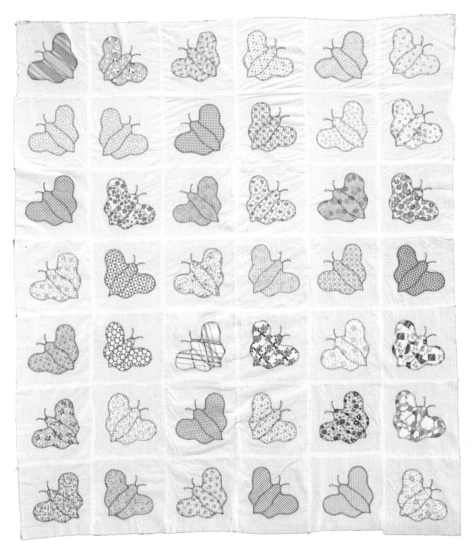

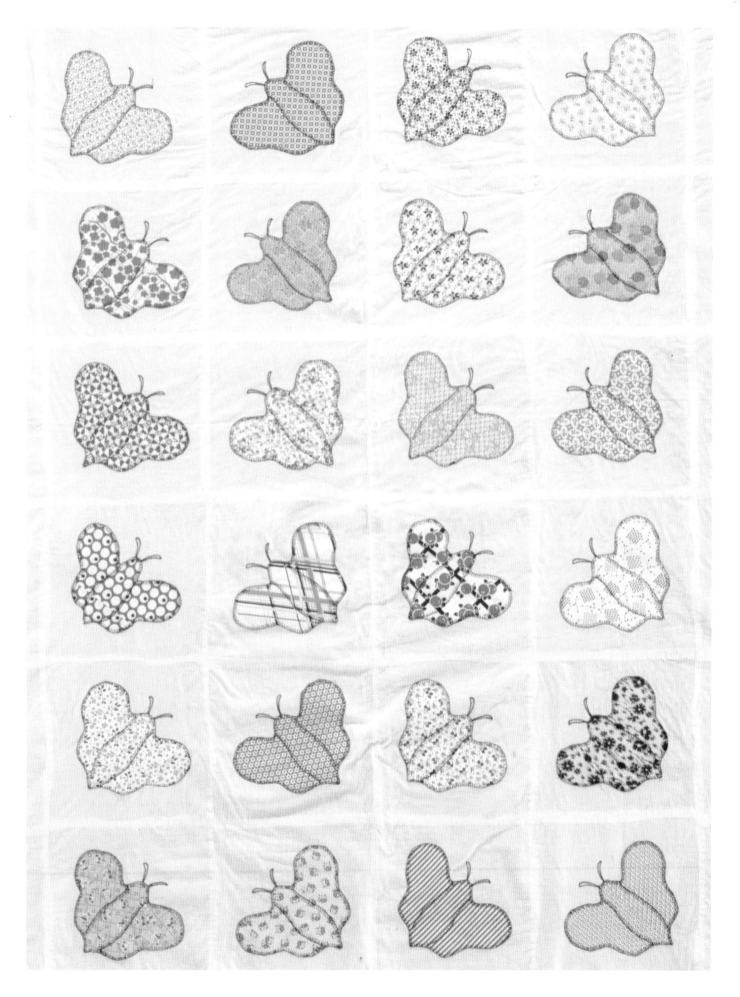

Cotton Gin and Farm (c. 1895)

Maker unknown

Most landscape quilts date from the 1920s, with large numbers being made today. Many examples combine patchwork with appliqué to great effect, with blocks such as Log Cabin (*see pages 32-43*) making up backgrounds or houses and overlaid with applied images. By the end of the twentieth century, the landscape quilt had become a standard part of the quiltmaker's repertoire, together with portraits and realistic natural forms.

This charming nineteenth-century "scenic" quilt was made in Pennsylvania and is a masterpiece, both in terms of the wonderful texture it displays and in its depiction of a prosperous Mid-Atlantic farmstead of the late 1800s. The barns, houses, and mill are fashioned from cotton and silk, while many of the figures—animal and human—and numerous details like the smoke billowing from the gin smokestack have been embroidered with brightly colored silk thread. Others have been appliquéd, and some of them are padded with stuffing to give them a realistic three-dimensional look. The detail is magnificent, from the sun setting between the mill and the big red barn, to the doves standing on the barn roof and the child sitting on the fence. Vines clamber up the side of the house, and in the bottom right-hand corner a rider struggles to control his horse, frightened as it must be by the strange mechanical tractor-contraption coming toward it. Flowers bloom along the beautifully executed fences, with heads larger than those of the children playing nearby. All life, as the quiltmaker knew it perhaps, is here, and welcome, if the open doors on all the buildings are anything to go by. The wide white border is elaborately quilted with mainly floral motifs.

Lunch M'Lady (c. 1995)

Patricia Allen

Texture on pictorial quilts can be created in a variety of ways. It can be mainly visual, with the images worked in two planes, or it can be realistically three-dimensional. It can come from surface stitching or from the way various elements in the design relate to each other. Manipulating the fabric by folding or ruching, stuffing shapes, and gathering pieces can all add extra dimension to fabric pictures.

British quiltmaker Patricia Allen made this delightful wall hanging with amazingly realistic texture. Her wheelbarrow, filled with fresh vegetables from the the garden, is made from hand-dyed fabric cut and pieced to give it depth. The produce has all been worked to make the effect as real as possible. The new potatoes at the bottom of the barrow, almost hidden by the dark green lettuce and the carrots, are actually part of the wheelbarrow fabric stitched, gathered slightly, and stuffed to create the lumps.

The leafy vegetable is veined with machine embroidery worked in metallic thread. Each carrot and radish is made and stuffed separately, with strips of raw-edge fabric for the carrot tops, and string—green for the tops and white for the roots—on the radishes, which are made in two shades of pink. Each bean is made and applied separately. The green thread tops and tiny gold dots on the strawberries create a crop that looks good enough to eat.

The white background, on which the abandoned garden fork has been laid, has been quilted in a slightly irregular diamond grid. The jagged green border, with a subtly placed hand-embroidered white daisy with almost invisible appliquéd leaves in the bottom left-hand corner, adds a finishing touch.

And the Nominations Are .... (c. 1995)

Claire Scott

Human figures and faces are among the most difficult images to get right on pictorial fiber work. When the portrayals are of famous people, especially the iconic faces from the world of film, it seems an almost impossible task. Claire Scott, a British quiltmaker, designed this prize-winning hanging by combining the classic image from three dozen of the world's favorite movies into a reel of film that surrounds the larger

image of a lame Oscar, the golden statuette presented to winners of Academy Awards in Hollywood each year. Virtually every image is immediately recognizable to movie fans the world over, due to the maker's clear and clever use of particular props or costumes to help identify each frame. The composition balances the color values, the shapes, and the overall effect with great skill and panache.

From Mickey Mouse and Sally Bowles to ET and Auntie Mame, from Al Jolson to Laurel and Hardy, or Gene Kelly singin' in the rain and John Travolta in a Saturday night fever, the images are clear and beautifully executed. All of the elements are appliquéd, with surface embroidery and quilting to add detail and texture. Dorothy, the Tin Man, and the Straw Man, on their way to see the Wizard of Oz, are embellished with embroidery, and Marilyn Monroe's billowing skirt from *The Seven-Year Itch* is made from white chiffon, gathered and ruched to fly up and give us another glimpse of her lovely legs. Backs can be almost as expressive as the fronts of figures, and the climactic scene from *The Full Monty* shows how true this can be ... we see both the backs of the strippers on the screen as they look out at the audience watching their number, and the backs of the actual viewers of the film, watching attentively from their comfortable seats, doing what moviegoers do best.

Ex Libris (c. 1995)

Melyn Robinson

While most of the places pictured in quilts are outdoor landscapes or views of the outdoors seen from inside, glimpsed through a window or door, it need not be so. An indoor spot—quiet corner, a favorite room, a table set for supper, a cabinet or shelf full of souvenirs or books—can all be re-created in fabric to great effect.

In the wall hanging on the left, British quiltmaker Melyn Robinson has used strip patchwork to create the blocks that make up the bookcase and sashed them with wood-grain effect fabric. Each book has the title

and author printed on the spine using a computer. The fabrics were hand-dyed and fed through a printer set for a variety of typefaces, adding greatly to the realistic feel of the piece. The patchwork technique Robinson used was irregular Log Cabin block piecing, with background fabrics filling in gaps between books of widely differing sizes. Machine quilting in the ditch gives texture and shape to the backs of the books on the shelves, while the wide plaid border is worked in an abstract leaf and vine pattern.

Sunset in Africa (1990s)

Silvia Momesso Ranieri

Many pictorial quilts are made to commemorate or celebrate a particular place or event. An anniversary or a memorable vacation trip can be immortalized in fabric to evoke wonderful memories, with symbols that bring to mind what you were doing on a particular occasion or in a certain place. Choosing a design to provoke certain responses can be viewed as a process of elimination to get rid of complicated images that would confuse the response you wish to evoke.

Ranieri, an Italian quiltmaker whose family business was making silk ties, loves travel and the natural world. Her early introduction to silk has led her to use silk more than any other fabric, partly because she loves the way it feels when she is working, partly for its brilliant hues, and partly for the wonderful texture that is created when it is hand quilted.

She wanted to commemorate a trip to Africa with the quilt below, and the two images that she particularly wanted to convey were a long crane flying above the landscape and an ancient tree rooted deeply in the earth below.

She used the English paper-piecing method (*see pages 20-21*) to make the background, lit with the rich colors of the setting sun, positioned just off center. It casts

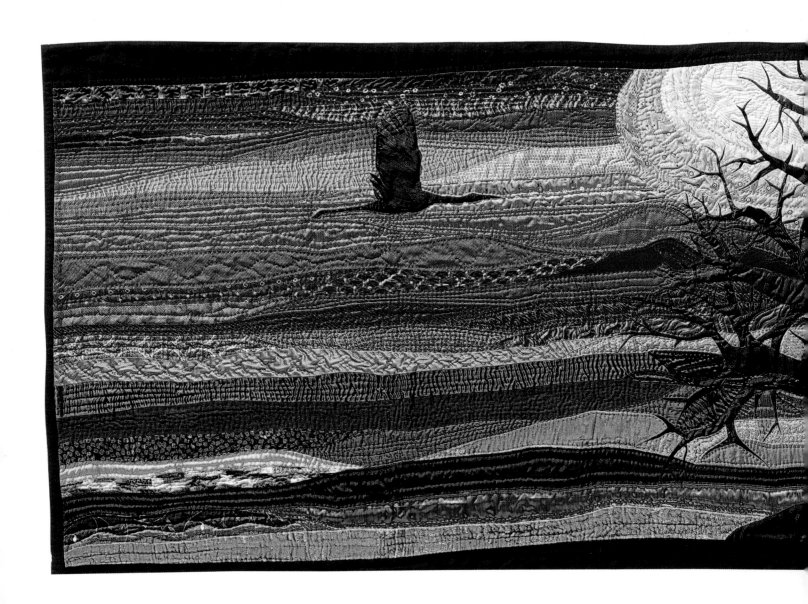

into silhouette the bird in flight with its upswept wings and the leafless tree, both pieced from several different dark fabrics, and makes them stand out against the vastness of the African plain. The blending of background colors is so subtle that it is impossible to tell where the horizon is, exactly as we might expect at sunset in such a place. The hanging is outlined by a thin black irregular border that adds to the effect of looking out at the view.

LETTERS/ALPHABETS

ABC Baby Quilt (c. 1990)

Cheryl Fall

Alphabet samplers have been made for several centuries, most by young girls learning to embroider. The first samplers were simply examples of various stitches, and were kept close at hand as a memory aid in the way that we today have books of stitches to look at if we forget how to work one in particular, or wish to try something new to create a particular effect or simply for a change of pace. Alphabet samplers were used from the seventeenth and eighteenth centuries to teach girls their letters and numbers in an era when few girls were formally schooled, and many never learned to read and write. Childhood in Europe and America was short-lived until Victorian times. Children were viewed as functioning members of society who needed to be trained as early as possible to be productive, and many beautiful samplers were made by children under the age of ten.

Alphabet quilts are found dating from the 1800s, when learning and executing high-quality needlework was much more important for girls than reading and writing, but the quilts made at the time—when a young woman was expected to have completed several quilts for her dowry chest by the time she married—were more often patchwork blocks or traditional appliqué patterns. Quilts with alphabets became much more popular in the twentieth century, and the crib quilt on the right is a delightful version which could be used to help a preschool child learn letters. Each letter is made from a different fabric and appliquéd on a contrasting block, again all different, blanket-stitched in place. The rounded, chunky letters would be simple to cut out and stitch, and the effect is totally charming. Stars and hearts fill the blocks in the four corners to balance the letter blocks, and they are sashed with plain white strips. Multiple borders—dark rose, black, and bright blue—enclose the design. Simple quilting is used throughout, and a white binding finishes the edges.

  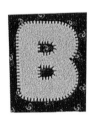  

Little acts of kindness
Little words of love

Make our earth
like our Heaven

Is our
Home a
Heaven

Heaven
is our
Home

Be still Peace

Kind
words
Never
Die

forgi
as yo
hope
forgi

Earth has
no sorrow
Heaven
cannot
heal

Be still
and know
that I am
God

thy will
be done

Oh sacred
Patience
with my
soul abide

There
maci
kinbr
that sr
from ak

Maria
Cadman
Hubbard
aged 79

If you can
not be a
Golden Pipp
indon't turn
crab apple

Love one
another

184

Pieties (1848)

Maria Cadman Hubbard

American Folk Art Museum/Gift of Cyril Irwin in loving memory of his parents, Cyril Arthur and Elise Macy Nelson

We know that Maria Cadman made this extraordinary quilt in 1848 because she dated it. She also wrote her name and age, in the style of needlework samplers made in earlier times by children learning their alphabet and numbers, so we know she was born in 1769. The entire quilt, probably made in Austerlitz, New York, is pieced, from the letters—somewhat eccentric in their formation but entirely readable—to the sawtooth edgings around each block and in the border. Quilt historian Barbara Brackman suggests that the fashion for making these elaborate zigzag borders started to decline very shortly after the date on the quilt.

Turkey red and white make a highly graphic combination, and it has been used to great effect here. The "pieties" all have biblical references, except for my personal favorite, "If you cannot be a golden pippin, dont turn crabapple." The balance of colors and design, and the execution of the piecing, make this a wonderful piece of work. It has recently gained attention as an exhibit in a museum show where it could be seen and appreciated by a wider audience.

Admiral Dewey Commemorative Quilt (1900-1910)

Mite Society (Ladies' Aid), United Brethren Church

American Folk Art Museum/Gift of Janet Gilbert for Marie Griffin

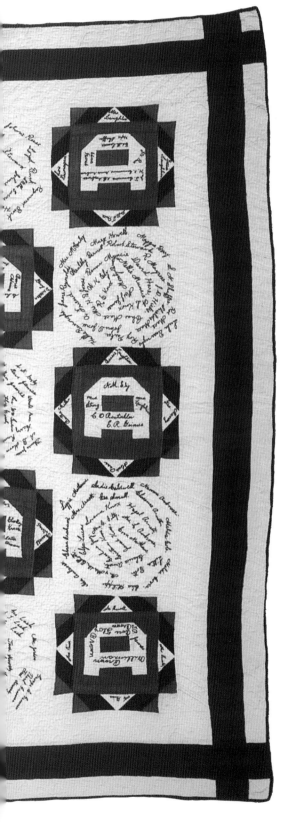

Alphabet quilts are sometimes made from repeating blocks of one or more letters. The designs can be intriguing, and this quilt is a fine example. It is a signature quilt made, it is thought, by the ladies of the Mite Society of the United Brethren Church in Center-Point, Indiana, and several of the spacer blocks between the blocks of pieced letter Ds have been signed in a way that creates embroidered letter Ds.

Admiral George Dewey, to whom the quilt is inscribed, was an American naval officer who had served in the Union Navy during the Civil War, but who won his place in history as the hero of the battle of Manila during the Spanish-American War of 1898. His defeat of the larger Spanish fleet in the bay of Manila without the loss of any of his sailors endeared him to the American public, and among other honors, ordinary people contributed funds to buy him a home in Washington, DC, when he returned from the war. Raising money with signature or autograph quilts (*see pages 332-337*) was a common practice from the mid-1800s, and it is likely that this quilt was made to gather funds for the war effort, or even to help pay for the admiral's house. The size of a contributor's donation often determined the size and location of their signature on the quilt. The finished article was sometimes raffled to add to the fund-raising effort, or presented to a worthy recipient. This quilt was probably a very successful effort judging by the large numbers of signatures.

So popular was the admiral that patterns were published for so-called Dewey quilts around the turn of the century and the idea for embroidering the signatures in the shape of the letter D may have come from one of those. The patriotic red, white, and blue cotton blocks place the letters in a diamond and signatures are worked in red floss. A border of deep burgundy crosses itself at the corners of the quilt, which is quilted in a straightforward way with slanted parallel lines. The quilt has great charm in spite of, or perhaps because of, its eccentricities, such as the fact that if the center block, which is embellished with an inscription to Admiral Dewey, is turned the right way up, the single letters will be back to front.

Bible Verses Quilt (c. 1922)

Jemima Patton Clark

Courtesy of Quilts of Tennessee

Mrs. Clark, from Christiana,
Tennessee, made this charming and
highly geometric quilt to raise money
for her church's missionary society.
As is the custom with fund-raiser
quilts, she charged a set amount to
embroider the donor's favorite Bible
verse on one of the rectangular
blocks, either blue or white, which
she then put together into a stepped
Brick pattern quilt. The embroidery
is worked in red floss on the white
blocks and in white floss on the blue
ones, and she frequently sent her
grandson William F. Clark II to the
store to buy more thread. It was
probably a successful money spinner,
but it also involved many hours of
work. The blocks are just under 4 x
8" (10 x 20 cm), and many of them
are filled edge to edge with the
embroidered quotation. The backing
fabric is a blue and white print and
there is no border, only a bias binding
of blue. The quilting is admirably
simple, consisting of horizontal rows
spaced an inch (2.5 cm) apart.

Blessed is every one that feareth the Lord that walketh in his ways
Be not deceived God is not mocked for whatsoever a man soweth that shall he also reap
But the path of the just is as the shining light that shineth more and more unto the perfect day
For it is better if the will of God be so that ye suffer for well doing than for evil doing
It is better to trust in the Lord than to put confidence in man
Who will have all men saved and come unto the knowlege of the truth
Jesus Christ the same yesterday and today and for ever
For man looketh on the outward appearance but the Lord looketh on the heart
The way of the wicked is as darkness they know not at what they stumble
I will love thee O Lord my strength
O give thanks unto the Lord for he is good for his mercy endureth for ever
But be ye doers of the word and not hearers only deceiving your own selves
I will lift up mine eyes unto the hills from whence cometh my help
If ye shall ask any thing in my name I will do it
For as the heaven is high above the earth so great is his mercy towards them that fear him
Love is the fulfilling of the law
Fret not thyself because of evildoers neither be thou envious against the workers of iniquity
For by grace are ye saved through faith and that not of yourselves it is the gift of God
I will sing unto the Lord because he hath dealt bountifully with me
The just shall live by faith
Freely ye received freely give
For God loveth a cheerful giver
Whatsoever ye would that men should do to you do ye even so to them
Prepare to meet thy God
For where your treasure is there will your heart be also
Better is a little with righteousness than great revenues without right
Be not overcome of evil but overcome evil with good
And now abideth faith hope love these three but the greatest of these is love
Do all things without murmurings and disputings
I am the good Shepherd the good Shepherd giveth his life for the sheep
And lo I am with you alway even unto the end of the world
Jesus wept
Who forgiveth all thine iniquities
Who healeth all thy diseases
The Lord is my light and my salvation whom shall I fear
It is a fearful thing to fall into the hands of the living God
The desire of the wicked shall perish
Take my yoke upon you and learn of me
For my yoke is easy and my burden is light
Judge not that ye be not judged
She hath done what she could
Marvel not my brethren if the world hate you
I can do all things through Christ which strengtheneth me
The Lord is my shepherd I shall not want
For our God is a consuming fire
Rejoice in the Lord alway and again I say rejoice
Set a watch O Lord before my mouth keep the door of my lips
The effectual fervent prayer of a righteous man availeth much
I have no greater joy than to hear that my children walk in truth
Blessed are the pure in heart for they shall see God
Casting all your care upon him for he careth for you

EMBELLISHED

Redwork Quilt (c. 1890)

Maker unknown

Embellishment on quilts can take many forms, and embroidery is one of the most popular. A machine that stamped patterns onto paper or cloth was invented during the latter half of the nineteenth century, and soon printed embroidery motifs were being sold in large numbers in stores and by mail. The vogue for red and white quilts, made practical by the invention of a colorfast red dye called Turkey red, was also enjoying one of its peaks in popularity, and many of the printed embroidery designs were worked in red floss and incorporated into red and white quilts like the one on the right. Many of the designs had great charm, and a good number of them have been reproduced in books or as individual patterns for today's quilters who also enjoy embroidery.

Redwork quilts, as they were known, were most often made by one person. Each of the six blocks on the quilt shown here contains nine different motifs. There are two floral blocks, two animal blocks, and two with children. One of the latter panels shows children carrying out everyday tasks, the other has children dressed in national costume. The wide red and white triple sashing with plain white corners separates the blocks emphatically, and the idea is repeated in the border, but some of the piecing is not consistent. Perhaps it was the unknown maker's way of introducing a superstition block into the work.

Some Are Born to Sweet Delight (c. 2000)

Frieda Oxenham

This wall hanging was pieced using a Crazy Log Cabin technique to make the square blocks, with random strip-piecing for the filler triangles around the blocks, which are set on point. Cotton, silk, velvet, and synthetic fabrics, prints and solids, in bright colors from white and yellow to orange, pink, and red alternate with dark blocks. Each of the four dark blocks has a single piece of brightly-colored fabric inserted, seemingly placed at random. The triangles are made from the same dark shades, again with slashes of brights at irregular intervals. Running, herringbone, and interlaced buttonhole stitch highlights the seams, and beads and sequins are used both to embellish and to tie the layers together.

Blossom by Blossom the Spring Begins (c. 2000)

Frieda Oxenham

Four Crazy Log Cabin roses pieced from hand-dyed cotton fabrics make up this small wall hanging. The brilliantly colored blocks are joined together with beaded buttonhole stitches, which make a ridge down the middle of the piece in both directions. Some of the strips are beautifully decorated with buttonhole-stitch stars and beads, and each one is outlined with machine embroidery just inside the edge of the strip, which serves as the quilting. Small squares of frayed transparent fabric were applied to several areas of the piece before the quilting was worked, to give an extra layer of texture to the work.

Flour Mill Trademark Quilt (after 1933)

Maker unknown

Courtesy Merikay Waldvogel

During the days of the Great Depression that swept the world in the 1930s, flour, sugar, and meal as well as animal feed, fertilizer, and seeds, were sold in cloth bags. As hard times bit into the lives of millions of people, these feedsacks became a useful source of fabric for making clothing, mainly for children, and quilts. Manufacturers began printing their bags in bright patterns to reinforce customer loyalty, and thousands of quilts were made over the next years with immediately recognizable prints.

The quilt shown here is an interesting twist on the feedsack boom. The unknown maker, who was possibly from Murfreesboro, Tennessee, has used twenty different white cotton flour sacks to create a unique piece of work of great charm. She has embroidered each of the trademarks in pearl cotton and combined them into a quilt with pink sashings and blue corners. Simple straight lines have been used to quilt the sashing, with individual motifs of forks, spoons, and scissors in background areas.

All but two of the flour mills that are represented on this quilt are in Tennessee; the other two are in nearby Kansas. The block in the upper right-hand corner contains, in its upper left, a very faint impression of the eagle insignia of the National Recovery Administration, which was formed to help areas that had been particularly hard-hit by the depression. The NRA, as it was known, was formed in 1933, so the quilt must have been made some time after that.

The D.O.T. Straightens Things Out (1999)

Terese Agnew

Milwaukee Art Museum, Gift of Suzanne & Richard Pieper

The D.O.T. is the Wisconsin State Department of Transportation, which in Terese Agnew's contemporary work has created a grid of straight roads through the pristine forests of her midwestern homeland.

Agnew describes her work as "painting with thread," and she has embellished this piece with machine embroidery to make a landscape of trees and ferns. But overlaying this idyllic picture is a grid of paved roads, complete with yellow center lines and lane markings—as well as white directionals in the border— and with thread-painted cars, which becomes a window on our relationship with the natural world, both in form and substance.

To make the road, the artist coated gray denim with melted wax, cracked it (outdoors in the bitter cold of a Wisconsin winter), and then dyed everything black. The result is a fabric that looks very cracked, unevenly-colored and grease-stained, just as a real road should.

Agnew said of her work: "My subject matter is about the fragmentation of the natural world and of people"—here a lone man walking through the woods. "I want to create a memory of the dualities that surround us in both the real space and mental consciousness of our everyday lives... There is often a presumption that human development will inevitably order nature into rigid boundaries; calculated parcels, designated air space, classified regions, etc. My hope is that by comparing an ancient organic living process such as a forest to the linear constructs of society, our imprint will seem more recent, temporary and thus more flexible. Our participation in the world can all still be rethought and done again."

CONTEMPORARY

Blessèd Trinity (1999)

Louise Mabbs

Contemporary quilts do not always go on beds. This brightly colored wall hanging is the sixth in British quiltmaker Louise Mabbs "Creation" series, all made in the same colors but in very different designs. Originally designed for Clapham United Reform Church in London, it was transferred to St. Andrews Church nearby when the two congregations were amalgamated. The series is based on ideas from a mathematical coloring system that Mabbs has developed. The first piece in the series consisted of squares and half-square triangles, which created a single cross that shone out from a rainbow of semicircles. The second hanging developed the same theme, while in the third Mabbs took ideas from the first piece but put the design into perspective with each triangle distorted into a different shape while retaining its straight edges. A happy consequence of this development was the illusion of curves caused by the changing shapes of the triangles. The fourth piece was based on a clamshell design.

Soon afterward, Mabbs began designing on a curved grid, and when she was invited to submit a piece to the Quilter's Guild of the British Isles 1990s collection, her spiral designs started to emerge. She also changed her technique from standard piecing to a version of foundation piecing on interfacing, which she has refined with each new project. The quilt shown here is made from foundation-pieced cotton fabrics and is hand quilted.

Blessèd Trinity was the second spiral quilt Mabbs made. The title comes from the three yellow crosses that spiral out from the center, which represent both the holy Trinity and the three crosses of Jesus and the two thieves. After she had finished this piece, she went on to make a double spiral, called Infinity, and then a very challenging triple spiral version, Infinity 2. She is also developing other spiral designs, which are mainly based on the Fibonacci number system that often occurs in nature.

Crazy Crib Quilt (c. 2000)

Anne Hulbert & Audrey Kenny

Contemporary quiltmakers use many different materials in their work. There is a wide range of choices to experiment with, and fleece fabric, made from synthetic fibers and available in a heady selection of solid colors and prints from all areas of the spectrum, can be one of the most interesting. It is easy to work with when making complex designs, especially curved ones, because the edges do not fray in use and it is usually reversible.

For this baby quilt, it was a good choice because it is also warm and snuggly. The quiltmakers designed the blocks by drawing random swirling lines across squares of paper, twenty-four in all. The resulting shapes were then cut out and used as templates to make the curving shapes, nine in each square. Seam allowances were unnecessary since the raw edges of fleece do not ravel, and the shapes simply abut each other. The shapes were mounted on square pieces of compressed batting (wadding) that served as the foundations. They were machine-stitched in place, and the finished blocks were then joined, again by machine and again with the edges simply abutting.

The crazy-quilt arrangement using both plain and printed versions of fleece means that every block is different, but using primary colors and repeating some related fabrics from block to block means that the design is both visually coherent and pleasing.

The quilt is backed with a red marbled cotton fabric that has been turned to the front to create the binding as well. The layers were tied at the corners of each square block to hold them together.

Joining Forces 4—Tarantaal (1990s)

June Barnes & Leslie Morgan

Ethnic themes and fabrics from around the world have become much more widely available during the past few years, and a number of contemporary quiltmakers have experimented with them to very great effect. June Barnes is a British quiltmaker who was born in Africa, and much of her work has its roots in the vivid colors, patterns, and textures of that continent.

She and Leslie Morgan have worked together to develop a technique they call "Stitching to Dye, Dyeing to Stitch," and in this wall hanging they have used genuine African fabrics, which can now usually be readily purchased in both Europe and North America.

Barnes pieced this quilt using a random crazy patchwork method, from fabrics that include black and white prints, silk, satin, velvet, and viscose. When the stitching on the quilt was finished, Morgan added dye to the fabric in various shades of orange, and created accent areas of pink and green in places, to enhance the impression of an authentic African cloth.

Katsuri Star Throw (1999)

Janet Haigh

Katsuri is the Japanese name for a tie-dye technique in which the natural-colored yarn used for the warp thread in a woven fabric is tied at various points before it is dyed. The tied areas resist the dye, leaving fairly regular areas of natural yarn along the length of the skein. The resulting patterns, whether they are simple or complex, have a hazy appearance with slightly blurred edges. The fabrics, which are usually cotton, are used to make kimonos and other clothing, but they can work very well in quilts.

British quiltmaker Janet Haigh has used some of these fabrics to make a beautifully patterned throw in which she has placed plain hexagons in rows alternating with pieced six-sided stars in four different configurations. A column of whirling, bicolored hexagon stars made in white and a subtly striped dark blue marches down the center. Small

hexagons cut from katsuri fabrics and surrounded by a larger six-sided ring in white, with plain dark points all around, make the rows on either side of the center. Down the right-hand edge is a column of dark hexagons surrounded by white points, and the left side contains stars formed from three dark equilateral triangles that meet in the center and alternate with six white diamonds. Each star is separated from the next by a plain dark hexagon and the spaces between the hexagon shapes, which occur at regular intervals, are filled with red equilateral triangles. The same red fabric has been used to make the inner border, and a black outer border encloses and finishes the piece.

Solomon and the Shulammite (c. 1990)

Diana Brockway

Finding source material to provide ideas and inspiration is the first important step in designing a quilt. To assemble the images for an art quilt such as the one on the right by British quiltmaker Diana Brockway, may require several representations of various different elements in the quiltmaker's mind, while sometimes a single source has all the right components.

The inspiration for this sumptuous piece was a wood engraving made by the quiltmaker's son (*see below*), which was used as an illustration for the "Song of Solomon" in a modern edition of the Bible. It was necessary to adapt the original woodcut design very slightly, by enlarging and

modifying some of the elements to make the transfer from hard wood to soft fabric more successful.

The image was first divided into three separate parts: the right-hand side including most of Solomon, the left-hand side including most of the Shulammite, and the center portion, which includes the challenge of the two crossed arms. Each portion was assembled from the selection of wonderfully rich silk fabrics that have been used, and fully completed before the three separate pieces were carefully joined together. Shading was created, both in fabric and by adding embroidered areas—such as the shadows on the two bodies—to make the picture look quite likelike.

You Go First, I'll Follow (c. 1995)

Helen Keenan

Many contemporary quilts are pictorial in nature, and among the most effective are those that show clear simple images worked in strong, carefully chosen colors. Keeping the main body of a piece simple can allow the quiltmaker to add a complex border as well as plenty of embellishment. Here, two playful lizards dash across the surface, glowing red, in a bold wall hanging. Quiltmaker Helen Keenan likes image-based work and bold designs, and she has created an exuberant piece that fulfills both of those

criteria. She and her family were so entertained by the antics of two lizards they encountered on a hot summer vacation that she decided to memorialize them in fabric.

Both the lizards and the star flowers that pop through the surface, including in all four corners of the border, are worked in reverse appliqué on the fiery background that evokes the heat the family encountered, while the warm dusty colors in the border add to the overall effect. The top and bottom borders are pieced from blocks made

of diagonal strips cut into squares, while the sides are irregular Log Cabin blocks made from the same fabric selection of random-sized strips. A different fabric has been used in each of the corner star-flower blocks, chosen to coordinate with the color of the flower.

The main images are outlined with machine quilting, and the entire surface, except for the lizards and star flowers, is heavily meander-quilted with a brassy gold metallic thread. An earth-and-sand colored binding finishes the edges.

MOLAS

Angel de la Guardo (1960)

Maker unknown

Museum of International Folk Art

The "Guardian Angel" on this reverse appliquéd mola was worked in cotton, and the Kuna needlewoman who made it must have wanted to make absolutely sure there there could be no mistake about what was depicted—she worked the title twice, top and bottom, in wonderfully intricate, multicolored letters.

   The chains of flowers along each wing and on the angel's bodice are chain-stitch embroidery, and the straight lines of the "feathers" on the bottom edges of the wings are multicolored chain stitch rows worked close together. The moon and stars (or is the right-hand one a comet with its tail?) are golden yellow, while the background is a riot of color. Note her fairy's wand, shown on the right-hand side of the piece and in the detail below.

Flying Lizards (c.1930s)

Makers unknown

The fanciful designs shown on the mola to the left, which probably dates from the 1930s, are most likely taken from known animals. Perhaps the central figure is a mythological creature or an ancient god. The figures in the top corners have flat tails, a bit like beavers, and the winged beast on the right might be an insect or a bird. The underlying fabrics have been laid down as scraps and have not been sewn together, so raw edges can be seen in places where they overlap. Embroidery, mostly chain-stitch, embellishes the detail areas on all the figures.

The upside-down flying lizard shown below is a rather later piece and it is much more finely finished. Each of the cutout strips, except for the lifelike eyes, is backed by a single color, and it appears that black was used for both the top and the bottom layers of fabric. The zig-zag white teeth look almost like rickrack braid. The lizard is rather more life-like than its cousin on the left, and the workmanship on this piece bears witness to the great skill of the unknown maker.

Crucifixion Mola (c. 1960)

Maker unknown

Museum of International Folk Art

The subject matter covered by the molas made in the San Blas Islands off the coast of Panama is wide-ranging and diverse in the extreme. Religious themes occur often, as do stylized natural forms of plants and animals, people, places, and even advertising motifs. This extraordinary piece of reverse appliqué is a local depiction of the crucifixion of Christ, complete with nails in his hands and in his crossed feet and a golden crown of thorns. The embroidered tears on the face of the Virgin Mary kneeling at the foot of the cross, can be clearly seen. The rickrack-style border around the cross is also worked as reverse appliqué.

Woman's Blouse (c. 1965)

Maker unknown

Museum of International Folk Art

This exuberant mola blouse is typical of clothing made by women of the Kuna Islands off the coast of Panama. The islanders traditionally wore little until the arrival of European settlers, but decorated their bodies with bright-colored designs. By the nineteenth century, the designs had been moved onto fabric using reverse appliqué techniques, and garments were fashioned from the cloth.

On this blouse a large fish is eating a surprised octopus with tentacles decorated with multicolored "suckers." Fishermen stand on the shore with their lines and venture out in boats to snag the catch, while smaller fish swim nearby.

SASHIKO

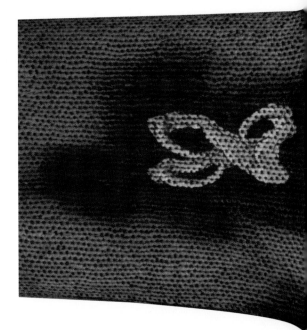

Fireman's Coat (late 1800s)

Maker unknown

Museum of International Folk Art

Sashiko stitching has been used in Japan for centuries to create work clothes and protective garments. Several layers of cotton fabric are stitched together to make thick padded clothes that were worn by farmers in the fields and firemen, who often soaked their coats in water before donning them to help keep them safer from the heat and debris when they were fighting fires in Japanese cities, where most of the buildings were built of wood. Farmers wore sashiko garments to shield themselves against the cold, and they believed that the indigo dye that was used in most sashiko cloth kept them safe from the poisonous snakes that they might encounter while they were tilling the land.

Sashiko techniques developed from the sixteenth century, and as society became more urban and organized in towns and cities, the members of the firefighting companies changed from volunteers to professionals. The garments remained more or less the same for many years, but became more uniform within a resident company and were worn with great pride. Much sashiko work is highly geometric (*see pages 226-227*), but the stitching was also used to create pictorial designs, especially on the clothing worn by firemen, which was usually reversible, with the company's unique design stitched on the outside and decorative images on the inside. The outside was worn when the fireman was working, and the inside turned out for special celebrations or other events, including visiting the victims of fires to convey condolences.

The coat here is shown from the inside. Its outside is stitched in a simple design, but the "off-duty" side has ferocious dragons fighting the black clouds around them with vicious claws and fiery blasts from their open mouths. The significance is clear: the dragon represents two aspects of the firefighter's job—a protective force to keep the wearer safe as well as the destructive force of the fire itself.

Kamon I (1990)

Janice Gunner

British quiltmaker Janice Gunner made this Sashiko sampler after she had attended a workshop taught by Rosemary Muntus, another well-known British teacher. The designs are based on traditional geometric sashiko patterns and Japanese family crests known as *mon*. Worked with white thread on indigo-blue cotton fabric, the piece won two first prizes at the Great British Quilt Festival in 1990, the first of many major awards won by the artist.

The pattern at the top of the piece is Hemp Leaf, or *asa no ha*, while the bottom design is a Wave pattern, known in Japanese as *hishi seigaiha*.

Hemp is a strong plant that grows abundantly in certain areas of Japan. It produces the fibers from which linen is made, and the Hemp Leaf pattern is considered a very auspicious design. However, it is not an easy pattern to work, unlike the Wave pattern below, which is quite straightforward to create and is often used to decorate many other items found in a Japanese home, from plates to metalwork. The individual motifs in the piece are taken from *mon* family crest designs, while the two background areas to be seen on each side are based on standard geometric patterns.

EASTERN TRADITIONS

Kantha Quilt (1900-1950)

Maker unknown

Joss Graham Oriental Textiles

Kantha embroidery is considered quilting because it comprises decorative stitching that holds together several layers of cloth, often old, worn saris. The region of Bengal in Bangladesh, where the technique originated and which is still the center of kantha-making, is one of the poorest places on earth, so recycling is a necessity, but the designs created by generations of needleworkers are still worked today.

Many of the motifs on this piece are traditional, from the central lotus flower to the intricate borders that frame the medallion area. The colors —red, yellow, black, and blue worked on a cream background—are also quite typical.

In the middle area around the central lotus, much activity is taking place. Fanciful birds hover around floral designs the relative size of trees, and the leaf-shaped motifs known as paisleys, which appear on fabrics of the same name, are scattered around. A man rides an elephant, another is astride a horse with a servant following behind. Both riders wear European garments. On the opposite side of the quilt are a man and a woman smoking a hookah. She stands while he sits in a European-style chair. In the corner inside a smaller square, fish—a quite frequently seen motif in the low-lying coastal area of Bengal—swim among more flowers.

Saami Quilt (undated)

Maker unknown

Joss Graham Oriental Textiles

A community of itinerant religious mendicants who live in small groups along the waterways of Sindh province in Pakistan has developed a unique style of quiltmaking within the local tradition known as ralli quilts. These Saami quiltmakers use rectalinear designs for their quilts, which like kanthas, are made from recycled fabrics, which have religious associations thoughout the area. A limited number of embroidery stitches are used to sew the layers of fabric together, which is done after the pieces of cloth are patched together. The quilting is worked from the outside of the piece to the middle, and the simple running stitches that are the most often seen are given great variety in size and spacing as well as the color of the threads used.

Like many ethnic quiltmaking traditions today, Saami quilts have been compared to modern art, especially color-field painting, but quilts made today are still based on the old traditions, using recycled fabric and stitched in the old patterns used for generations.

Ralli Quilt (c. 1900)

Maker unknown

Joss Graham Oriental Textiles

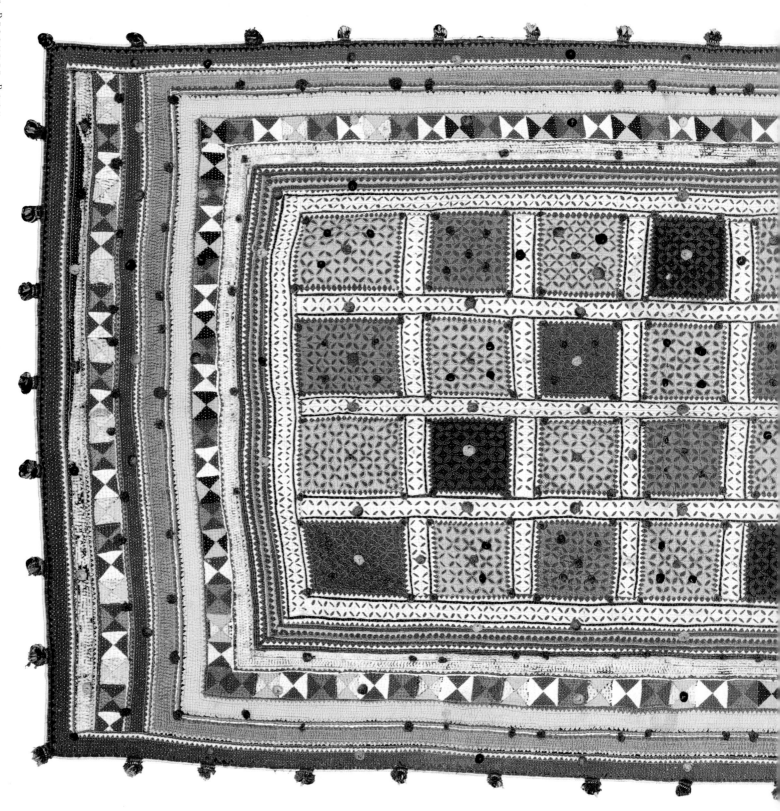

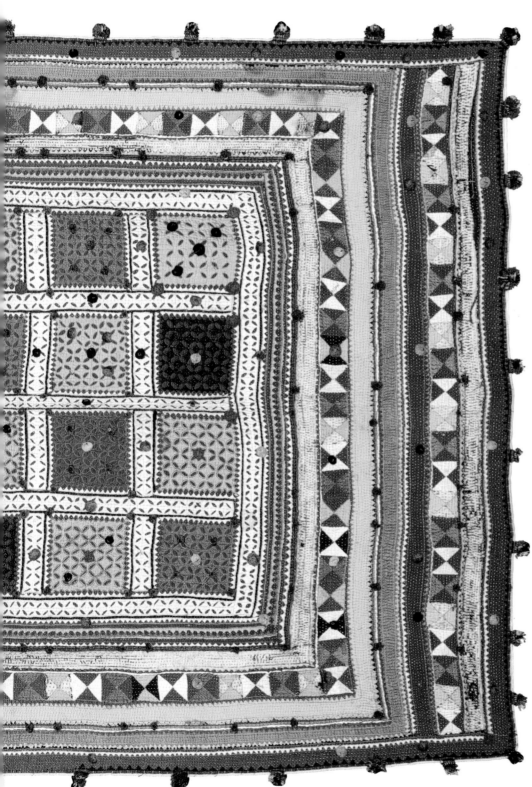

The ralli quilts made in the Sindh province of Pakistan are mainly used as household textiles, but some are used ceremonially. Their uses include bed covers as well as sheets, table covers, door curtains or canopies, tablecloths, cradles, and carrying cloths. They are sometimes used as prayer mats, and have even been put to use as fans in the hot, humid climate. When they are too worn out to be used in the home, they become blankets for farm animals, cushions for manual workers to sit or kneel on, or cloaks for beggars.

Ralli quilts are, like kanthas and Sammis, traditionally made from old cloth, but unlike the neighboring traditions, they are generally pieced from many small patches that are torn to make them the right size and sewn together by hand. The top and bottom layers of a ralli quilt are called the *purr*, and the quilt is padded with several layers of scraps laid out as evenly as possible to cover the bottom *purr*, which are then basted in place until the top layer can be stitched down properly. Some rallis are batted with cotton or wool fibers for extra warmth.

The colors of the quilt shown here are typical. Red symbolizes life and death, yellow is the happy color, associated with the sun. Black symbolizes the earth and decay; white the heavens and goodness. The stitching is dense, and there is fine appliqué work in some areas and decorative cotton tufts. An inner border of hourglass shapes surrounds the central area, which is filled with a checkerboard of yellow and black squares sashed with strips of white, and is repeated at each end.

PATCHWORK TEMPLATES

Basic Patchwork Shapes

Most patchwork blocks are based on geometric shapes. Many patterns can be cut from strips using a rotary cutter and ruler, but multi-sided forms can be easier to cut using a template. The shapes shown here can all be enlarged or reduced to the size you desire. Remember to add seam allowances all around.

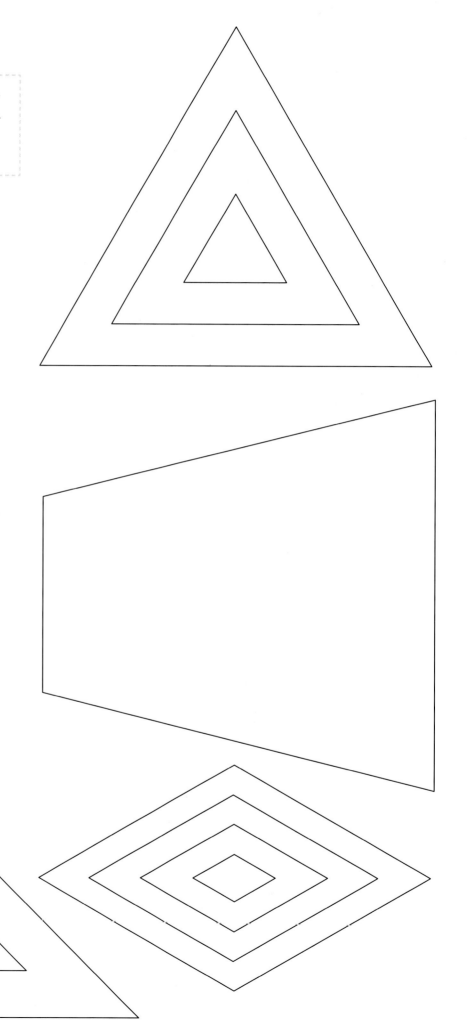

Four-Patch

There are a huge number of Four-Patch patterns, made in multiples of four. They can range from the simple—four squares in alternating colors—to highly complex groups of four. The small shaded diagrams beside each block here and on the following pages show the individual elements needed to make the block.

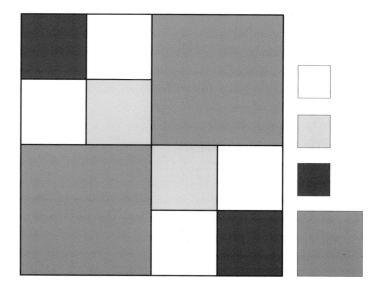

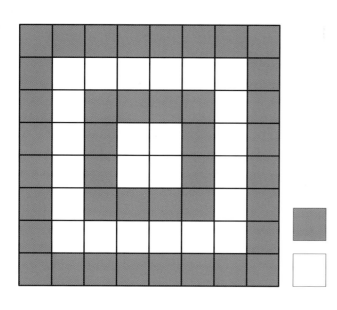

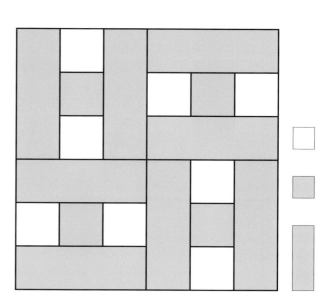

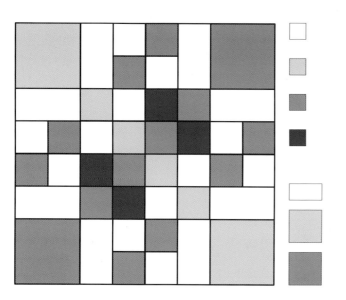

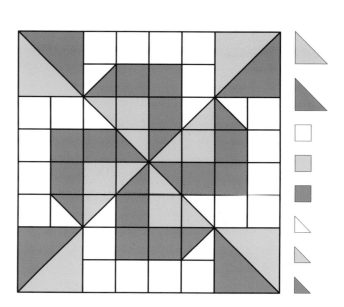

Nine-Patch

Nine-Patch patterns are, like Four-Patch, made up of geometric shapes. They are based on a 3 x 3 grid, and are among the most common of quilt designs. When nine small Nine-Patch blocks are combined into a larger block, it is known as Double Nine-Patch.

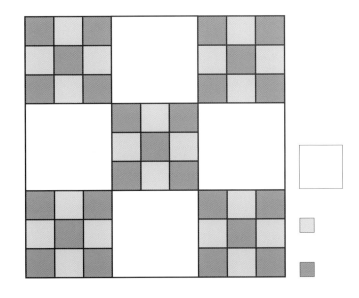

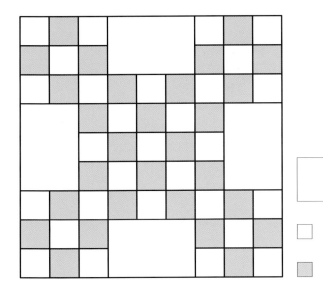

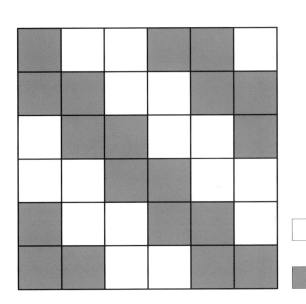

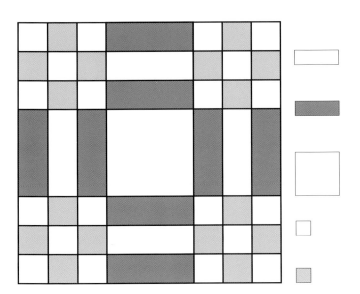

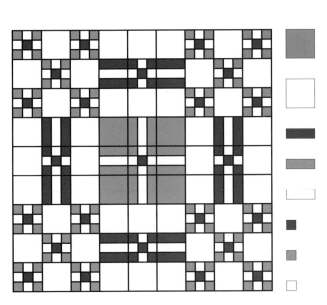

Triangles and Diamonds

Triangles come in a variety of shapes and with varying angles, but the most often seen in patchwork are the equilateral, or 60-degree, triangle; the right-angle, or 45-degree, triangle; and the isosceles, in which two sides are the same.

Diamonds occur as 60-degree diamonds or 45-degree diamonds, and are different from squares that have been turned on point. Sometimes triangles can be set base to base to make a diamond shape.

The range of patterns that include triangles is astonishing, and designs

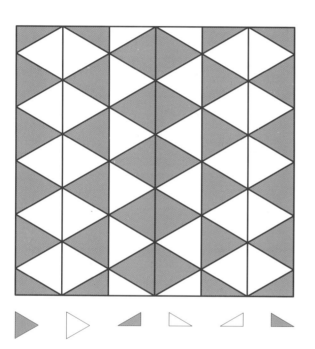

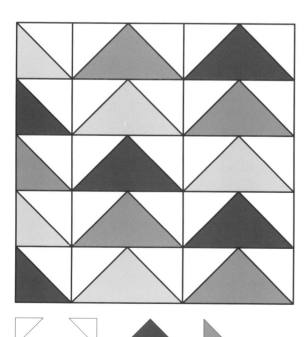

that include both triangles and diamonds can become highly intricate and fascinating.

Remember that when you cut either triangles or diamonds, two sides will be on the bias and are liable to stretching when you are working on a block. Even a minor distortion can cause problems in fitting shapes together properly.

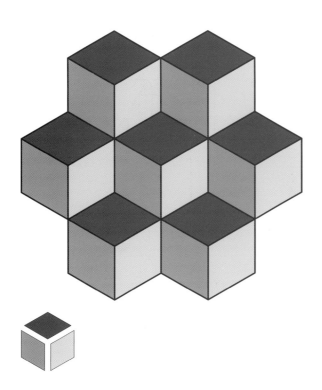

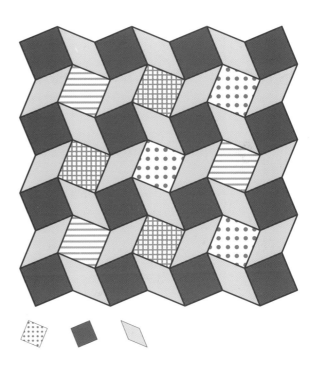

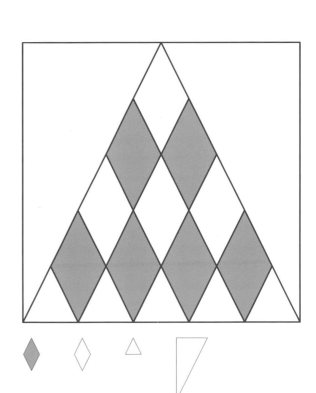

Stars

There are far too many star patterns to count, and their variety is simply amazing, ranging from the simplest of triangles arranged into basic four-pointed blocks to Mariner's Compass blocks of 64 or more points. Stars occur in profusion as Four-Patch and Nine-Patch patterns, but the most intricate and interesting designs frequently depend on making accurate templates before cutting out the pieces. Based on triangles and diamonds, often with both used in combination, these stars can really twinkle on a quilt.

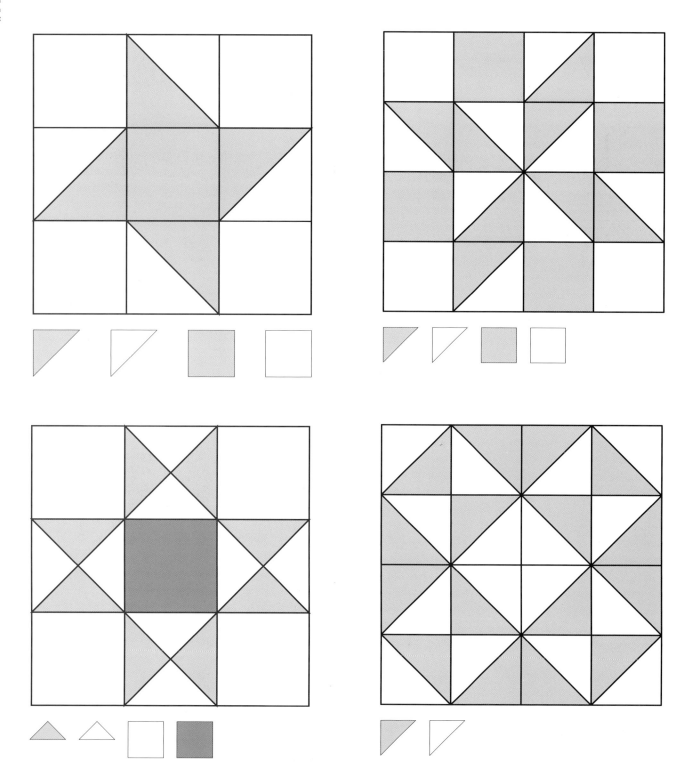

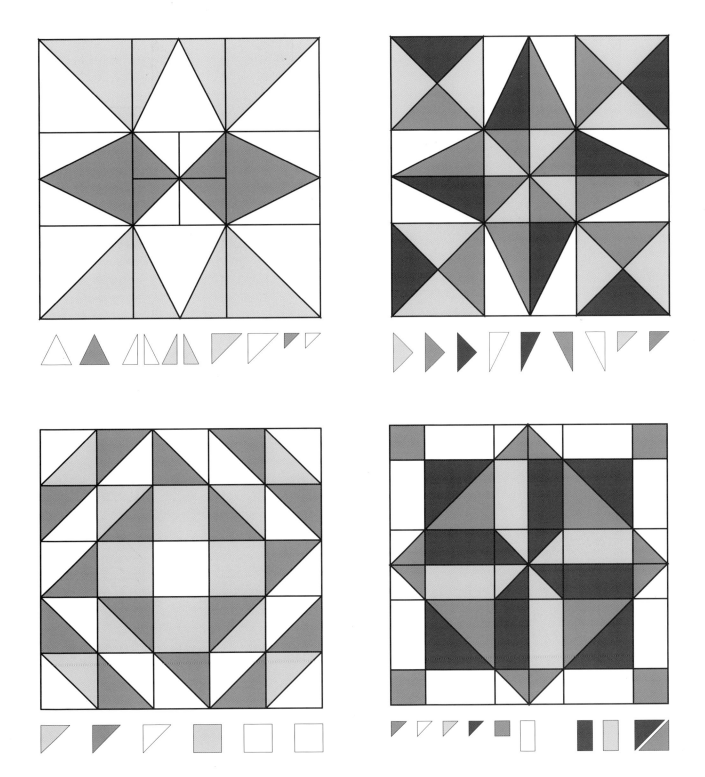

Curves and Circles

Many people avoid curved patterns because they can be tricky to piece, but their sense of movement make them worthwhile. Quite a few curved patterns are probably best pieced by hand, but several of the most popular are not difficult to work on the machine, provided you are careful not to stretch them out of shape as you work. Almost all of the best-known curved patterns need to be cut using templates, many of which are available to purchase, or you can make your own from template plastic or a suitable weight of cardboard.

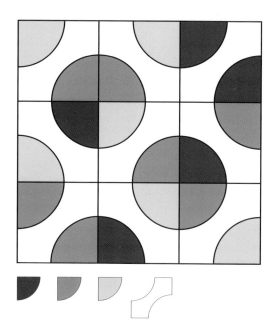

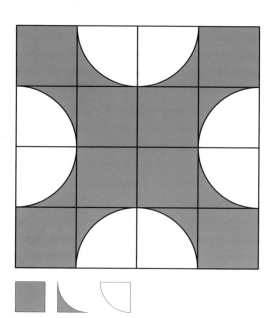

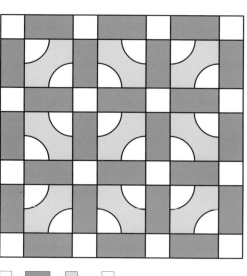

Alphabets

Letters and numbers are fun to work with, and there are a number of patchwork alphabets available. The version shown here is based on a Four-Patch block, but many others exist, from Five-, Seven-, or Nine-Patch configurations. It can also be fun to create your own letter and number blocks, and use them on baby and children's quilts and as monograms on clothing—or to make quilt labels.

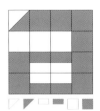 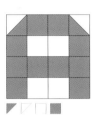 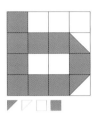 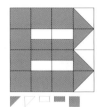 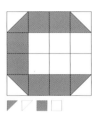 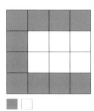

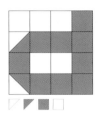 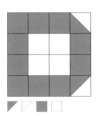 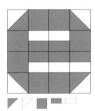 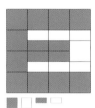 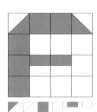 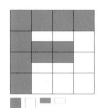

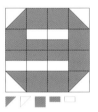 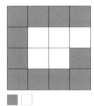 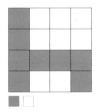 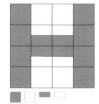 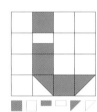 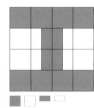

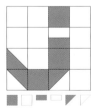 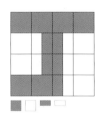 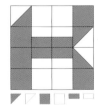 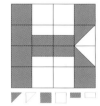 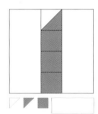 

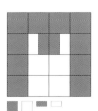  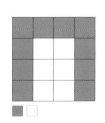 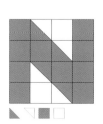 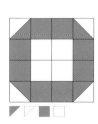 

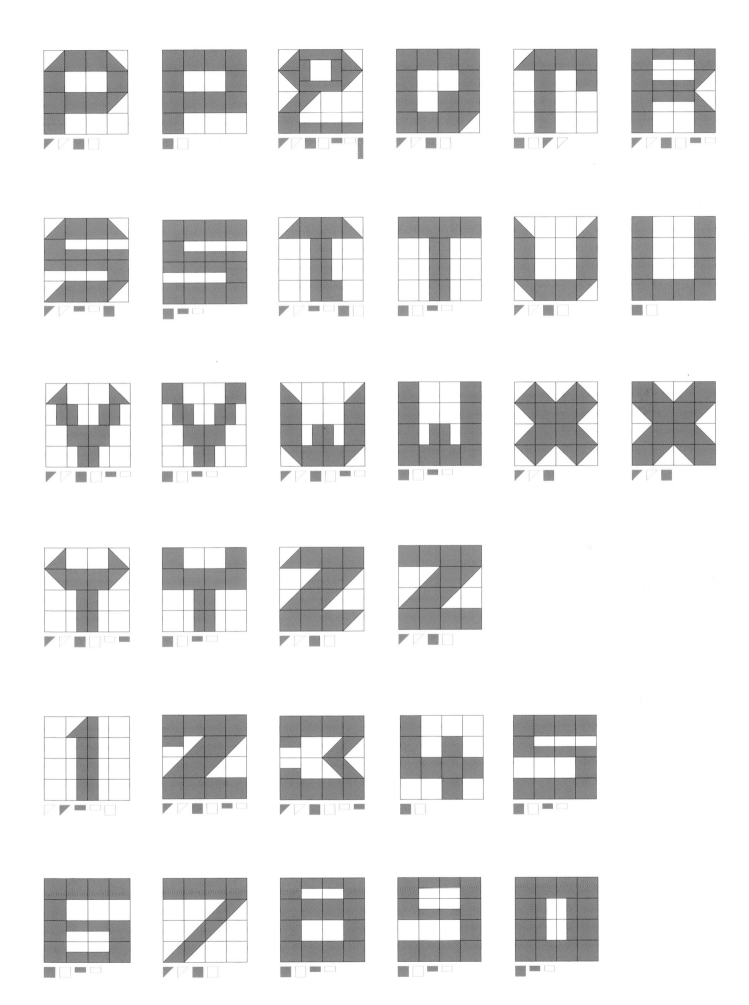

QUILTING TEMPLATES

Quilting Patterns

Since quilting is the "glue" that holds a quilt together, it is a crucial part of the quiltmaking process. The possibilities for quilting patterns is truly endless, but designs need to reflect the pattern of the quilt top, whatever technique has been used to make it, in terms of scale, balance, and overall feel.

There is a wide choice of background grid patterns, which can be worked to cover an entire quilt, or just parts of it. Many of the patterns can just as easily be stitched either by hand or by machine—as can the block motifs that stand alone—or they can be placed side by side for an overall effect.

Block motifs are perfect for giving texture and subtle pattern to plain spacer blocks, or can be used to frame areas of appliqué, or they can be stitched instead of a background grid on patchwork blocks.

There are entire books of quilting patterns, and making your own is not difficult. Adapting designs is also straightforward—doubling a single line in a motif is one simple method for enhancing a pattern. Just remember that overly complicated designs are more difficult to sew, and they will be lost if the fabric in the quilt is patterned. They will also disappear in designs made up of many small pieces.

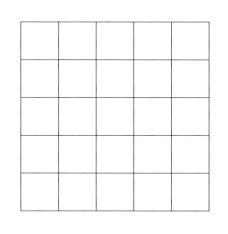

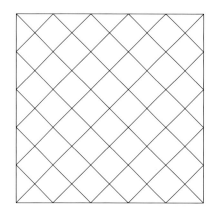

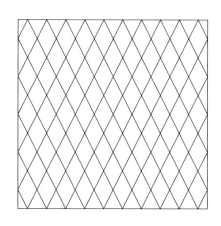

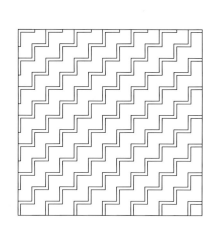

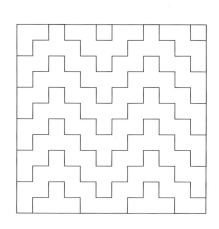

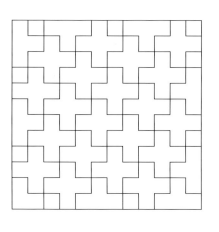

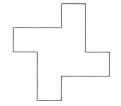

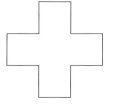

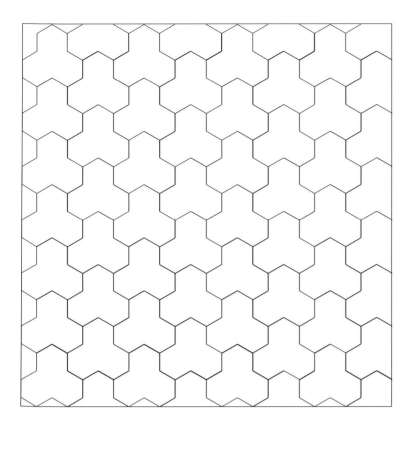

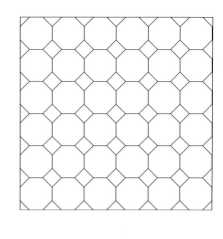

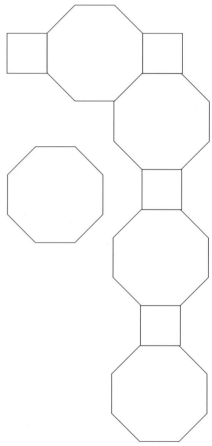

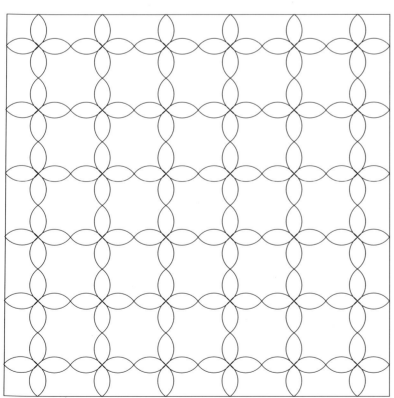

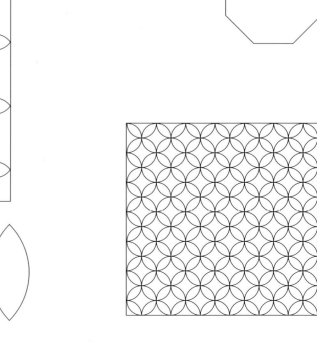

Borders

Most traditional quilts have one or more borders around the main part of the quilt. They frame the design and add definition to the pattern displayed on the top. Borders can be, and often are, pieced, but the majority are simply strips cut in widths to balance the overall design, and many are made of solid-colored fabrics that pick up colors in the quilt top. With no competition from the patterns of print fabrics or pieced edgings, the viewer's eye is free to examine the border quilting more freely.

Border quilting is usually worked in lines—some straight, some curved, some in combination—that appear continuous to the eye. Many are actually under-and-over or braided patterns that must be worked in the correct sequence to maintain their effectiveness. Planning the order of stitching is essential on these designs.

Many border patterns are suitable for working on the machine, which is certainly quicker than hand stitching. Here, too, planning the sequence of working is necessary, to try and avoid as much stopping and starting as possible.

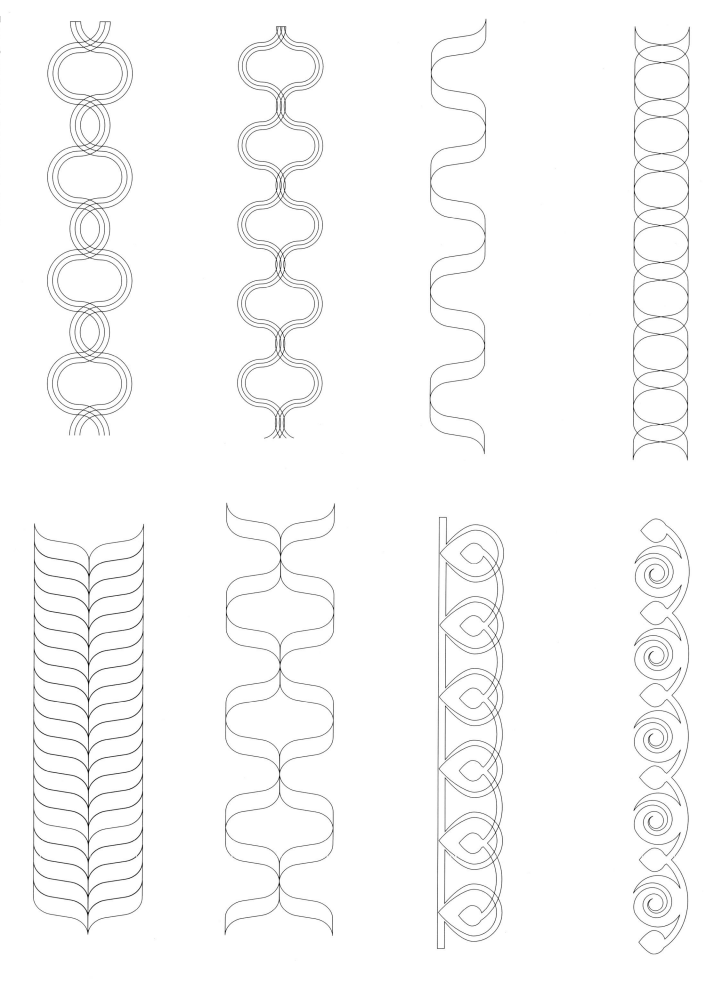

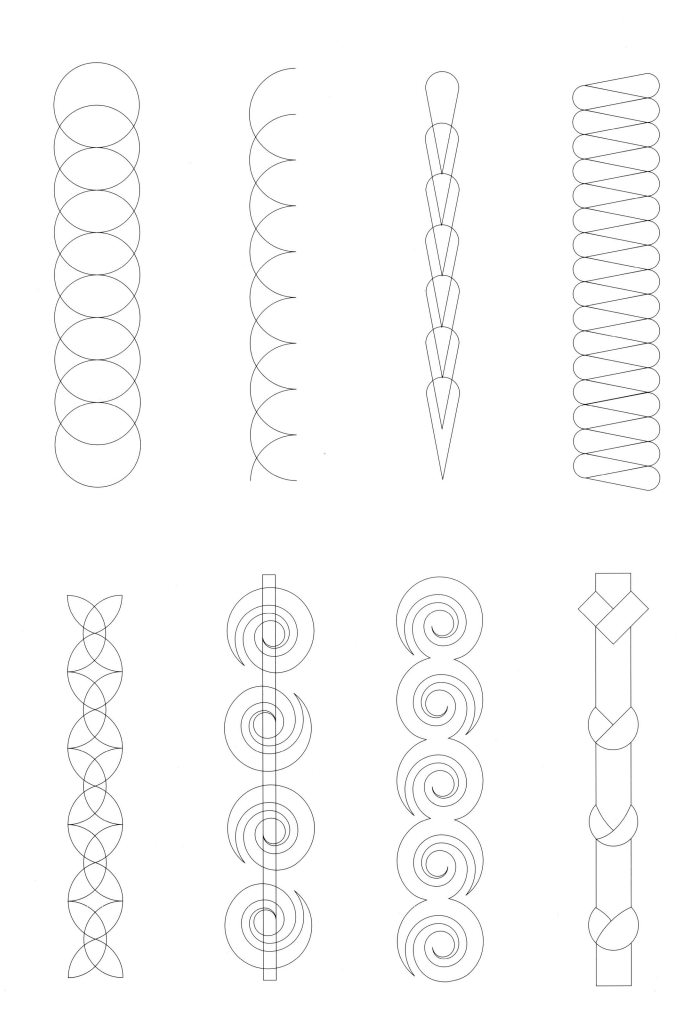

Corners

One of the problems about quilting borders is that quilts have corners, and making the continuous designs that comprise most border patterns turn these corners neatly can be a challenge. With a little planning, though, corners can be arranged to fit neatly into the bend, adding greatly to the overall effect of the quilt. Sometimes the best plan is to start with the corner and extend the design to fill the border. In other instances, a border can be given a right-angled corner by drawing a line at a 45-degree angle across the design and reproducing its mirror image. If you move a small frameless mirror along the pattern, it is easier to decide the point at which the corner should occur.

Corners can also be filled with a different or related motif, especially if the quilt has separate blocks in the corners. In this case, start planning the borders in the center of each side and make sure they end at a suitable, and attractive, point when they reach the corner blocks.

Index

THE QUILTER'S RESOURCE BOOK

Acknowledgments

With thanks to David for his patience.

Additional picture research by Marion Haslam.

A special thanks to Patricia Cox, and to all the quiltmakers who have generously loaned their quilts for use in this book, and also thanks to the team at Collins & Brown, especially to Marie Clayton.

The publisher wishes to thank the organisations listed below for their kind permission to reproduce the photographs in this book. Every effort has been made to acknowledge the pictures, however we apologise if there are any unintentional omissions.

Unless otherwise noted below, all photographs copyright © Chrysalis Image Library

B = bottom; L = left; R = right; T = top.

All American Crafts 180,181; **America Hurrah Archive** 50, 238, 246/7, 260/1, 292/3, 294, 296/7, 300, 305, 318/9, 328, 330/1, 340/1, 342/3, 344/5, 348, 349, 350, 351, 362/3; **Anne Hulbert & Audrey Kenny, photographed by Michael Wicks** 390/1; **Bowes Museum** 194, 195, 248, 249, 250/1; **Beamish North of England Open Air Museum** 237, 244/5, 259, 262/3, 281; **Carol Clay** 60; **Cheri Stearns** 141; **Christie's Images Limited** 145; **Christine Moulin** 72, 208/9; **Clare Everard** 118/9; **Collection of American Folk Art Museum, New York** 34, 41, 82, 93, 126/7, 152/3, 168/9, 242/3, 299, 301, 302/3, 332/3, 346/7, 374/5, 376/7; **Collection of Vera Moles** 104; **Corbis/ Robert Holmes** 326/7; **Collection of the Tinwood Alliance** 6, 258, 306/7, 308, 309, 312/13; **Deidre Amsden** 100; **Eiko Okano & Hisae Machiaoka** 207; **Frieda Oxenham, photographed by Michael Wicks** 382, 383;

The Heritage Center of Lancaster County 63; **House of White Birches** 179, 372/3; **Jan Jefferson** 12, 56, 77, 98/99, 196, 295; **Janice Gunner** 184B, 185, 188, 408, 408/9; **Jennifer Cooper** 120; **Collection of the John Michael Kohler Arts Center/ Eric Dean** 172/3; **JP Morgan Chase Art Collection** 322/3; **Joss Graham** 159, 228, 229, 230, 231, 410/1, 412/3, 414/5; **Judy Mathison** 74/75; **June Barnes & Leslie Morgan, photographed by Michael Wicks** 392/3; **June Colburn** 171; **Louise Mabbs** 140, 388/9; **Maggi McCormick** 212, 402/3, 403; **Magie Relph** 54; **Marie Clayton** 215, 220; **Martha Gin** 107; **Merikay Waldvogel** 274/5, 356, 384/5; **Milwaukee Art Museum** 3T, 3C, 3B, 84/5, 129, 201/2, 240, 241, 386-7; **Minnesota Historical Society Museum Collection** 10/11, 33, 36, 37CR, 38/9, 43, 49, 61, 67, 69, 73, 86/7, 89, 106, 131, 132/3, 138, 161, 164, 205, 236, 239, 252/3, 272/3,

276/7, 316/7, 336, 337, 360/1; **Courtesy of Michigan State University Museum** 320, 321; **Munni Srivastava** 2, 136/7, 183T; **Museum of International Folk Art: Girard Foundation Collection/ Michel Monteaux** 174, 400/1, 404; **Neutrogena Collection/Pat Pollard** 227, 405, 406/7; **Powerhouse Museum, Sydney, Australia** 352/3; **Quilter's Guild of the British Isles** 286, 287, 288, 289, 290, 291; **The Quilter Magazine, photographed by Danny Israel** 150; **Quilts of Tennesse** 56, 310-1, 314/5, 378/9; **Royal Berkshire Hospital Collection** 70; **Sandra Wyman, photographed by Michael Wicks** 130; **Toyoko Miyajima** 199; **University of Nebraska-Lincoln** 96, 124, 176, 197, 202, 206, 210.

Woodcut on page 396 by Harry Brockway, originally published in *The Reader's Digest Bible*, illustrated edition (1989).